THE OLD WAYS OF CUMBRIA

HISTORY & LANDSCAPE

BETH & STEVE PIPE

AMBERLEY

Every attempt has been made to seek permission for copyright material used in this book. However if we have inadvertently used copyright material without permission or acknowledgement, we apologise and will make the necessary correction at the first opportunity.

First published 2019

Amberley Publishing, The Hill, Stroud
Gloucestershire GL5 4EP

www.amberley-books.com

British Library Cataloguing in Publication Data.
A catalogue record for this book is available from the British Library.

ISBN 978 1 4456 8678 3 (print)
ISBN 978 1 4456 8679 0 (ebook)

Typesetting by Aura Technology and Software Services, India.
Printed in Great Britain.

Appointed GPSR EU Representative: Easy Access System Europe Oü, 16879218
Address: Mustamäe tee 50, 10621, Tallinn, Estonia
Contact Details: gpsr.requests@easproject.com, +358 40 500 3575

CONTENTS

	Introduction and Acknowledgements	4
1.	The Old North Road	7
2.	The Cistercian Way	15
3.	Roman Road Part I – Penrith to Ambleside	24
4.	Roman Road Part II – Ambleside to Ravenglass	32
5.	Carlisle to Bowness-on-Solway	41
6.	Martindale and Patterdale	50
7.	Kentmere and Longsleddale	59
8.	The Three Passes – Garburn, Nan Bield and Gatescarth	68
9.	Haweswater to Shap – Old Corpse Road	77
10.	Longsleddale to Wet Sleddale – The Old Quarrying Routes	86
	Bibliography	95

INTRODUCTION AND ACKNOWLEDGEMENTS

This book has been several years in the planning. We initially had the idea back in 2014, but it's taken a bit of refining to get it to what you're holding now. The journey of this book is almost as interesting as some of the routes within it. When we were researching an earlier book, we came across a small book from 1996 by Jack Woods titled *The North Road*, which describes in detail the route of the old road from Kendal to Shap. In the introduction he mentions that he sent an early draft to Alfred Wainwright, who replied with a very complimentary note and mentioned how it inspired him to publish a small book he'd been working on for some time, *Old Roads of Eastern Lakeland*.

As big fans of ancient routes we tracked down a copy of Wainwright's book and, as we began exploring the routes, we realised that more people would be interested in what we were discovering. The original book was, as the title suggests, very focused on the eastern part of the county, so we combined a few of his routes and added a few extras of our own – The Cistercian Way, Ambleside to Ravenglass and Carlisle to Bowness-on-Solway were our additions.

We have walked all of the routes described and, although this isn't strictly speaking a walking book, the routes we took should be easily identifiable from an OS map. We've added large-scale maps to give you a rough idea where the routes are but do please take your own. When exploring the old routes, we were struck by how practical they were; this wasn't a time of walking for pleasure, this was about getting from A to B in the most efficient manner, so the routes tend to stay low as long as possible, before nipping up and over the high parts.

There was also a lot of incredibly interesting history to be found along each and every route that it's been a challenge to cram it all in. While we've mentioned the better-known stories and events, we've tried hard to dig out lesser-known facts and focus on activities that we can still see evidence of today.

As well as thanks to Jack Woods for his original book, and, of course, to Wainwright, a huge debt of gratitude is owed to the many local history groups who conduct valuable research and make it freely available online, particularly Patterdale Today, who were immensely helpful when it came to my unhealthy obsession with Chapel-in-the-Hause! Enormous thanks are also due to Cumbria Libraries who are under-resourced but are an absolute treasure trove of information, help and support.

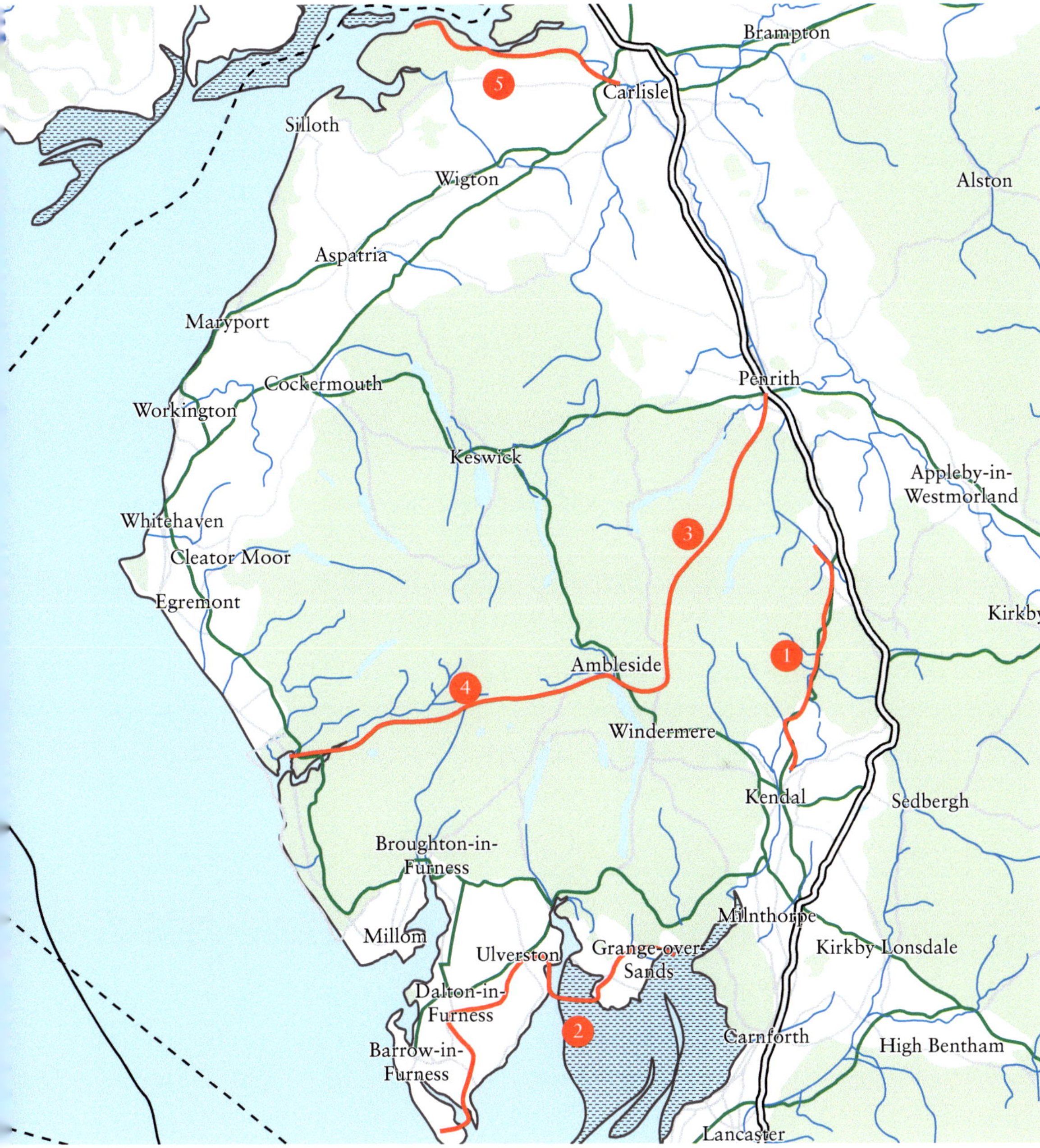

Key

1. The Old North Road
2. The Cistercian Way
3. Roman Road Part I – Penrith to Ambleside
4. Roman Road Part II – Ambleside to Ravenglass
5. Carlisle to Bowness-on-Solway

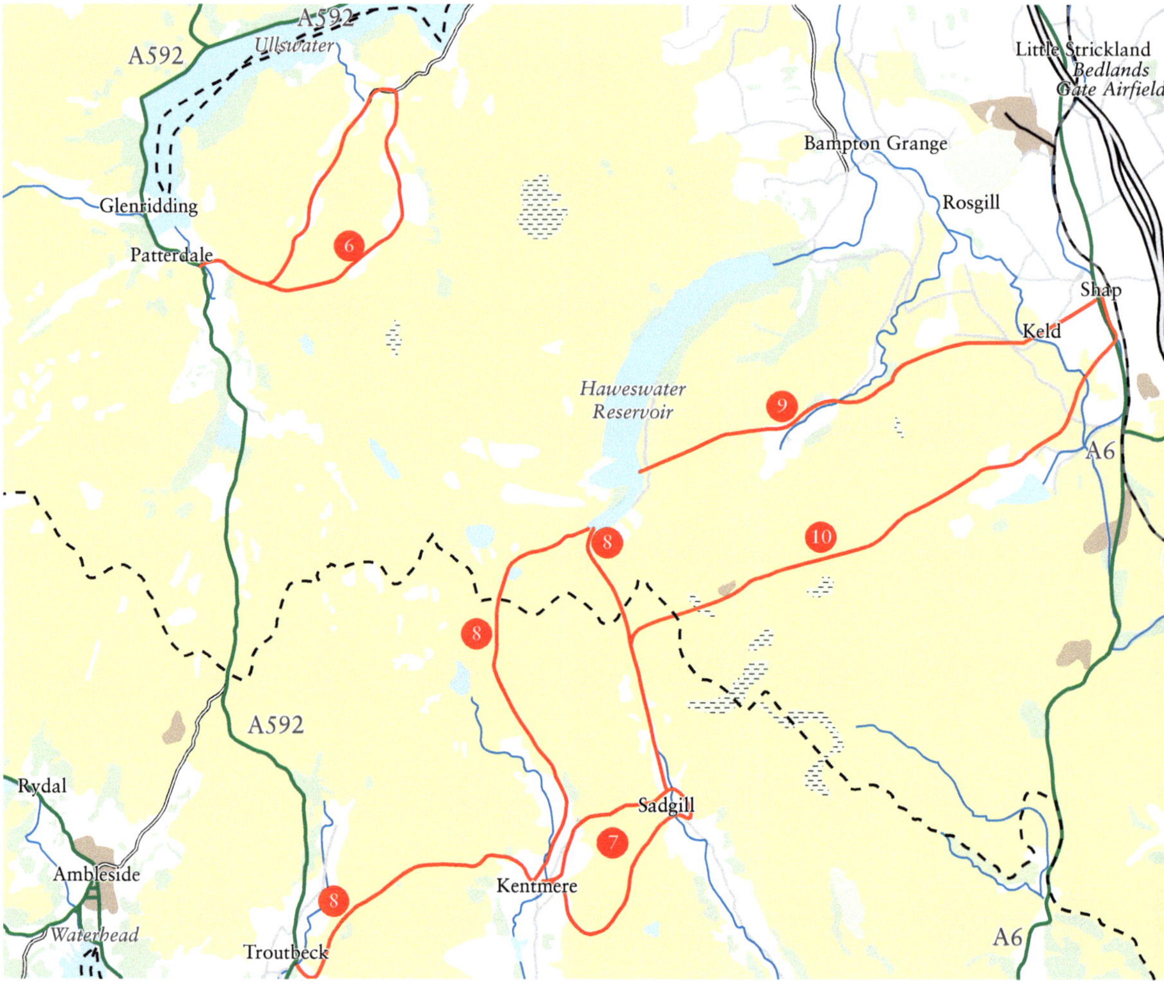

Key

6. Martindale and Patterdale
7. Kentmere and Longsleddale
8. The Three Passes – Garburn, Nan Bield and Gatescarth
9. Haweswater to Shap – Old Corpse Road
10. Longsleddale to Wet Sleddale – The Old Quarrying Routes

1. THE OLD NORTH ROAD

Introduction

We have long been fascinated with this route and it's fairly easy to pick it out on an OS map, as it winds back and forth across the present-day A6. Pretty much all of it is still accessible to walkers, and regular buses run between Shap and Kendal if you only fancy doing 12 miles one way or don't want to juggle cars. We walked it from Kendal to Shap but there's a lot more downhill if you walk it the other way around...

The Route

We started at Otter Bank where there's a large layby and a clearly signed path leading off parallel to the A6. Wainwright's account begins just to the south of Plough Farm, and the buildings there can be seen on Ogilby's Britannia Map from 1675, although it wasn't a farm

Bannisdale.

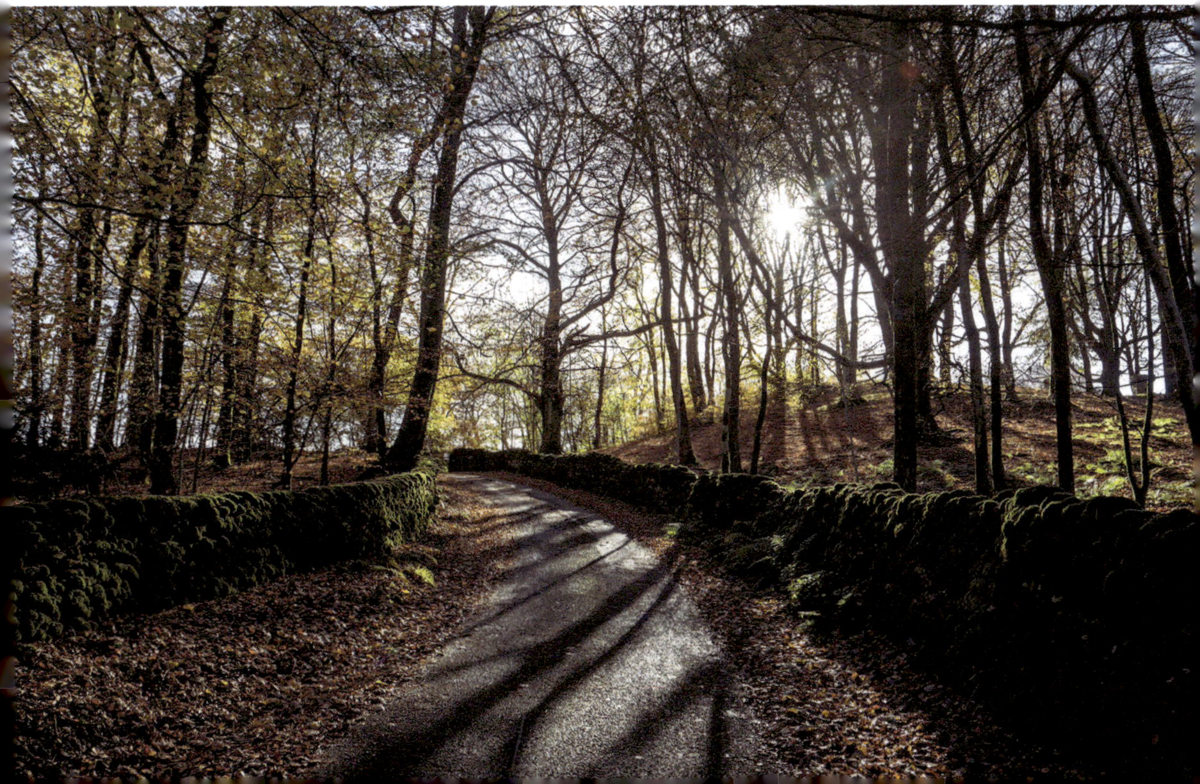

back then; it was an inn providing much needed refreshment for the weary traveller. Today the modern road turns sharply left while the old road continues straight on, through open fields, to Bannisdale and the site of another old coaching inn, The Bay Horse. According to one source, Bannisdale got its name from an early Nordic settler who was somewhat feisty and regularly invoked the gods to curse anyone he fell out with. His nickname was 'Bannandi', meaning 'the man who curses', and the area became known as 'Bannandi's Dale' and later Bannisdale.

From there, the route takes a sharp left at Thorn Cottage, before rejoining the A6 near Kids Howe, and continuing north over High Borrow Bridge to Hause Foot.

After heading up to the TV Repeater Station and crossing the A6 again, the Old Road throws up a few reminders of life before the petrol engine. Half buried in the grass on the right of the track is an ancient mile marker; Wainwright mentions that it's possible to make out the number '10' on it but although we found the stone, we struggled to decipher anything legible. Then there's Packhorse Hill on the left, where the horses, having slogged all the way up the valley, would have been allowed to take a short break before a nice downhill stretch to the beautiful Wasdale Old Bridge.

After rejoining the A6, the last stretch of the Old Road forks off right, before looping down through the site of Shap Granite Works and continuing north under the new A6. Our route ended in the centre of Shap, where there's a decent car park, a bus stop and an award-winning chippy.

Ancient mile marker.

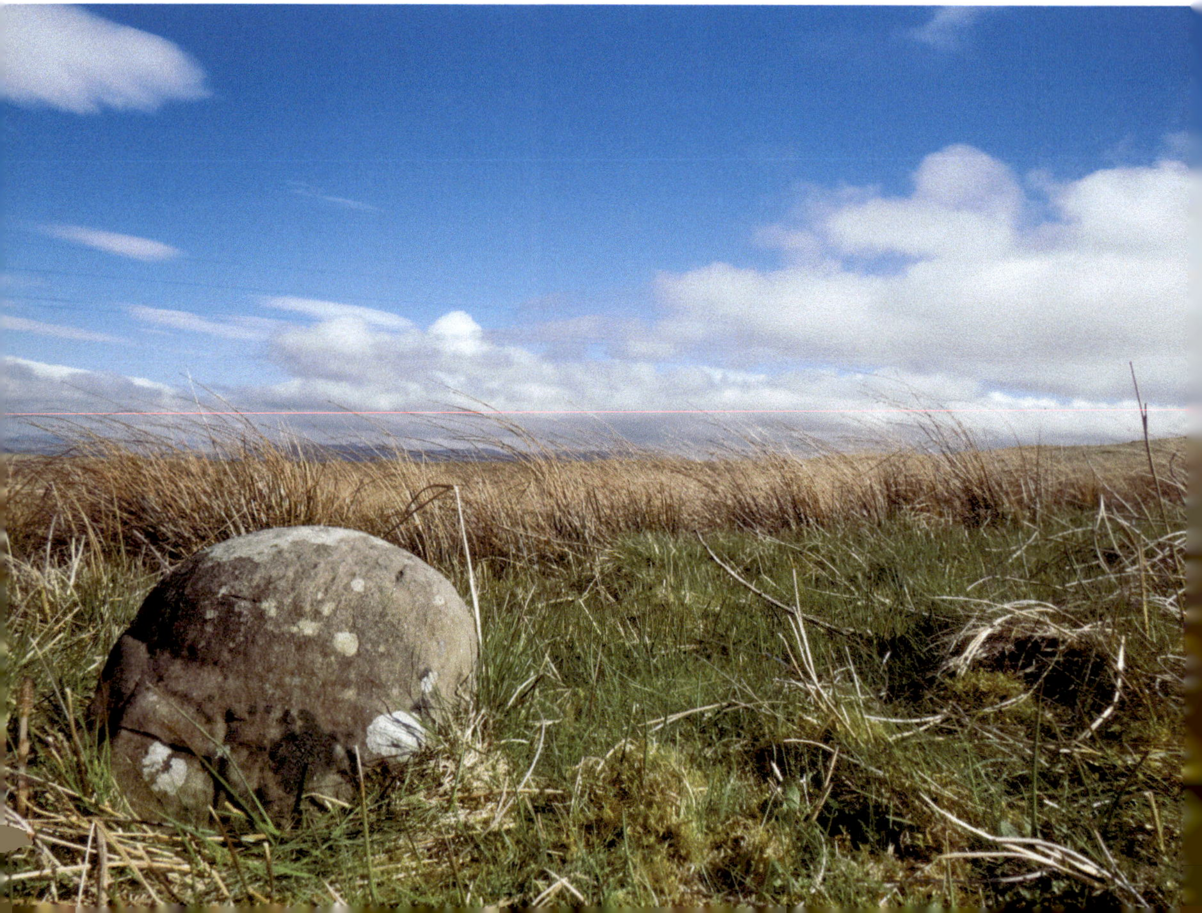

The History

Sometime during the thirteenth century, a landowner in Shap provided land for a road to be built southwards towards Kendal. This was no easy undertaking, as much of the area it needed to cross was either boggy, rocky or both. As with many old routes, it evolved from a combination of farm tracks and communications routes between local communities, which all joined together to create a long distance road, though we can't think of it in the same terms as a modern road.

'Roads' were originally meant for feet, packhorses and sleds – before carts became common place flat wooden sleds were the preferred mode of transport for peat, hay, mineral ores and slate. Outside of the towns, the responsibility for maintaining these roads fell to the local landowners who would be pressurised into keeping them in some sort of acceptable condition by the people who used them. Of course, they weren't always keen to maintain a route that they personally didn't often use, and records show regular court orders were made forcing them to resolve a particular issue or face a substantial fine. In 1669, the Kendal Quarter Sessions ordered the owners of land on either side of the North Road to '... cut and flash their hedges hanging into the way under pain of 10 shillings each'. They obviously didn't learn their lesson as the same order was made again in 1703.

There were no nice smooth surfaces either, meaning that in anything other than warm, dry weather the going would be difficult, however you were travelling. Back in the days before rubber wellington boots and raincoats, the lucky well-to-do folks would wear heavy woollen long coats with leather boots and the labourers would have to make do with wooden clogs bound with iron. Those travelling by coach would have had it a little easier but if the coach got bogged down in mud or snow, the passengers could often be called upon to help dig it out.

Old North Road and modern A6 near Huck's Bridge.

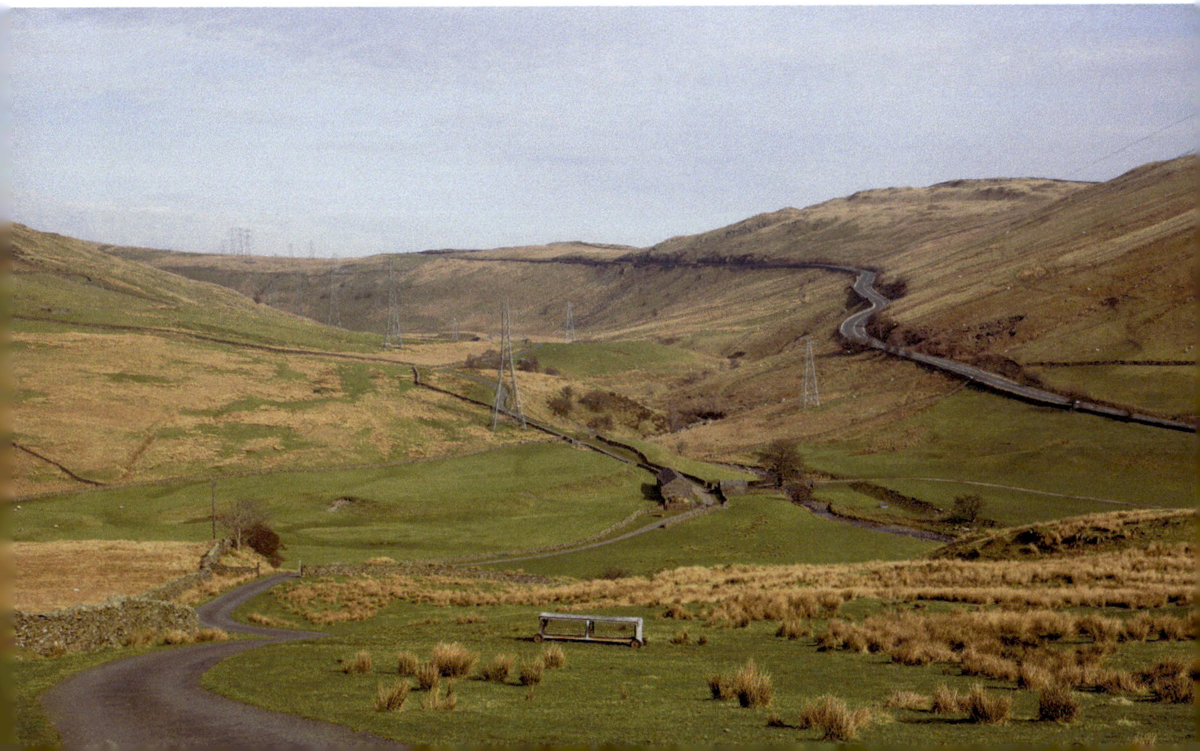

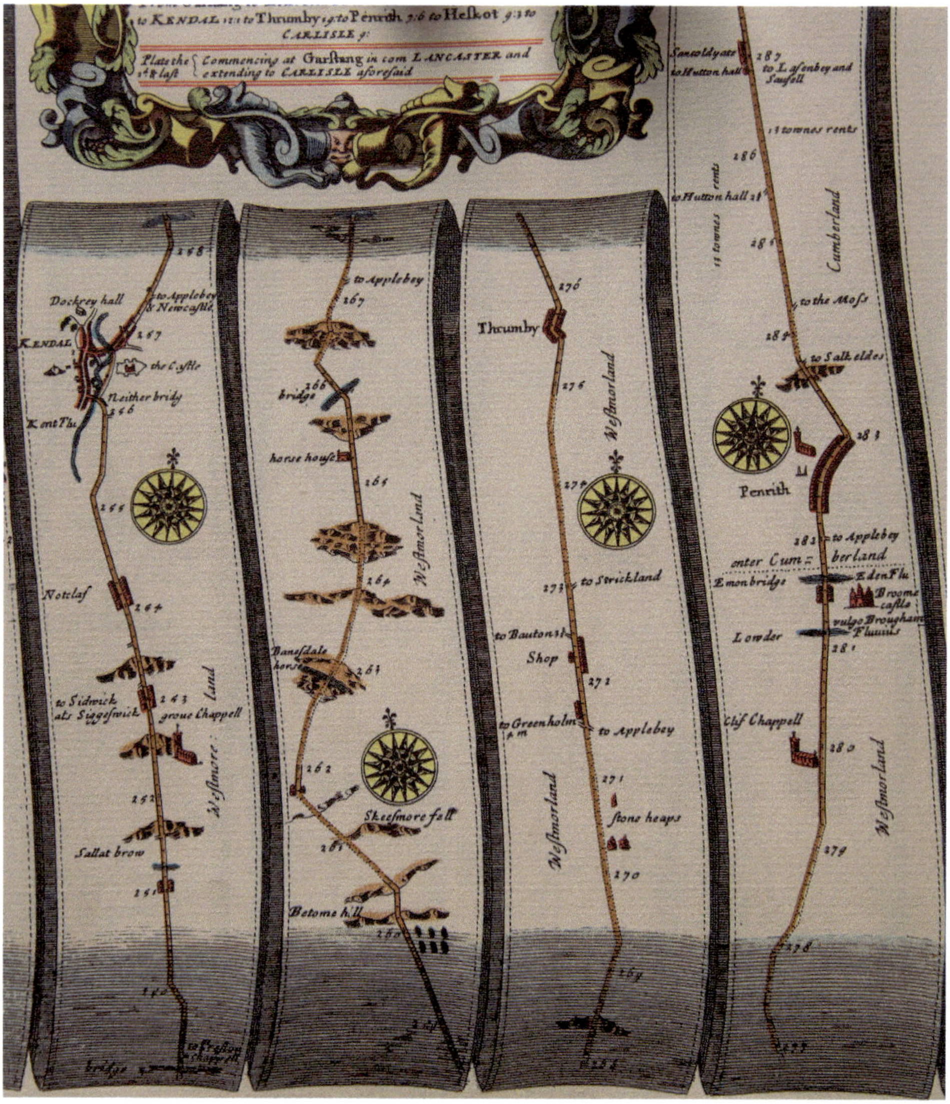

Old North Road in Ogilby's *Britannia*.

The route of the Old North Road was recorded in 1675 by John Ogilby in his spectacular book *Britannia*, the first map of all the major roads in England, and many of the landmarks he identifies are still visible today. It would be very easy at this point to get sidetracked into telling you a lot more about Ogilby and his fascinating past, which included using lottery winnings as a child to begin a career as a dance instructor in order to bail his father out of prison for debt, founding the first theatre in Ireland, narrowly avoiding getting blown up in the Irish Rebellion, getting shipwrecked, moving to London, and having his house burnt down in the Great Fire. All before being appointed 'His Majesty's Cosmographer and Geographic Printer' and producing *Britannia* in 1675. It was meant to be the first of three volumes but sadly he died the following year. Safe to say he had an interesting life and is well worth learning more about. But back to the Old North Road ...

Today we might walk from Shap to Kendal for pleasure or fitness, or to see wildlife, but that is a modern phenomenon. In the past walking was the only option for the majority of the population; coach fares were too high for regular working-class folks and carts, etc. were for transporting goods, not people.

Not that those journeys were always easy. The poor state of the Old Road has its place in British history, as it was used by the army of Bonnie Prince Charlie, fleeing the Duke of Cumberland's forces in 1745. The weather and heavy going caused a lot of problems for their carriages, and a number of them were bogged down overnight. Some lightened their load by dumping cannonballs into local lakes or paying 'sixpence to every man who could carry cannon balls'. It's said that some local farms still have cannon balls serving as ornaments and door stops.

In the late 1700s, the Turnpike Trusts were formed across England so the money raised from tolls would address these issues and pay for the upkeep of the roads. In 1815, the Heron Syke Trust, responsible for the Old North Road, borrowed £17,000 (over £1.4 million in today's money) to improve the road. There were two major roadbuilders to choose from at that time: Telford and McAdam. The trust selected McAdam on the grounds that he was the most cost-effective. He redesigned the route all the way from Heron Syke (near Burton, south of Kendal) through to Shap, and his key aims were to reduce the gradient of the road and improve the drainage, both of which he achieved.

Travel was very much improved and toll records show that traffic doubled in the years after the road was finished. The new road (now the A6) also cost a lot less to look after with maintenance costs falling by a third. It wasn't all good news though. For a start, speed wars broke out when, in 1823, the North Mail (a popular coach of the time) shaved forty-five minutes off the journey time from Kendal to Carlisle, reducing it to just five hours fifteen minutes. In 1831, it was reported that £2 10*s* had been collected from 'fines for furious driving'.

As the roads improved so more people used them, both tradespeople and visitors alike as, for the first time, it became easy for people from towns and cities to access more remote communities, and vice versa. New influences were seen in buildings, furniture, fashion and literature and, as is human nature, many people were resistant and suspicious of such

Near Plough Farm.

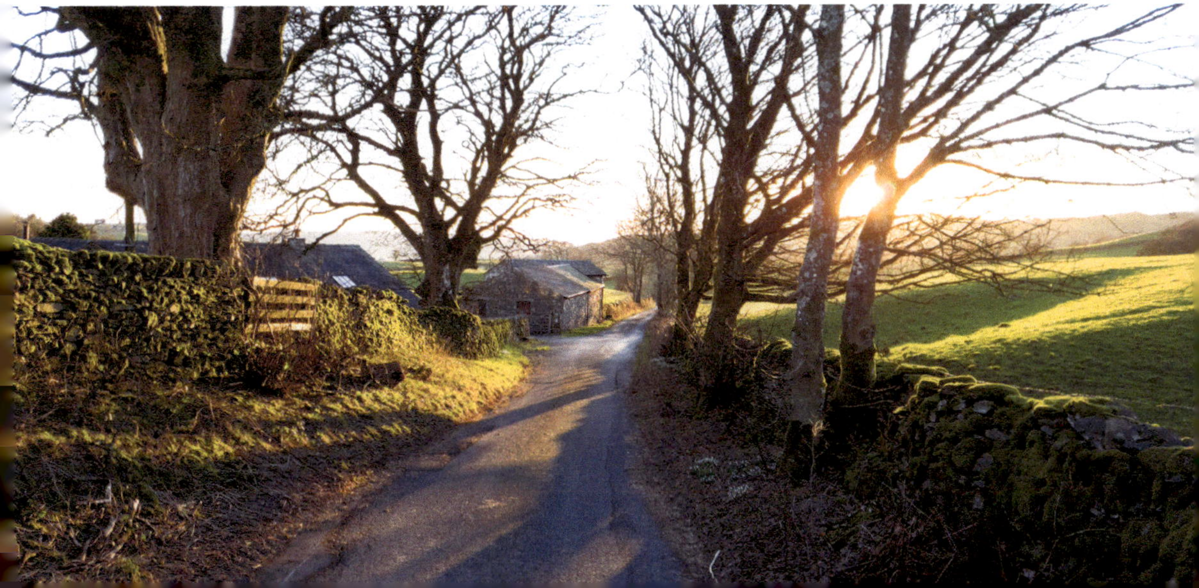

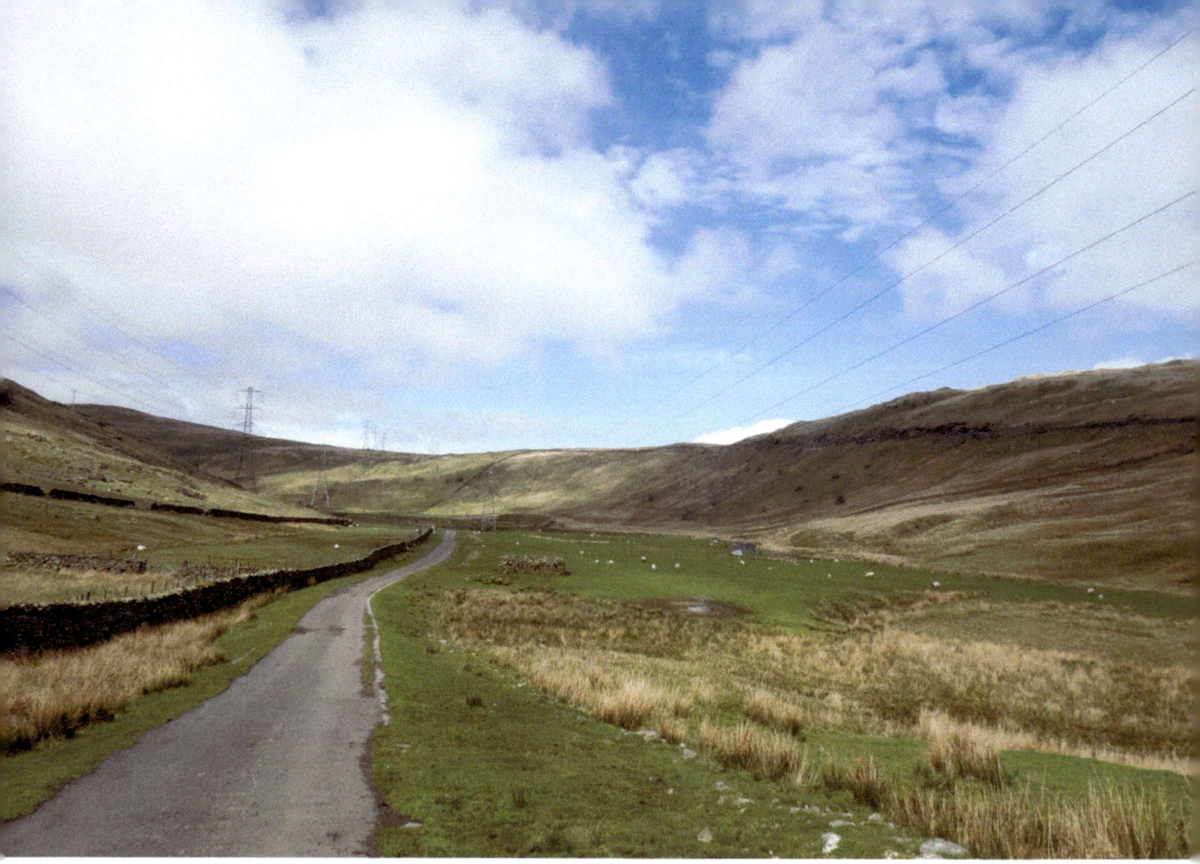

Above: Looking along old road towards the steep gradient at Hause Foot, and the gentle gradient of the new road along the hill on the right.

Below: High Borrow Bridge.

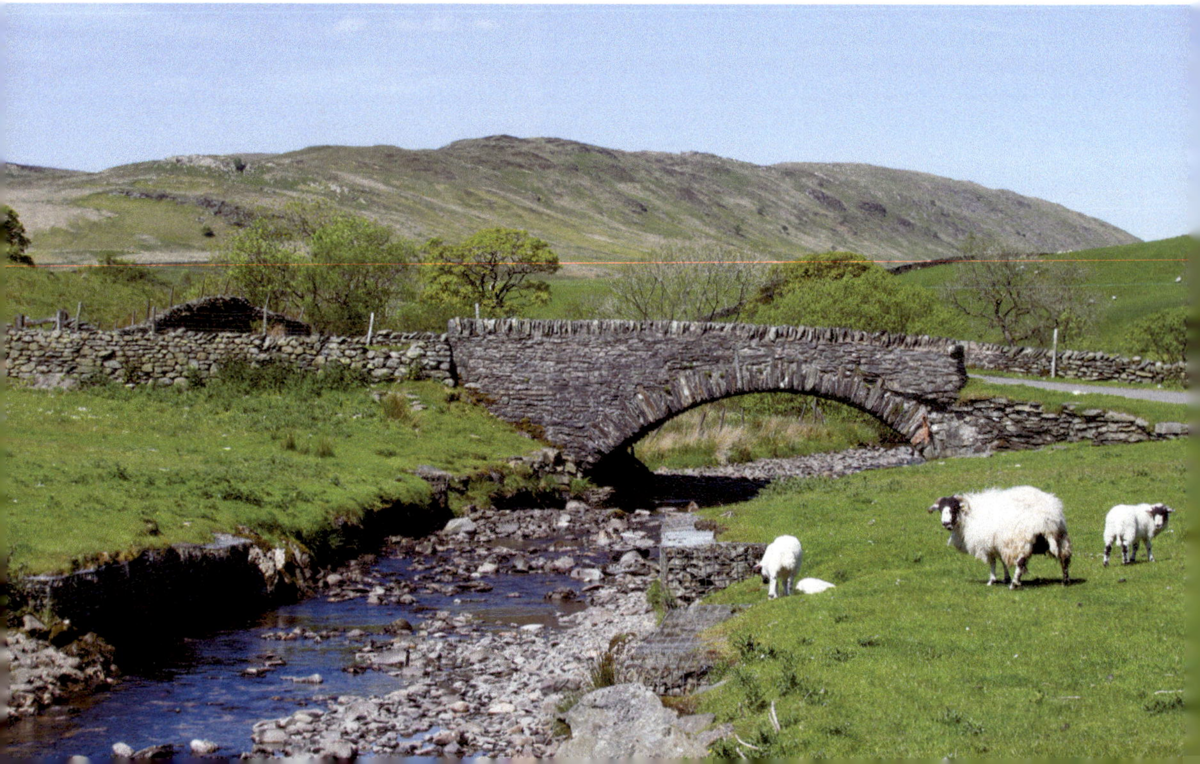

changes. On 17 April 1819, the *Westmorland Gazette* reported that 'We have not less than 60 arrivals and departures of coaches to and from this town in a week' and there's no denying that the increased visitor numbers were a benefit to the local economy in the same way then as they are today.

In an effort to boost the local economy still further some trades, such as those involved in the wool industry, were exempt from toll charges but the tolls were still not popular and some farmers preferred taking detours via Nan Bield or Gatesgarth Pass to paying the fees.

The heyday of the toll roads couldn't last forever, and in 1846 the Preston to Carlisle railway opened, providing a quicker and easier mode of transport. As a consequence, toll takings plummeted, although the A6 remained the main route from the north-west into Scotland until the M6 opened in the 1970s. People who travelled along it back then remember colossal traffic jams from Shap to Kendal caused by poor weather in the winter and visitor numbers in the summer.

Throughout its history it's been a hotspot for accidents with many coaching accidents occurring in the eighteenth and nineteenth centuries due to the poor conditions of the Old North Road. Even its modern replacement has been the site of a number of notorious incidents, including the worst road accident in the region, which occurred in August 1953 when a coach plummeted down the rocky hillside near to Huck's Brow, sadly killing seven people and injuring many more.

These days, with the majority of traffic now racing along the nearby M6, the A6 from Kendal to Shap is usually a pleasant and uneventful drive. If you don't fancy exploring the whole route, there are plenty of laybys where you can park up and wander along the quiet valleys on either side of the route. Near to the highest point on the road is a large layby on the right (as you're travelling north), with a lovely stone as a fitting memorial to all the people who helped make the route possible.

Wasdale Old Bridge.

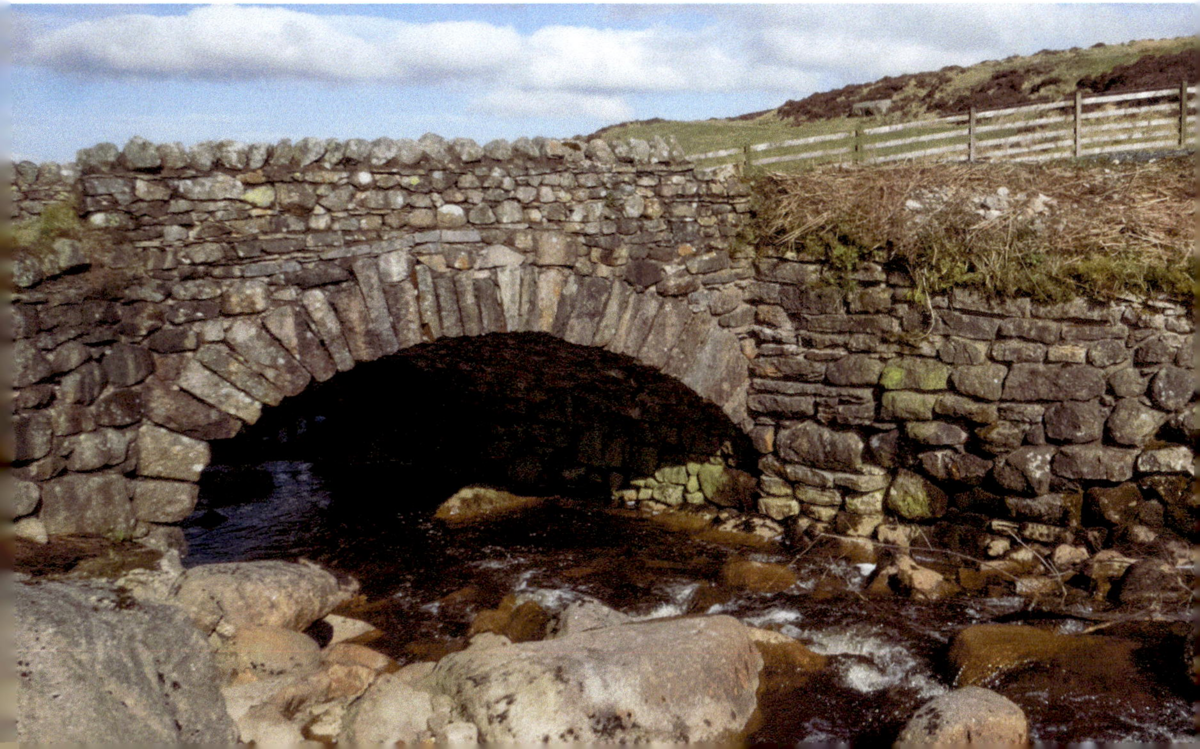

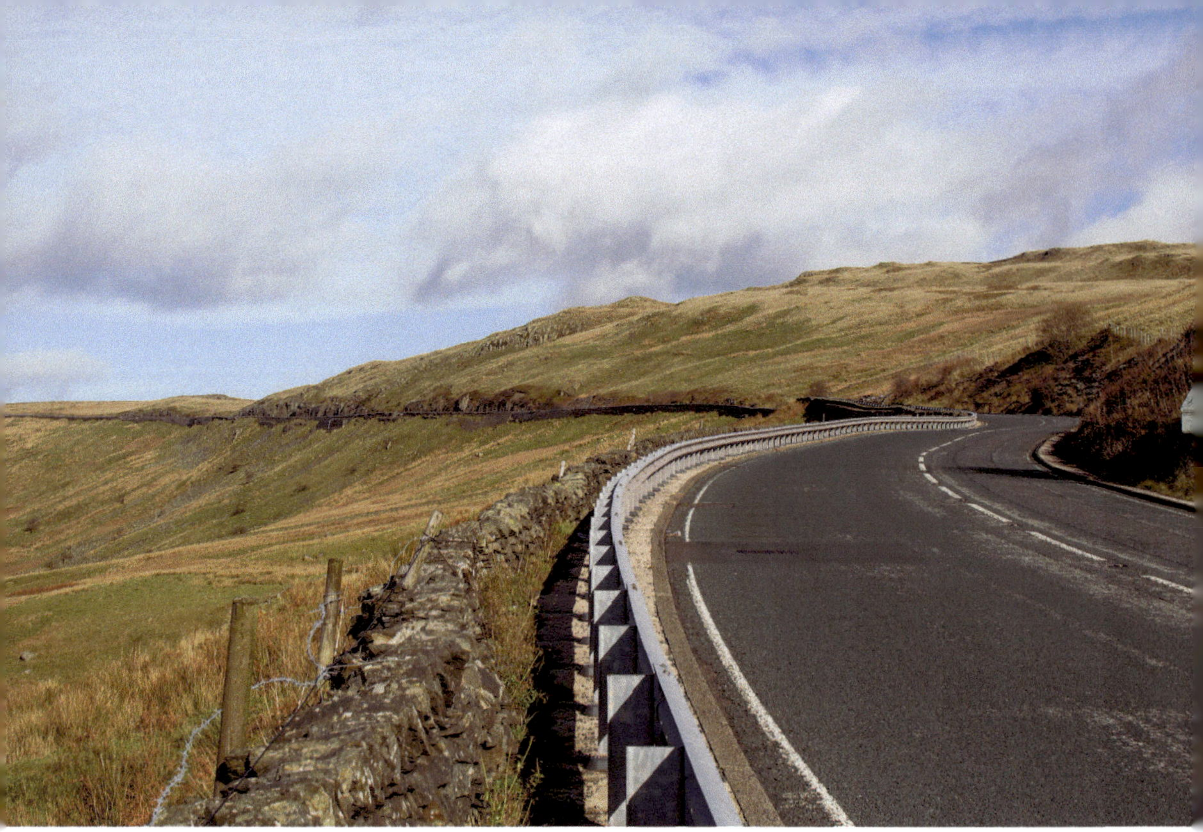

Above: Steep embankment near Huck's Brow.

Below: Memorial to those who created the new road.

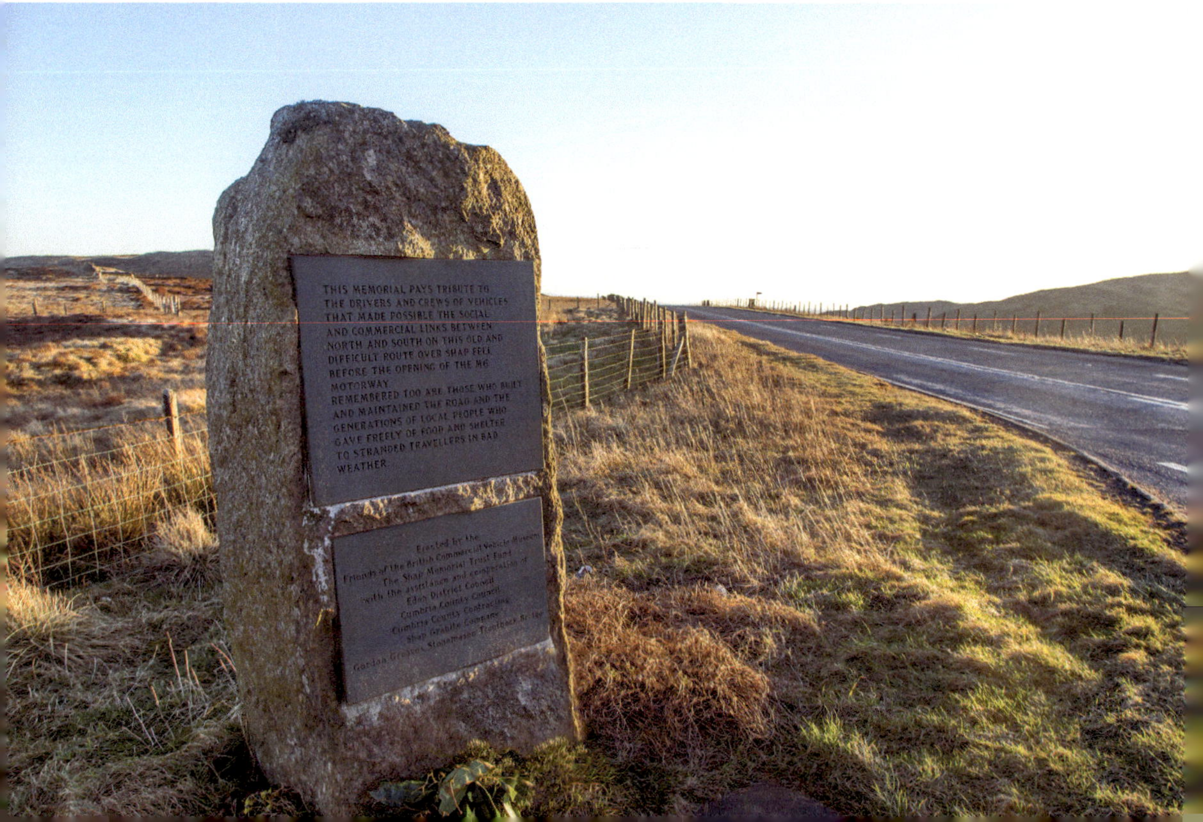

2. THE CISTERCIAN WAY

Introduction

The Cistercian Way is a 33-mile (53-km) route that winds along the south coast of Cumbria from Walney Island to Grange-over-Sands. It was once signposted throughout and featured on a series of promotional leaflets and materials produced by Cumbria County Council to attract visitors. However, the route fell out of favour, it is no longer marked on an OS map, many of the signposts have disappeared, and the route is no longer endorsed by the council, all of which is a huge shame because it offers miles of glorious views and plenty of natural and historical interest.

The Route

We took our version of the route from Ian Brodie's 1989 official guide, *The Cistercian Way*, except we didn't complete all of it and we did it back to front.

We began our journey on Walney Island but as the original route called for us to cross the sands, we opted to stick to dry land and instead headed around to Roa Island. From there,

Furness Abbey.

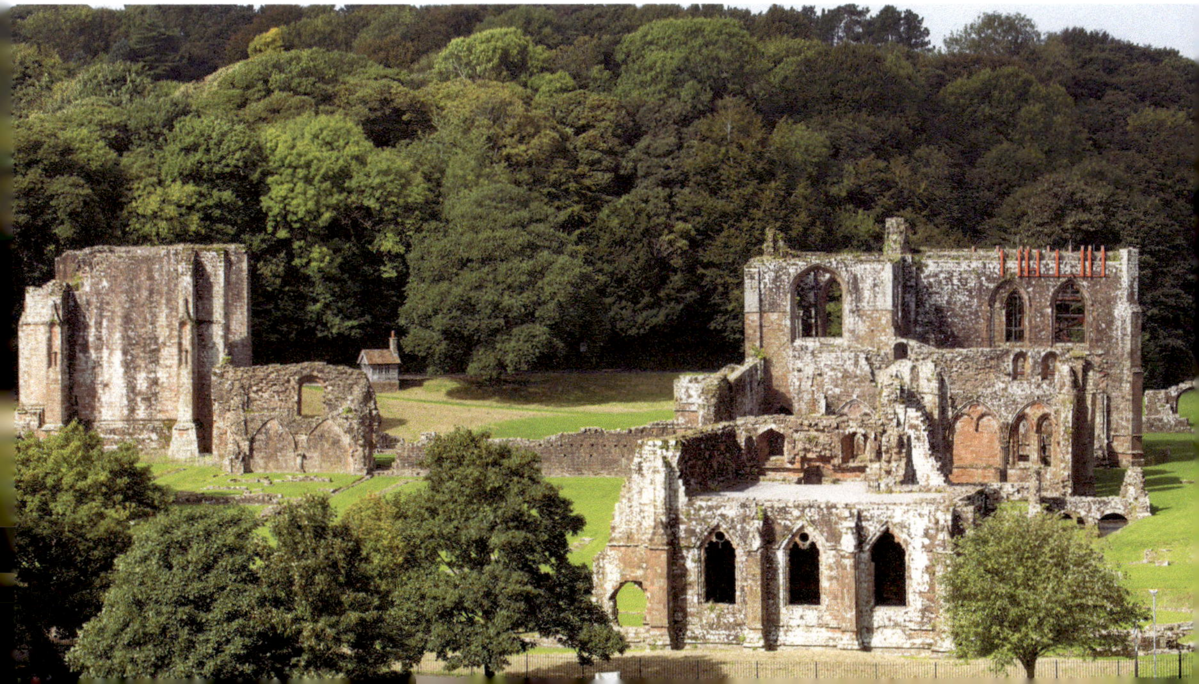

we followed the route described past Furness Abbey and on to the wonderful surprise that is Dalton Castle. Leaving Dalton, we wove our way through Little and Great Urswick and on, via Swarthmoor Hall, into Ulverston where we visited Conishead Priory before, again, sticking to the land and driving around to pick the route up again at Lenibrick Point near Cark. We did manage to nip over to Chapel Island as part of a guided tour though, which was well worth the effort and definitely recommended.

From Cark, we journeyed on past Holker Hall through the woods around and down into Cartmel. Much of the land the Cistercian Way passes over is owned by the Holker Estate, who are very keen to bring the route back into regular usage.

After pausing at Cartmel, it was a short push up over Hampsfell and back home to Grange-over-Sands. The route officially starts or ends at the railway station and, if you prefer to be based in one place, we found most of it to be easily accessible as day hikes, hopping on the train for the outward journey and walking back a couple of stations each time.

We've seen the route described as 'challenging' but most of it is low level with only a few small hills, and there are plenty of places along the way for provisions if you prefer a lighter backpack. A couple of small sections were a little trickier to navigate, but this is only because it has fallen out of use.

The History

It makes most sense to start with who the Cistercians were, as they give their name to the route and had a huge influence on the history of this area of Cumbria. The Cistercian Order was formed in 1908 at Cîteaux in Burgundy. The monks who initiated the order wanted to return to a life of simplicity and austerity, which is interesting to bear in mind when we see later how the monks of Furness Abbey operated. The Cistercians sited their abbeys 'far from the concourse of man' and they committed to spending their days in solitude, prayer and the study of the scriptures. The impact of the order on the region was so strong that even today there are many visual reminders of their existence.

Sheep Island, right at the start of our route, is, as Wikipedia informs us, 'an uninhabited grassy island of around 15 acres located ¼ mile from the shores of Walney Island'. Fair enough, there's not a lot there these days. In the past, it would have been used as a stopping off point on the walk across the sands from Walney to Roa Island and the mainland beyond. It was also once home to an isolation hospital, where sailors with nasty diseases were dropped off on their way in to Barrow, although this building has long since disappeared.

The next island over, Piel Island, is home to Piel Castle. At the time of the Spanish Armada (1588), the harbour was considered to be the finest between Milford Haven in South Wales and the Scottish Borders. The monks of nearby Furness Abbey owned the island and used it as a base for their lucrative import/export business. The castle was fortified in 1327 to protect it from the many Scottish raids occurring at that time, and the monks maintained the island and traded extensively through the port, becoming wealthy, influential and owning substantial areas of land across much of the region, somewhat removed from their original goals of austerity and simplicity.

Next up for us was Roa Island and it would be a shame to visit without also including a detour to Foulney Island. Roa Island was once a proper island before being bought by

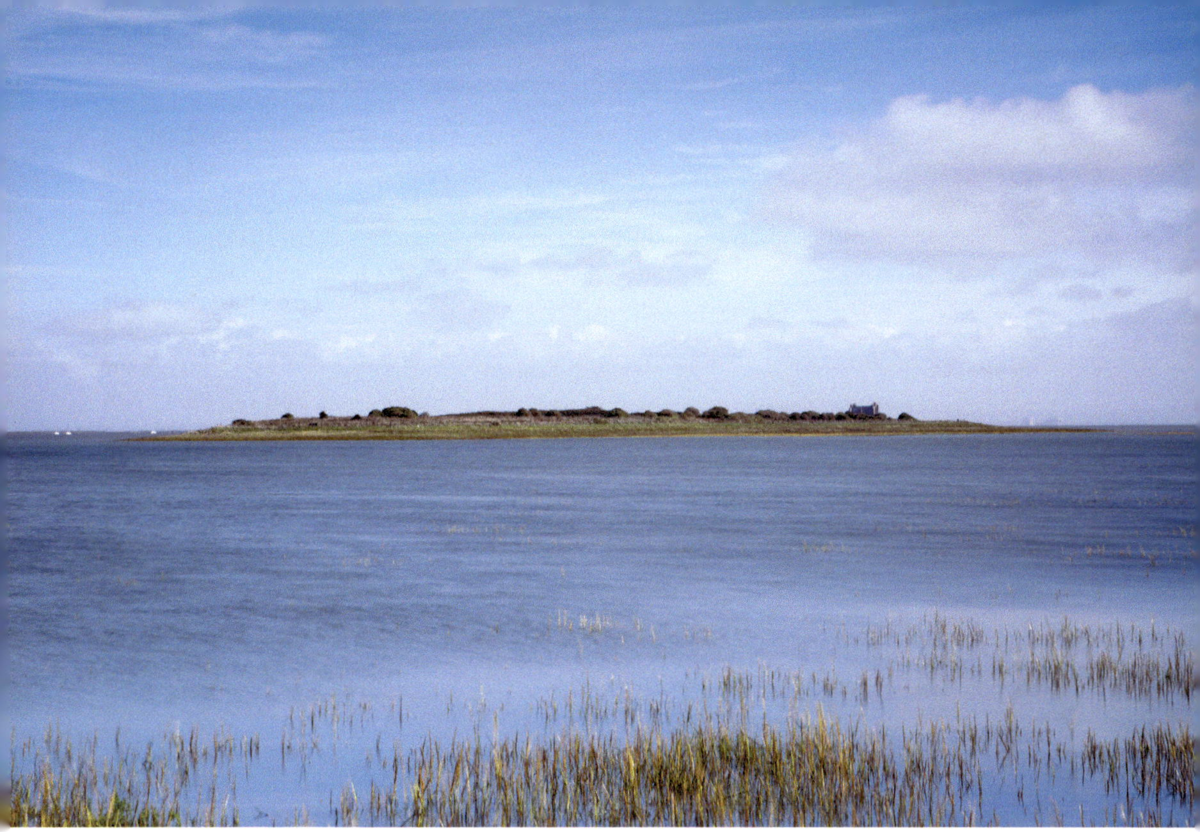

Above: Sheep Island.

Below: Piel Castle.

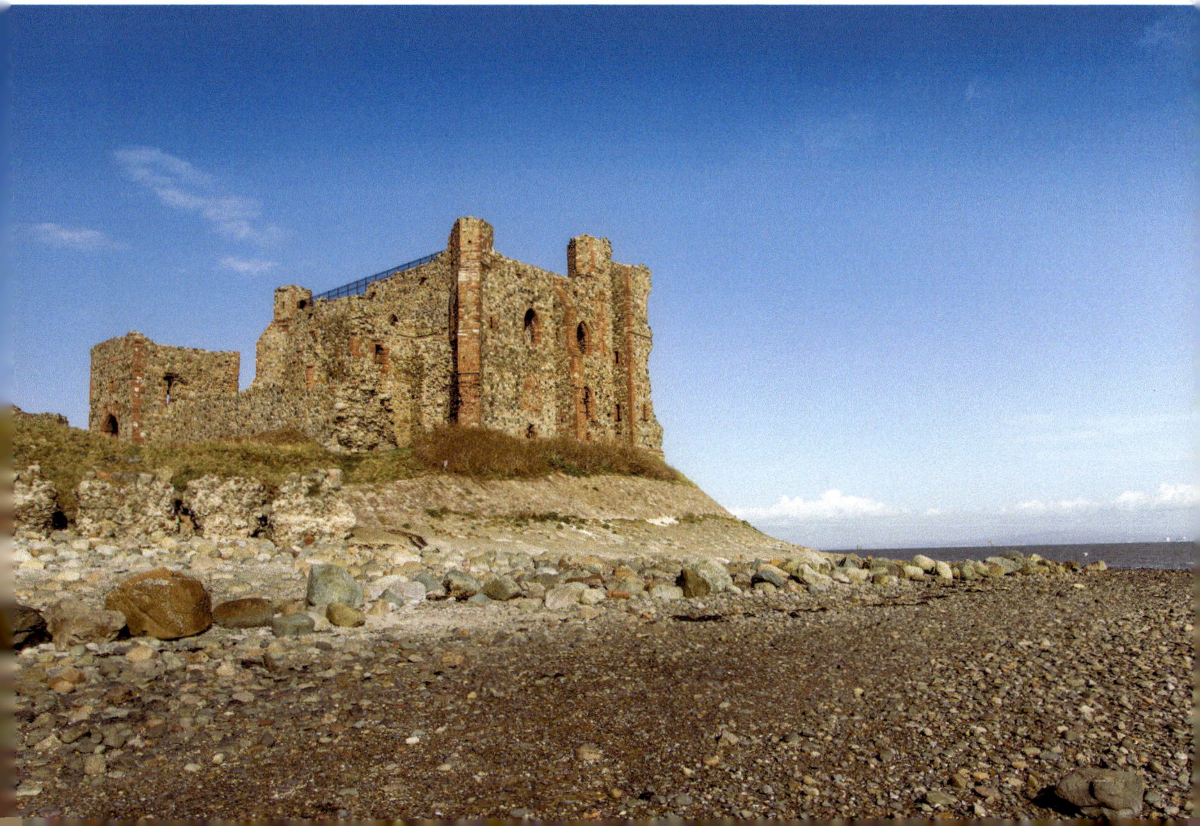

John Abel Smith in the 1840s. He envisioned creating a Harbour Company that he hoped would one day dominate the world and he got as far as building the permanent causeway to the island. In 1846, the Furness Railway Company (FRC) completed a rail connection to the island but they struggled to negotiate an acceptable deal with John Smith and it was not a happy relationship. In December 1852, a severe storm damaged the causeway that Abel could not afford to repair and the FRC happily bought him out for £15,000 (the equivalent of around £2 million today).

Nowadays Foulney Island is owned by Cumbria Wildlife Trust and is a haven for migrating birds and rare marine shingle plant life. It is regularly cut off by high tides and I can thoroughly recommend getting stranded there on a warm sunny afternoon with a good picnic and a pair of binoculars for a spot of very peaceful birdwatching.

Moving inland towards Furness Abbey, there is a spectacular viewpoint to be had from the stile just behind Bowesfield Farm (easy to spot on an OS map). From this vantage point, you can see both Furness Abbey and Bow Bridge nestled among the trees and it is particularly pretty during the autumn.

Approaching the abbey across Bow Bridge is an excellent way to get a feel for the site. The bridge was built in the fifteenth century with locally sourced sandstone and limestone and is a beautiful example of an old packhorse bridge. Although connected to the trading monks of the abbey, it also sits on one of the most important medieval trading routes in the North West and would have been a popular and much used crossing point for local traders.

When the abbey was constructed, the site would have been remote and untouched but with a ready supply of fresh water and timber nearby. There were no major towns in the area, and the easiest way to access the region would have been from the sea or the sands. The abbey was

Roa Island Causeway.

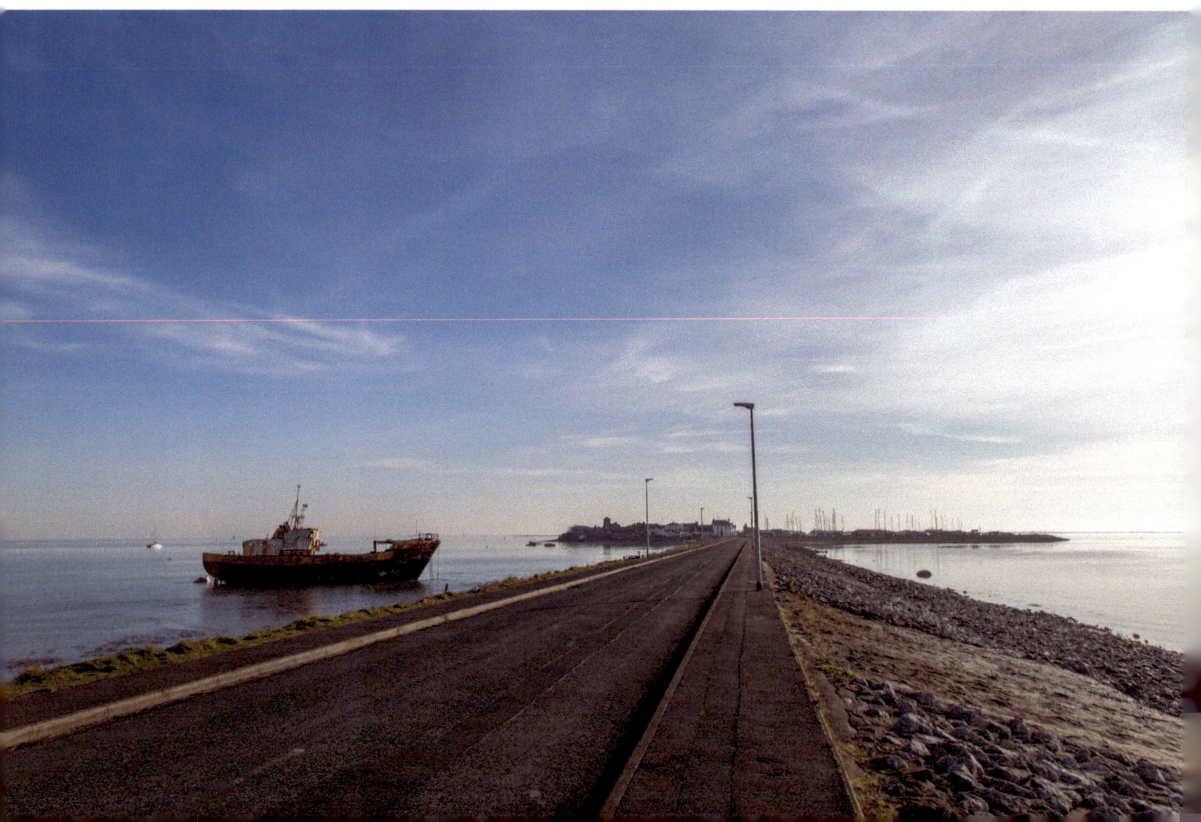

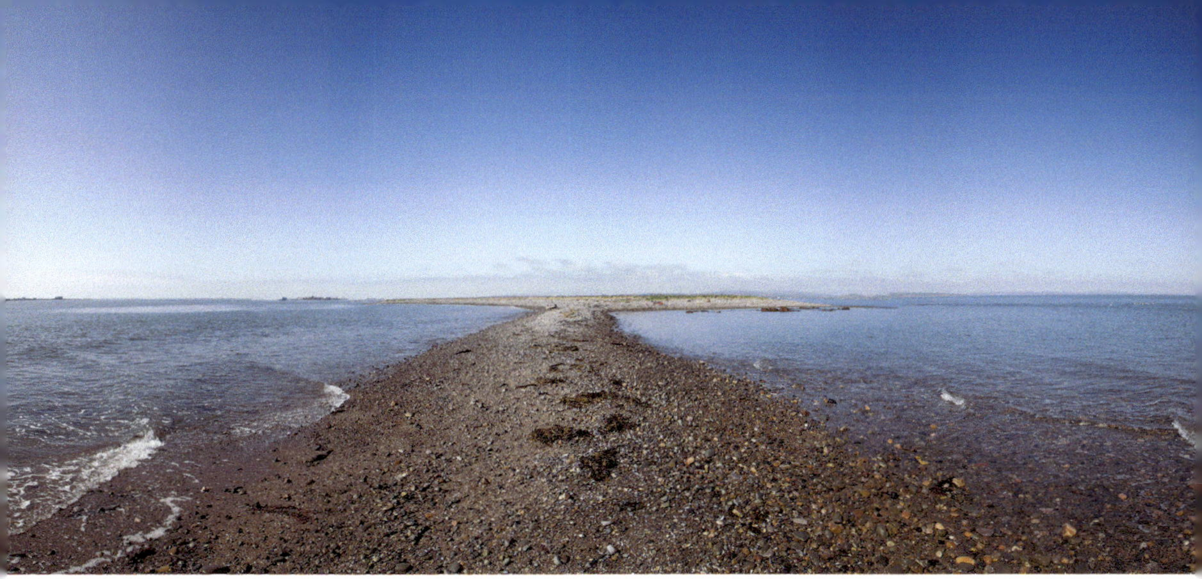

Above: Cut off by the tide on Foulney Island.

Below: Bow Bridge.

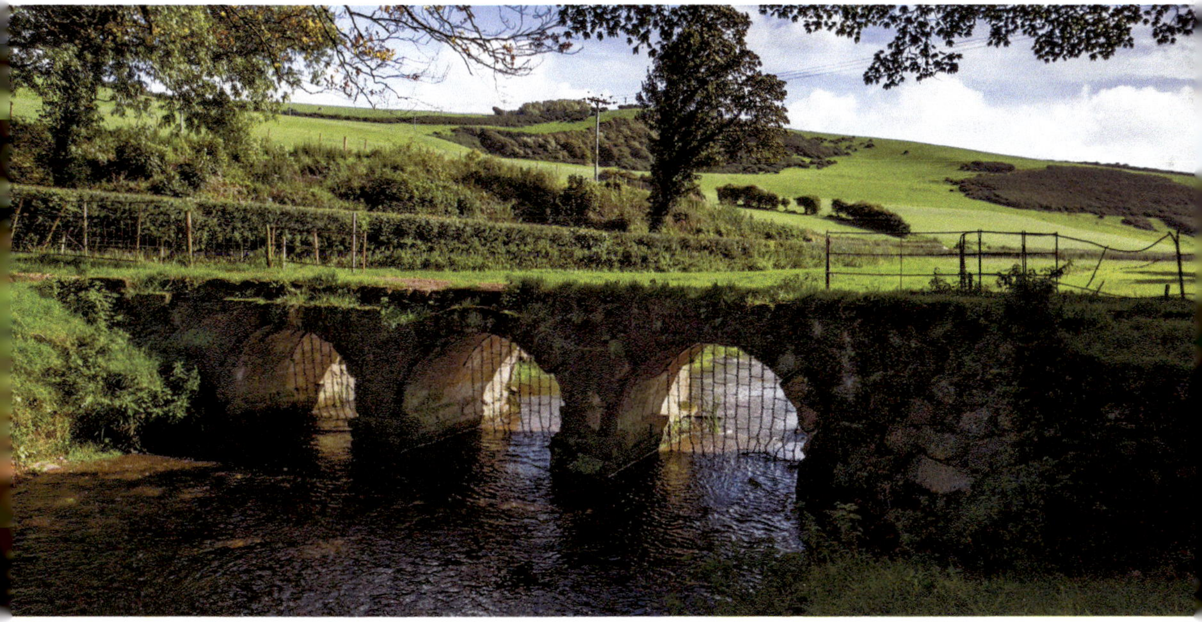

originally part of the Order of Savigny and was absorbed by the Cistercian Order in 1147. Although parts of the abbey existed at this time much more was added during the twelfth and thirteenth centuries. The abbey initially prospered before a series of crises (plague, famine and war with France) badly affected the Cistercian Order. During the fifteenth century the abbey was in decline with reduced land holdings, fewer monks and deteriorating relationships with local landowners. One local landowner took the abbot to court charging that 'the said Abbot and more than 22 of his monks behaved in a riotous manner'.

On 9 April 1537, Furness Abbey became the first of the major monasteries to be dissolved when the abbey was stripped of its assets and much of the building was dismantled. Over

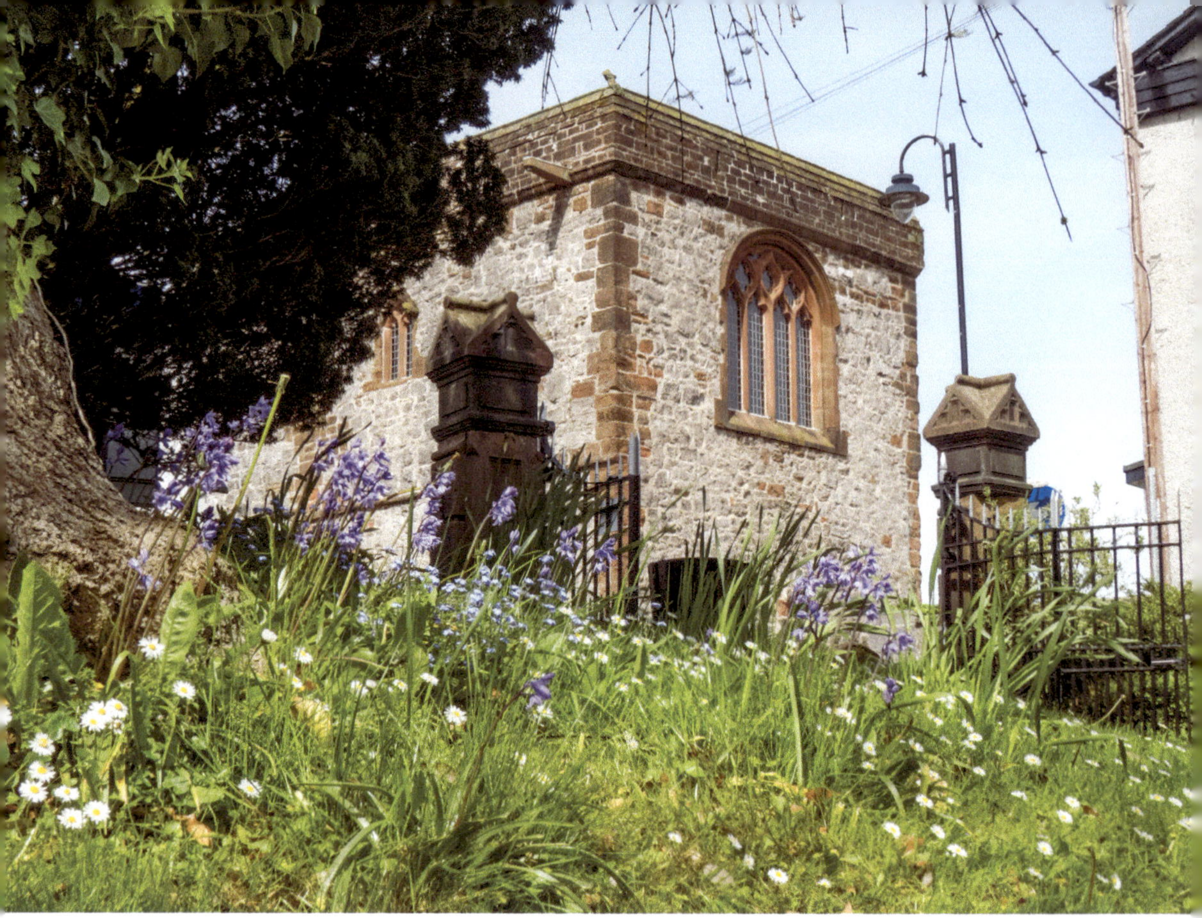

Dalton Castle.

the intervening years, it passed through numerous hands before arriving, by marriage, into the Cavendish family. In 1847, the railway was built right through the middle of the site, much to the consternation of many people, including William Wordsworth. The upside was that a lot of archaeological research was carried out during the construction of the railway, which in turn brought in many visitors and stimulated an interest to protect and preserve what remained. In 1923, Lord Richard Cavendish handed the remains of the abbey to the guardianship of the state, with the present car park and museum opening in 1982.

From Furness Abbey, it's a relatively short walk to Dalton-in-Furness and the castle tucked away at the top of the town. It's not open every day, so it's best to check ahead if you're keen to see inside. It's 45 feet high and 30 feet wide with walls up to 6 feet thick and was most likely built to defend the town from raiders from the north. It also served as the local courts of justice and prison and was overseen by the Abbot of Furness. It ceased holding prisoners in 1774 but the court leet (local court of record) was held there until 1924. These days, it's in the safe hands of the National Trust.

Having passed through Little and Great Urswick the route winds over a beautiful hill with far-reaching views before dropping down to Ulverston via the sixteenth-century Swarthmoor Hall, regarded as the birthplace of the Quaker movement. The hall was built by local lawyer George Fell in 1568 then passed to his son Thomas, a travelling judge. Thomas' wife Margaret was interested in the teachings of George Fox, one of the founders of the Quaker movement, and she persuaded Thomas to allow George to stay with them and hold meetings in the hall. Thomas died in 1658 and eleven years later Margaret married George and they lived in the hall for the remainder of their lives.

Down on the shores of the estuary is Conishead Priory, founded as a hospital in 1160 by the Order of Augustine and raised to a priory in 1188. It was seized and dismantled in 1537 then gifted by Henry VIII to William Stanley, who built a large private residence on the site. Having gone through several changes of ownership and been demolished and rebuilt, in 1878 it was bought by a Scottish syndicate who turned it into a Hyrdopathic Hotel, which was so popular it merited its own branch line, the remains of which can still be seen in the gardens.

From 1928 to 1972 it was owned by Durham County Miners Welfare Committee, where it provided a welcome retreat for miners and their families, apart from during the Second World War when it served as the largest military hospital in the North West. After that, the site remained empty for a number of years and it fell into disrepair. Some work was carried out in the 1980s before £500,000 was raised in 1991 to fully repair and restore the site. It is now owned and maintained by the Manjurshi Buddhist community, who host a number of international festivals and worship at the impressive golden temple now in the grounds.

Looking across the estuary you can't fail to spot the Levens Viaduct, originally built in 1857 and rebuilt in 1880. On 27 February 1903 it was the scene of a frightening train derailment, when an early morning mail train became stranded on the bridge and blown over in an almighty gale. Luckily the carriages all remained on the bridge and all of the passengers managed to crawl across the bridge to safety.

Holker Hall in nearby Cark is the present-day home to the Cavendish family. The first hall was built on the site in the sixteenth century and the hall we see today is the result of a

Conishead Priory.

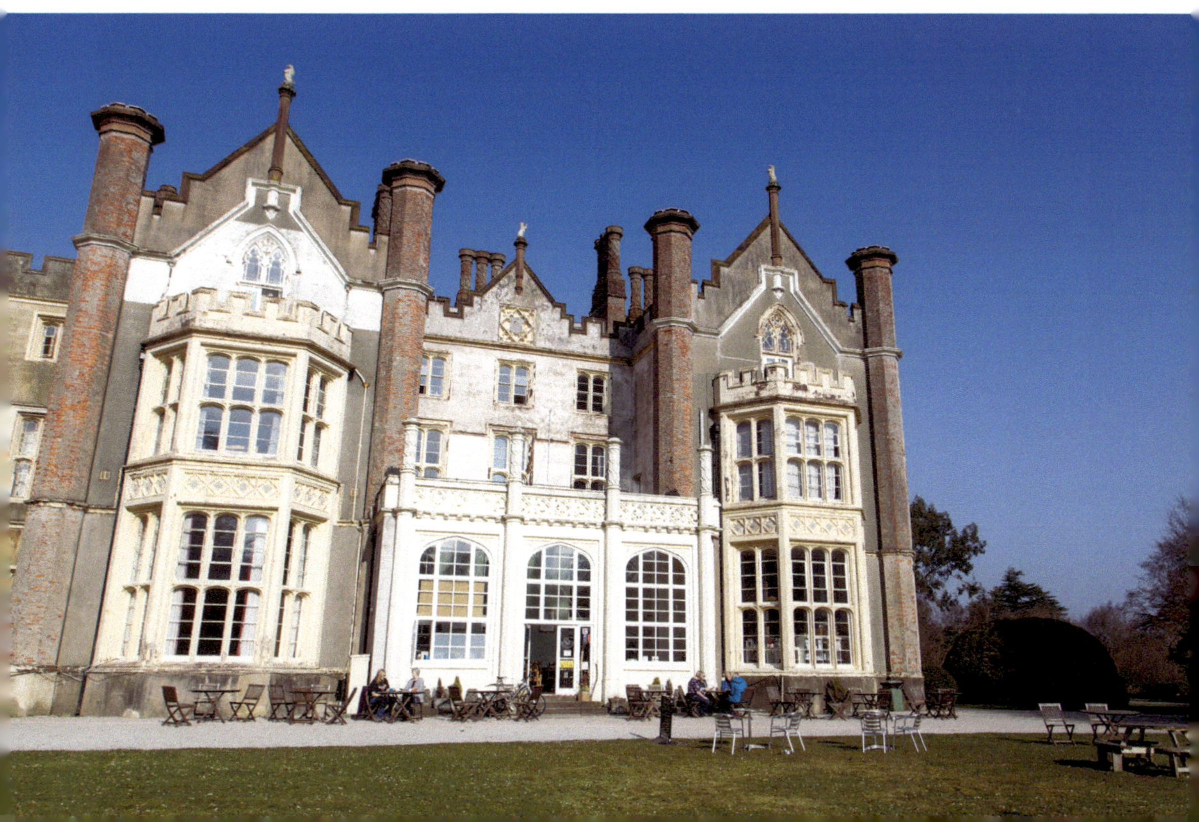

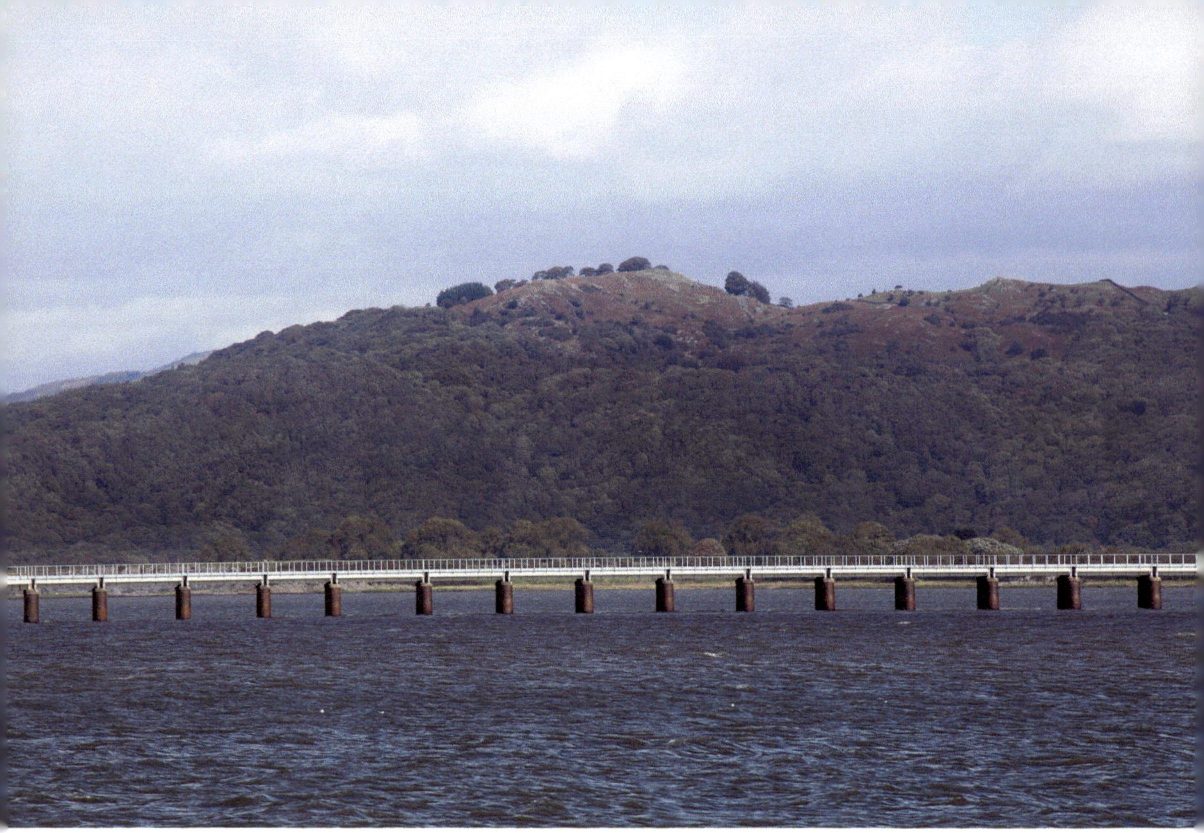

Above: Levens Viaduct.

Below: Cartmel Priory.

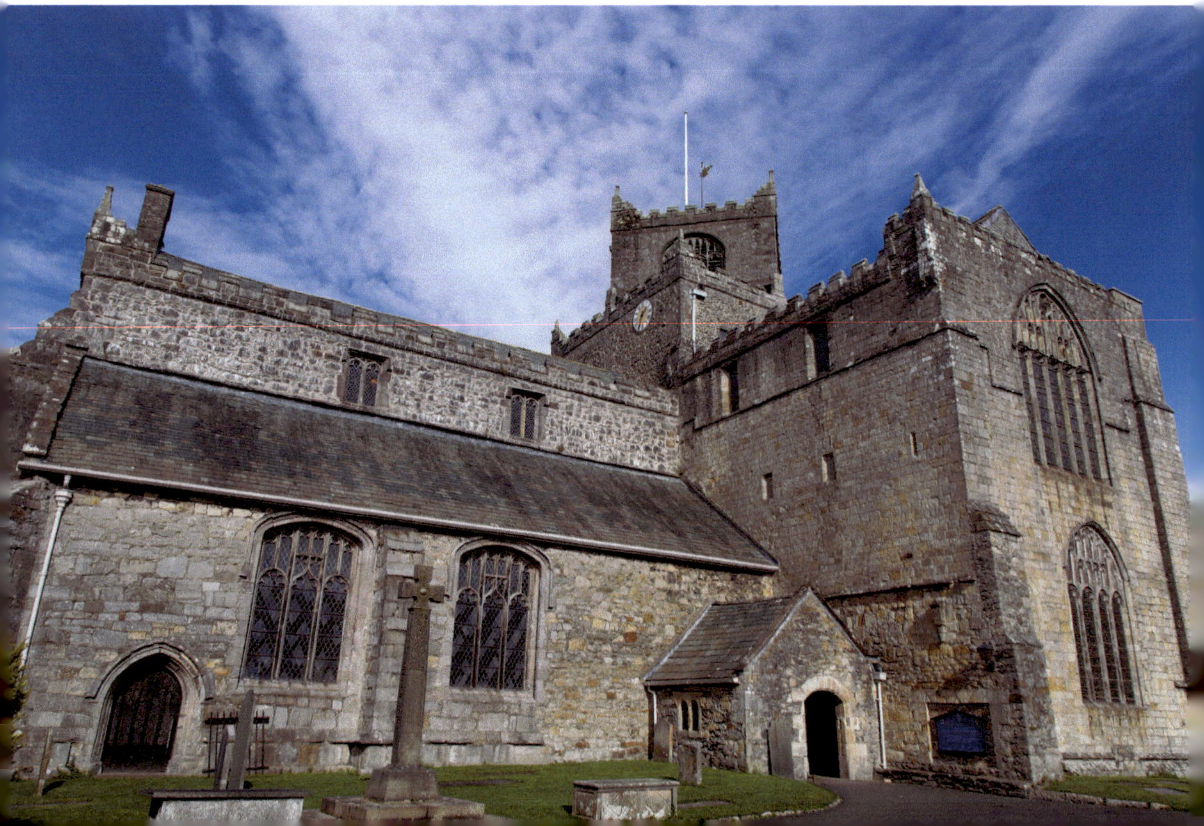

rebuild, following a disastrous fire in 1871. The grounds and hall are open throughout the year with a wide variety of fairs and festivals taking place.

The last major site of historic interest on the walk is Cartmel Priory. The priory was founded in 1189 by William Marshal, 1st Earl of Pembroke, and it was saved from the dissolution because he had been granted an altar in one of the chapels, allowing the locals to successfully argue that it was their parish church. It didn't escape unscathed though: the monks were expelled and the assets, including the lead roof, were stripped and ten laymen were hung, drawn and quartered at Lancaster for treason. The site has remained a place of worship throughout the centuries, ringing in the changes with electric lights being introduced in 1934, and is still the focal point of the beautiful village of Cartmel.

3. ROMAN ROAD PART I – PENRITH TO AMBLESIDE

Introduction

When we set out to walk this route, we planned it around the well-known old Roman road up and over High Street, but as we researched it, we quickly realised that the Romans were only a small part of the story. There were people here long before the Romans arrived and the landscape has continued to evolve thanks to all the people who came after. To be perfectly honest, we could have written an entire chapter just about Penrith but seeing as we'd gone to all the trouble of planning a route and booking accommodation, we thought we'd best crack on.

The Route

Although the Roman route starts from Brougham Castle, we travelled by train so started from the station. We wound down through the town passing St Andrew's Church and Dockray Hall, before picking up the A6 south and passing the old Plague Stone in the housing association grounds on our left. We carried on over Eamont Bridge

Brougham Castle.

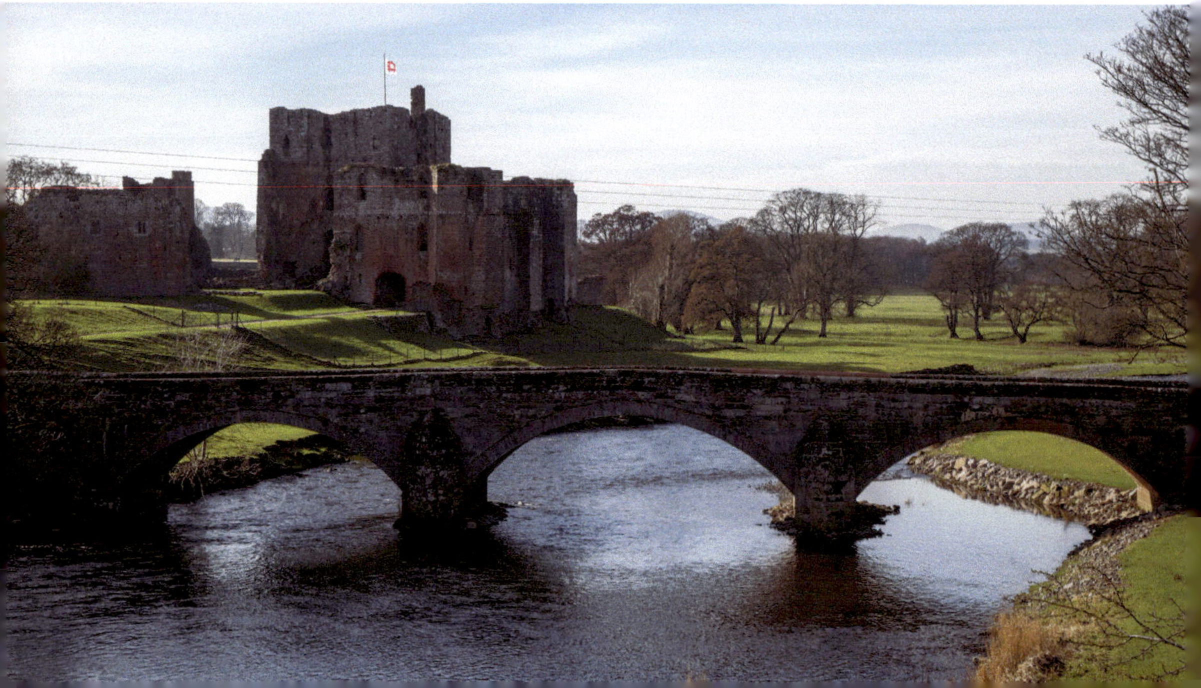

where we cheated and turned right past King Arthur's Round Table rather than head back to start at the castle (we'd already been there and had a long walk ahead of us!).

We continued on through Yanwath and Tirril, before picking up the road past Winder Hall and out onto the fell. We broke our journey at Pooley Bridge for the night before continuing up over High Street proper where, despite it being August, we were pelted by hail and strong winds, an apt reminder to always be prepared for anything on the high fells. Dropping down into Troutbeck via Beatrix Potter's old farm, we picked up Robin's Lane and followed it around the base of Wansfell and down into Ambleside.

On the whole the route is fairly easy to follow but there are sections up on top of the fell where the road becomes indistinct and later footpaths have taken precedence.

The History

This area is swathed in layer upon layer of history and rather than try to recount it chronologically we will, instead, piece it together as we follow the route.

First up is Penrith Castle, bang opposite the station. The castle was originally built in the fourteenth century by Ralph Neville on a site once occupied by a Roman fort and formed part of the defence of the Scottish border. His son, Richard, made it his headquarters and fortified it further. Following his death, the castle was granted to Richard, Duke of Gloucester and future Richard III, who lived there for several years making further extensive renovations. After he became king, the castle was no longer used as his residence and, barring a brief period of use during the Civil War, fell into disrepair. Parts of it were dismantled and, as was the custom at the time, the stones were put to good use in surrounding buildings.

Richard III is also involved in the second interesting site, Dockray Hall in the centre of town, where he lived while the castle was undergoing restoration work. For over 150 years, the hall was an inn known as the Duke of Gloucester in his honour and his coat of arms

Richard III's coat of arms on Dockray Hall.

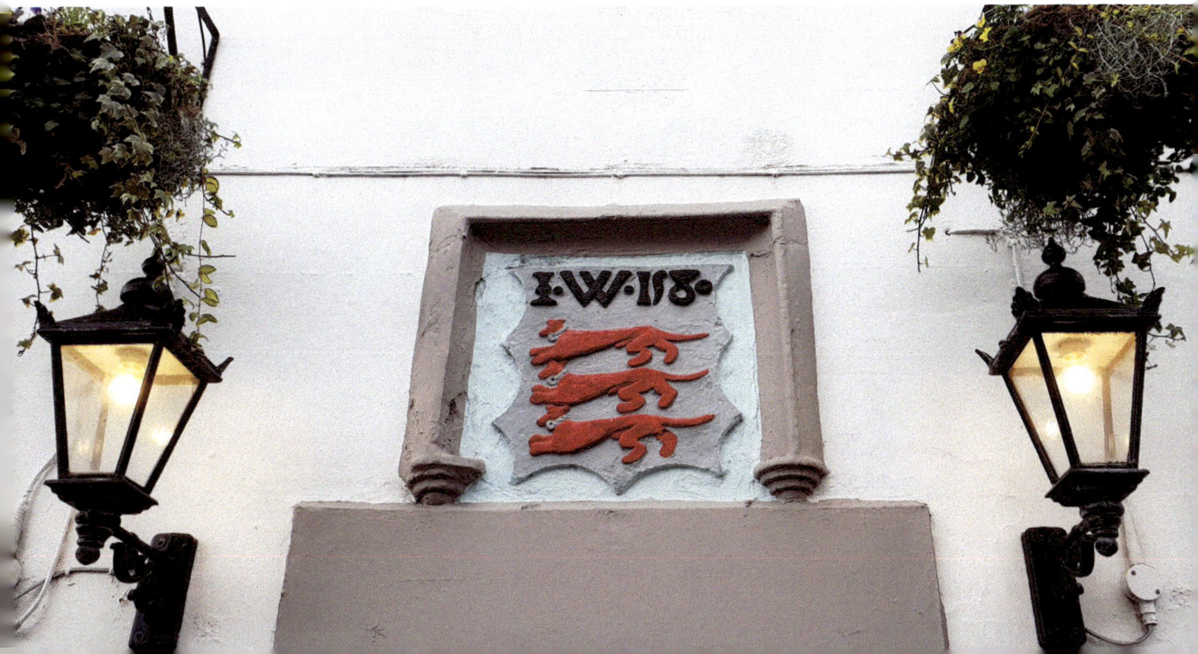

can still be seen above the doorway. It is said that the castle was linked to the hall by means of an underground tunnel over 300 yards long, which was used both as a means of escape if the castle came under attack and as a way to bring goods in and out away from watchful eyes.

A short walk from Dockray Hall is St Andrew's Church where you'll find an intriguing spot of Cumbrian folklore in the form of the Giant's Grave. The grave is marked by two large pillars with four smaller 'headstones' between them and early drawings show them to have originally been ornately decorated. It is most likely an early Christian burial site for a family or connected group of people but the folklore is far more entertaining. The story goes that the grave marked the final resting spot of Ewan/Owen/Hugh (depending which version you read) Caesarius, who towered over 17 feet tall and was renowned for hunting, fighting and killing wild boar.

Down along the A6 is the Plague Stone, a reminder of a turbulent time in Penrith's past. Between September 1597 and January 1599, 2,260 people in the town were wiped out by the plague, accounting for around one-third of the population. When towns were known to have the plague they were put into isolation, which made things like food difficult to come by so, on the outskirts of the towns, plague stones were placed where traders could leave food at a safe distance and the locals would drop their money into a hollow filled with vinegar to disinfect it. Penrith's stone survives and is now in the grounds of a housing association but easily visible and accessible from the road.

Eamont Bridge crosses what was once the boundary between Cumberland and Westmorland. The bridge itself is one of the oldest in the country still in regular use and it's thought that it was constructed during the fifteenth century before being widened in the nineteenth and twentieth centuries.

Brougham Castle stands on what were the remains of the ancient Roman fort of Brocavum and there are the remains of a small marching camp on the other side of the A66 (which broadly follows the route of another Roman road). Roman legionnaires were expected to be able to march 20 Roman miles (18.4 miles or 30 km) in a day and this fort sits 22 miles south of Carlisle and 20 miles north of Brougham Castle, with Ambleside fort 20 miles to the south-west.

Giant's Grave.

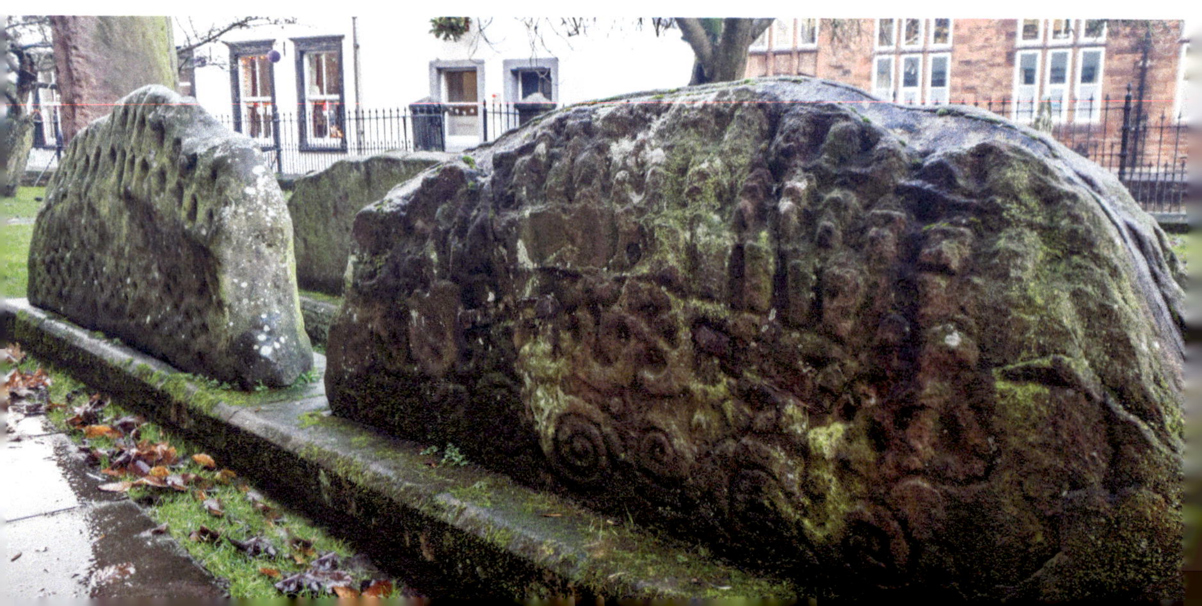

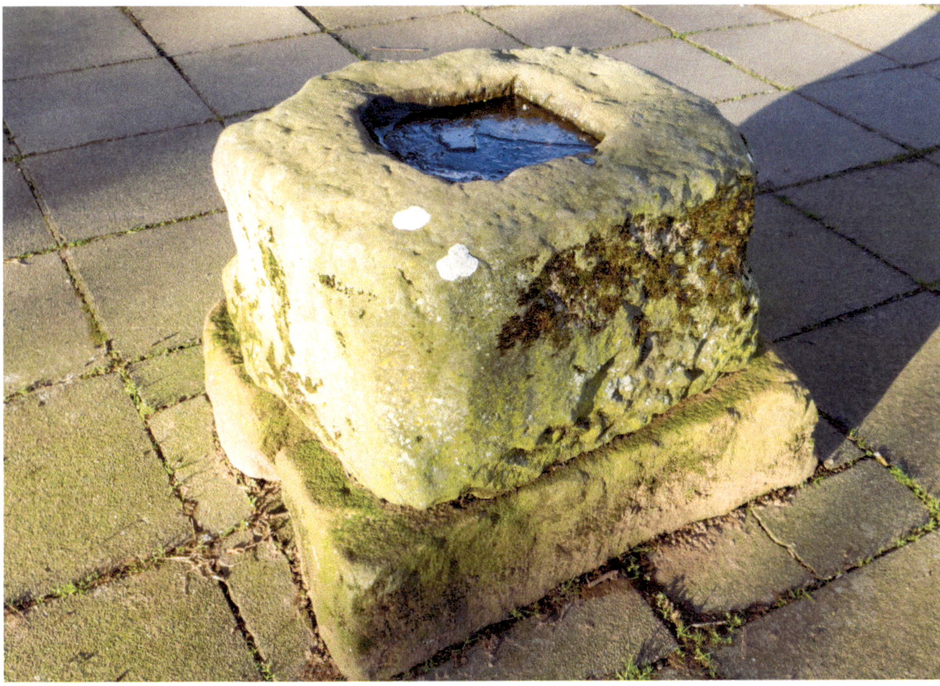

Plague Stone.

Marching 20 odd miles a day wouldn't have been much fun for them. The typical legionnaire would have worn underwear, tunic, hobnailed boots, sandals, armour padding, armour, two belts, a sword, a dagger, padded cap, helmet, shield and javelin. Then there would have been the yolk they had to carry with all their bedding, pots and food on it, with the whole lot weighing in at around 5 stone – and we were commenting that our backpacks were feeling a little heavy...

Around 1214, Robert de Vieuxpont acquired the land on which Brougham Castle is now built with the aim of protecting King John's land against raiders from the north, and stones from the old Roman fort were used in the construction of the castle. As with many castles in the region, it played many important roles in British history, including the Wars of the Roses. The castle fell into disrepair but was briefly revived in the seventeenth century when Lady Anne Clifford, an important figure in the history of the region, resided there and upgraded and improved the building. She was such a strong character that when it was suggested to Oliver Cromwell that he should stop her building, he replied, 'Let her build what she will, she shall not be hindered by me.' There is also reputed to be a skull hidden in the walls that keeps the ghosts at bay. Apparently, any time that a previous resident tried to remove the skull from the hall, the ghostly goings on increased dramatically until the skull was returned, so one resident buried it deep in the walls and they've had no trouble since.

Heading out towards High Street the road passes two sites that remind us of man's presence in the region long before the Romans: King Arthur's Round Table and Mayburgh Henge, both thought to be of Neolithic origin. Although the exact purpose of these sites will never be fully known, they were both clearly of huge significance and it's thought that jousting may have taken place at King Arthur's Round Table. Originally there were a series

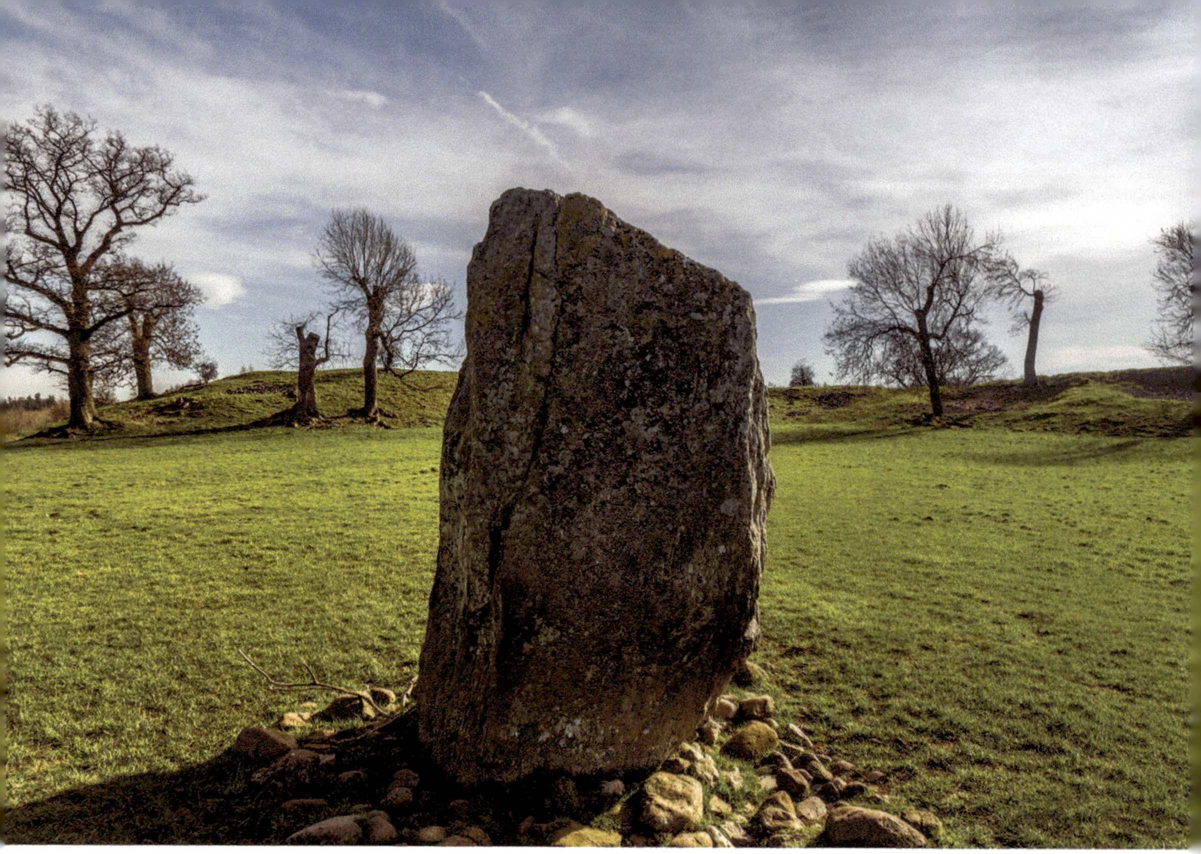

Mayburgh Henge.

of standing stones at Mayburgh Henge but now only the central stone remains with the raised bank surrounding it creating an ethereal amphitheatre.

Travelling out through Tirril and on to Celleron the Roman road finally leaves tarmac and climbs up past Winder Hall (an imposing seventeenth-century hall that is now a dreamy but expensive holiday let) and out onto Heugh Scar where there are some glorious views out over Ullswater. The poet Thomas Gray visited the area in 1769 and his descriptions were so vivid that artist Joseph Farringdon followed in his footsteps five years later to paint the views originally described. There is a peace and tranquillity to this spot that Farringdon captures beautifully, and although the local town of Pooley Bridge has grown, the view has lost none of its magic.

Soon the route passes through another Neolithic site, known as The Cockpit, on Moor Divock. Being broad and flat with rich soil and a good supply of running water, this would have made a great place for an early settlement. Numerous hut circles have been found together with a small stone circle and a number of tumuli. Some of the tumuli were opened during excavations in the early twentieth century and were found to contain Bronze Age remains and relics.

Apart from admiring the stunning views and wondering how on earth anyone could have ever considered turning Ullswater into a reservoir (which happened in the 1960s and was successfully defeated by Lord Birkett who sadly died two days after his victory and now has Birkett fell named in his honour), there's not a lot of other remains to explore up on the top of the fell. It's a fairly straightforward walk (apart from when you're getting hammered by hail) so there is plenty of time to enjoy your surroundings.

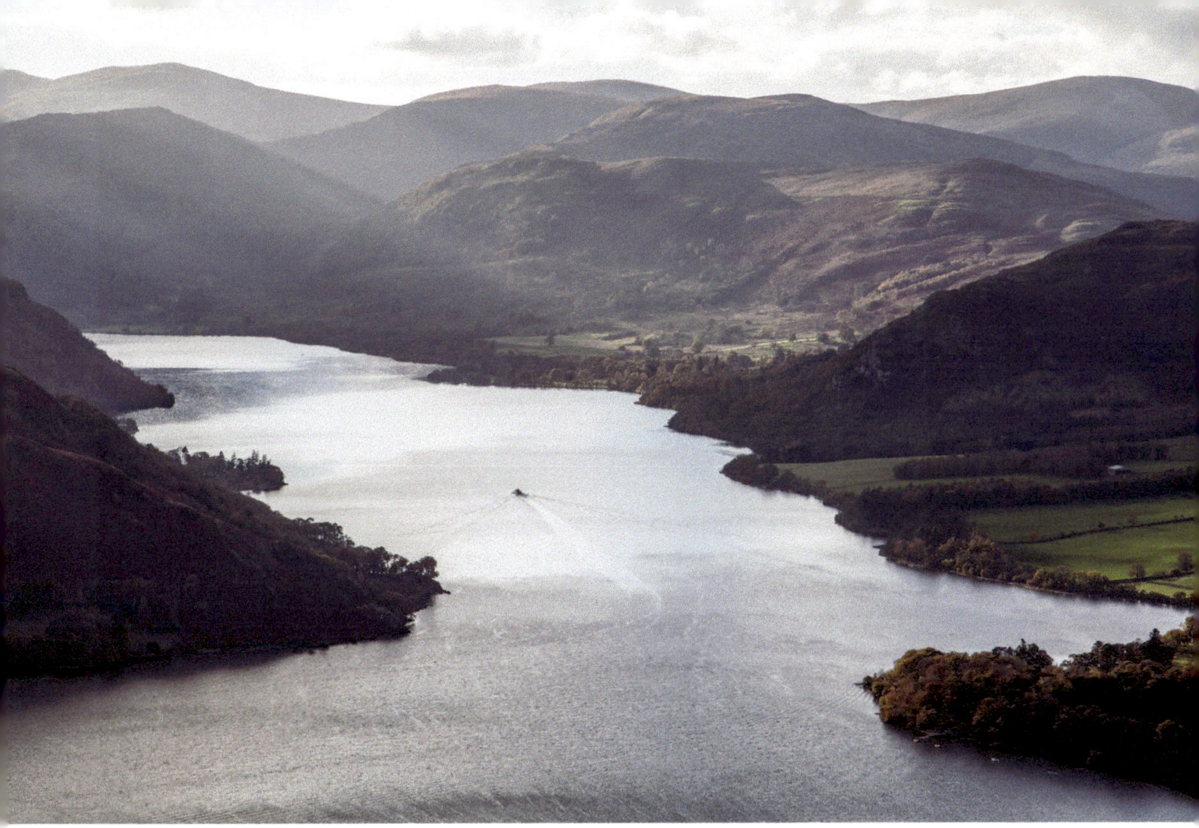

Above: Ullswater.

Below: 'The Cockpit' on Moor Divock.

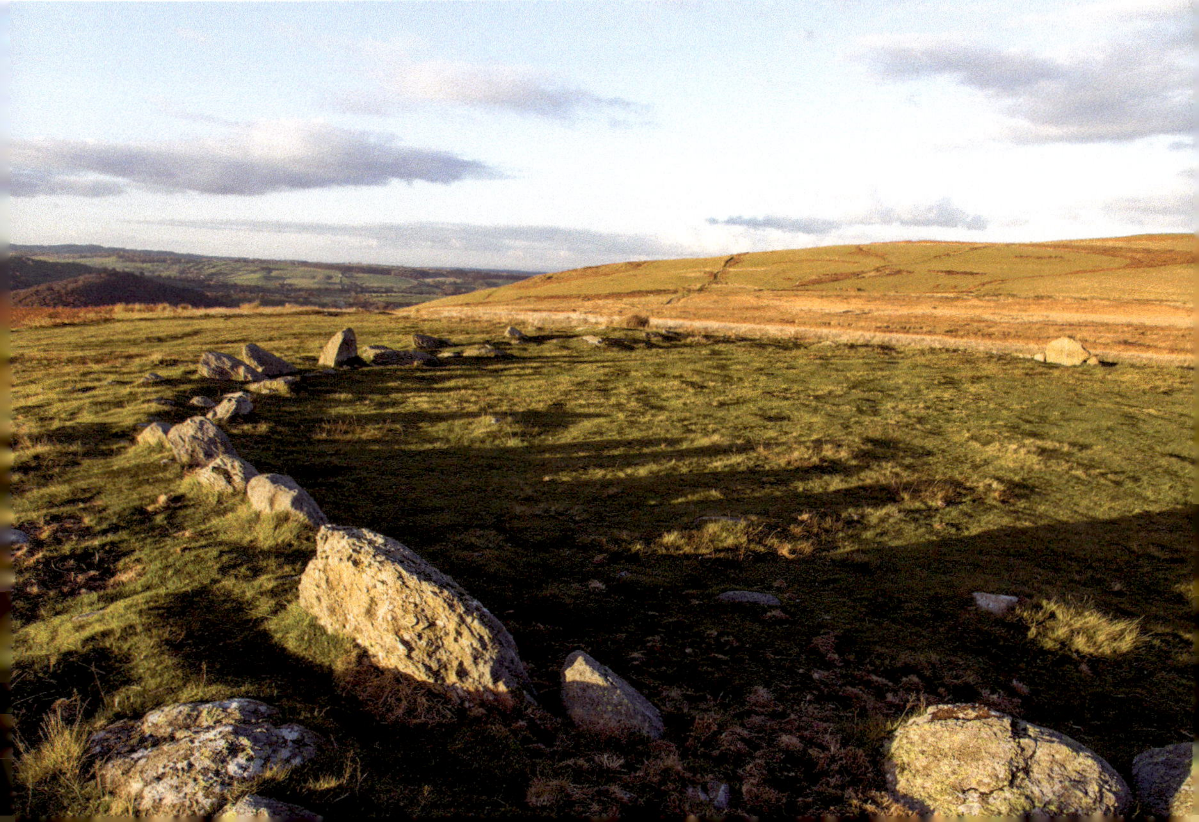

Racecourse Hill is so named because it really did hold horse races and fairs on its summit until the mid-nineteenth century. The site would have been a central meeting point and a vital catalyst for communication and trade in the days when valley communities were very remote.

As the Roman road drops down to the valley floor it passes Troutbeck Farm, which, in 1923, was bought by Beatrix Potter to protect it from development. From here, she successfully bred Herdwick sheep and became well respected in local farming circles, becoming the first female elected president of the Herdwick Sheep Breeders' Association in 1943. The house is not open to the public but there are plenty of gorgeous 'Herdies' grazing in the nearby fields.

Further along the valley is the beautiful Townend House. The house was built in 1623 by George Browne, who was an enthusiastic woodcarver, and it's well worth a visit to the house to see the many fantastic items he left his mark on. The house remained in the same family right the way through to 1923 when it was handed over to the National Trust – beautifully preserved and kept exactly as the Brownes left it. The distinctive Westmorland chimneys give it an imposing feel but inside its cosy and homely and the guided tours give a fascinating glimpse in everyday life in the house and surrounding valley.

The final section of the walk into Ambleside is a gentle leg-stretcher along a nice broad path. We've walked that way many times and have always wondered about a random stone pillar in a nearby field and have finally discovered what it is: it's apparently one of twenty-one viewing stations that were essential for all Victorians to visit. They were popularised in a guidebook of the era and those undertaking the 'grand tour' were required to visit each pillar and admire the views.

Racecourse Hill.

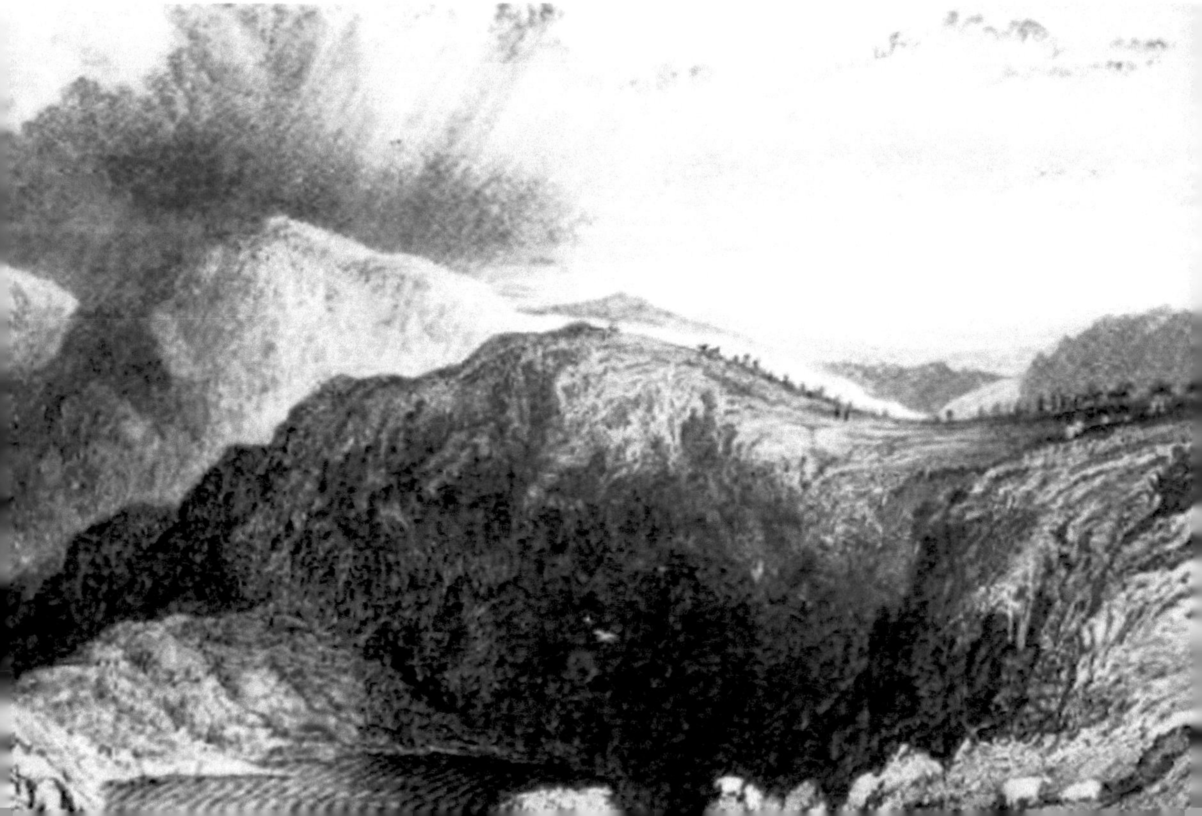

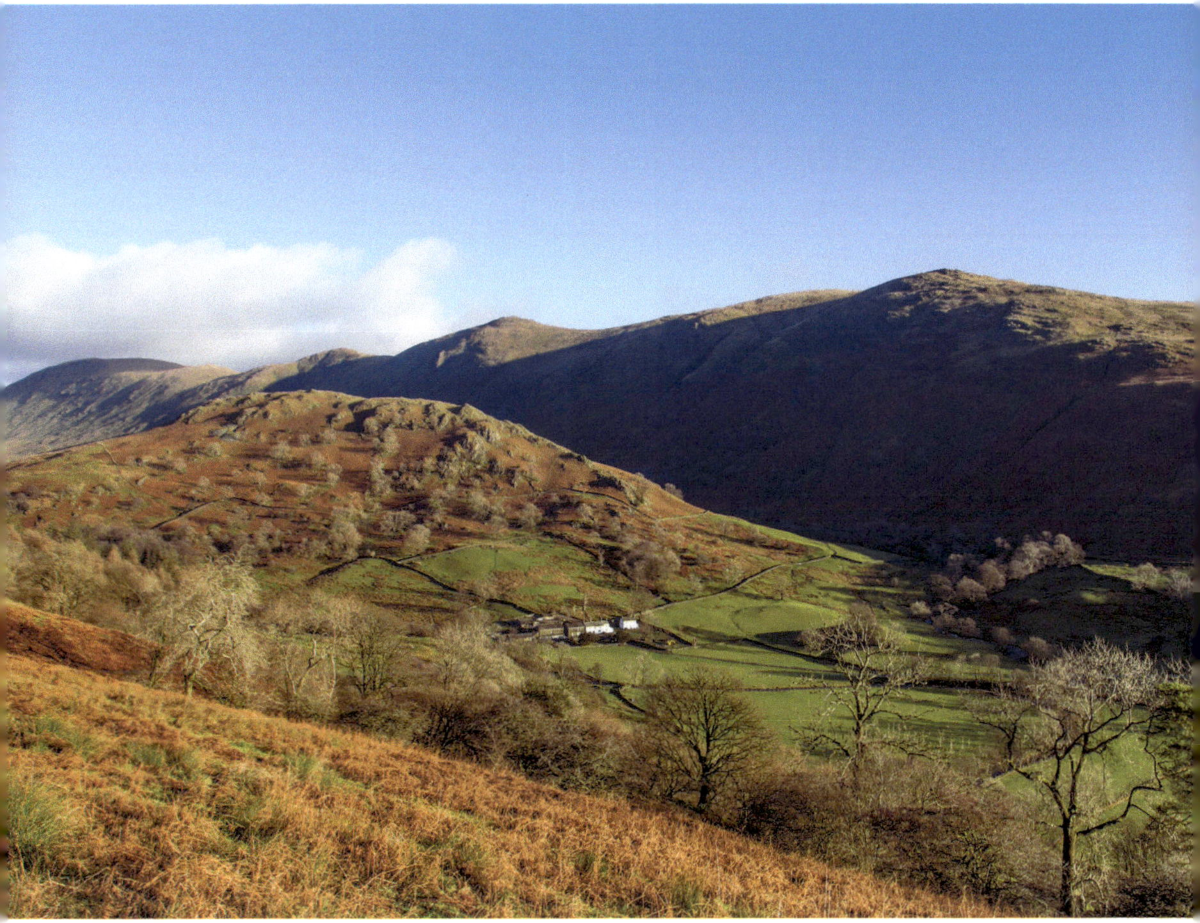

Above: Troutbeck Farm with High Street in the far background.

Below: Townend House.

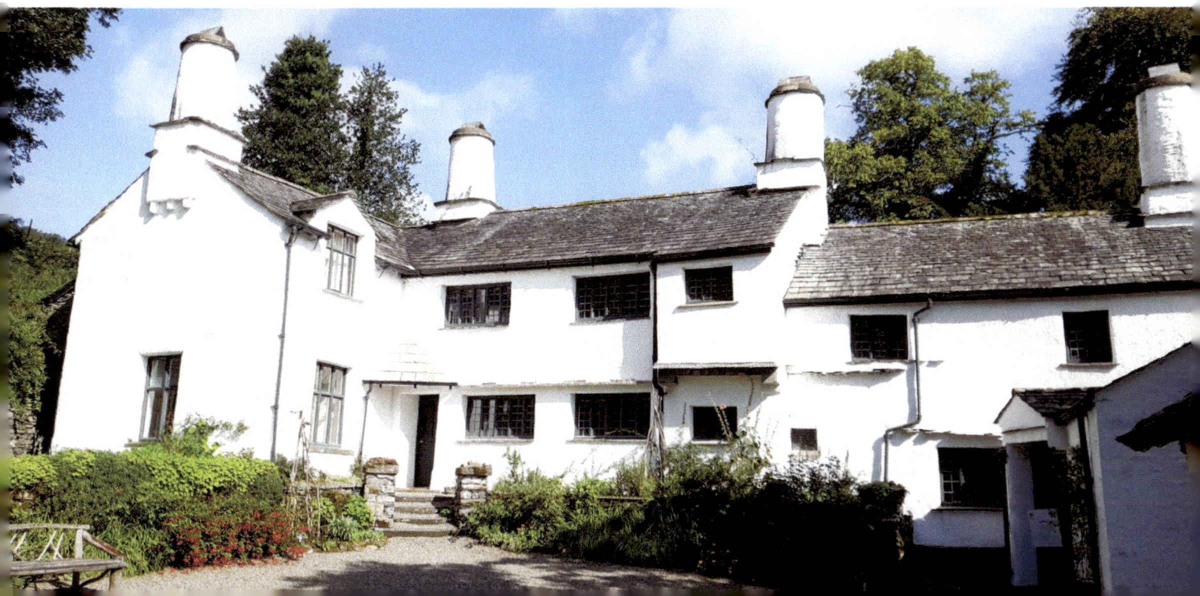

4. ROMAN ROAD PART II – AMBLESIDE TO RAVENGLASS

Introduction

This route is obviously the continuation of the route started in the previous chapter, but there's so much going on that we needed to split it into two. The local area is overflowing with fascinating history and sadly we can't cram it all in so these are our highlights. As with the previous chapter, although this is primarily known as a Roman route, if that was all we focussed on we'd be missing out on a whole pile of fascinating historical nuggets.

The Route

I'll be honest up front, we deviated from the original Roman road for a couple of main reasons – firstly because it poured with rain for the whole of the first day of our walk. We'd have loved to have the luxury of rescheduling but sadly that wasn't an option so we hauled

Wrynose Bottom.

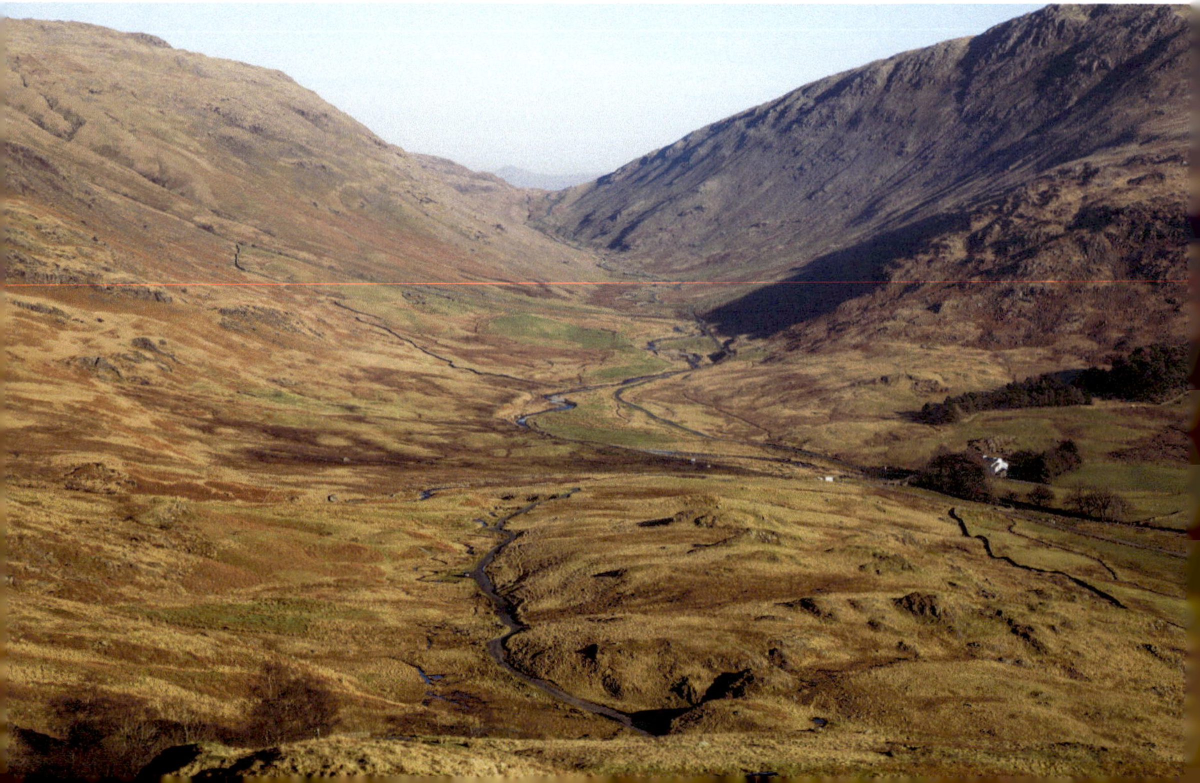

on the waterproofs and cracked on, avoiding a section of the walk at Hardknott Pass, which looked somewhat swampy, and stuck to the road instead. The other reason we deviated was that the original route passed over a stream and there was no footbridge. Given the pounding rain, the stream was in spate so we thought it unwise to attempt a crossing.

The actual route runs out of Ambleside through Clappersgate, then along the main road through Skelwith Bridge to Colwith Brow. From there it drops down to wind through High Park and Stang End into Little Langdale, where it gets a whole lot easier as it pretty much follows Wrynose Pass to Wrynose Bottom. Here the Roman road is clearly marked on the OS map but we stuck to the road for the reasons above.

The original road loops around the fort at Hardknott Pass, before following the modern-day road down to Eskdale Green. From there it winds along the base of Muncaster Fell and was still the main road in use through the eighteenth century. The road then passes through Muncaster Castle grounds and up through Dovecote Wood, dropping into Ravenglass via the Roman Bath House.

The History

Although this route isn't all about the Romans, the Roman fort in Ambleside is obviously a good place to start. It originally began as a small wooden fort in the first century but by the second century the stone fort was built and was in use through to the fourth century. Although marked on maps as Galava, it's not completely certain that this is the correct name for it.

Roman maps were rudimentary at best and there are several accounts of Romans getting lost as they generally relied on local information to find their way around. That said, they did produce basic maps but these were generally of a highly practical nature for military use, featuring the important roads and forts, and bore only a passing resemblance to the actual geography. The Peutinger Table, a thirteenth-century copy of an original Roman map, is fascinating to study but tricky to match up to present-day locations.

Ambleside Roman Fort.

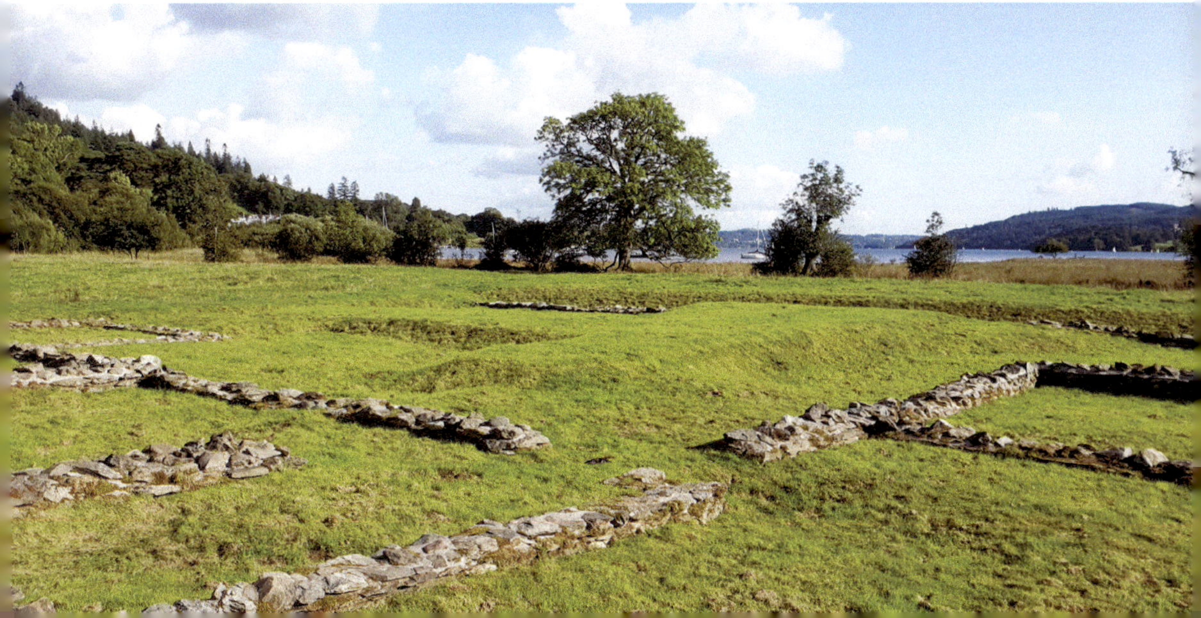

There is still plenty to see at the Ambleside site and there are lots of information boards that give a real feel for what life must have been like at that time. It is known that they used Windermere in some form, possibly for food and to move men and materials around the shores.

It's pretty hairy these days walking along the A593 with cars whizzing past, especially on the narrow sections, but it got us pondering how Romans built their roads and just how they got them to last so long, especially in such inhospitable places as the top of High Street and Hardknott Pass. Well, it turns out there were several stages to the building of the roads, which went something like this:

- Firstly army builders would clear the ground of rocks and trees – roads were always as straight as possible as it was the quickest route between two points.
- Next a large trench would be dug and filled with stones, pebbles and rudimentary cement on top. This would have been packed down as firmly as possible.
- Then would come a layer of more cement, possibly mixed with broken tiles.
- On top of this would sit paving stones, fitted together as tightly as possible and with a small camber to improve drainage.
- Lastly keystones would be slotted in onto either side to keep everything in place and a drainage channel cleared for water runoff.

You have to be impressed with how long their roads lasted, especially given the volume of roadworks constantly needed on today's roads. Though, to be fair, the Romans generally travelled by horseback, on foot or with oxen-drawn carts so the roads didn't have to contend with the volumes we see today.

Wrynose Pass leading up from Little Langdale.

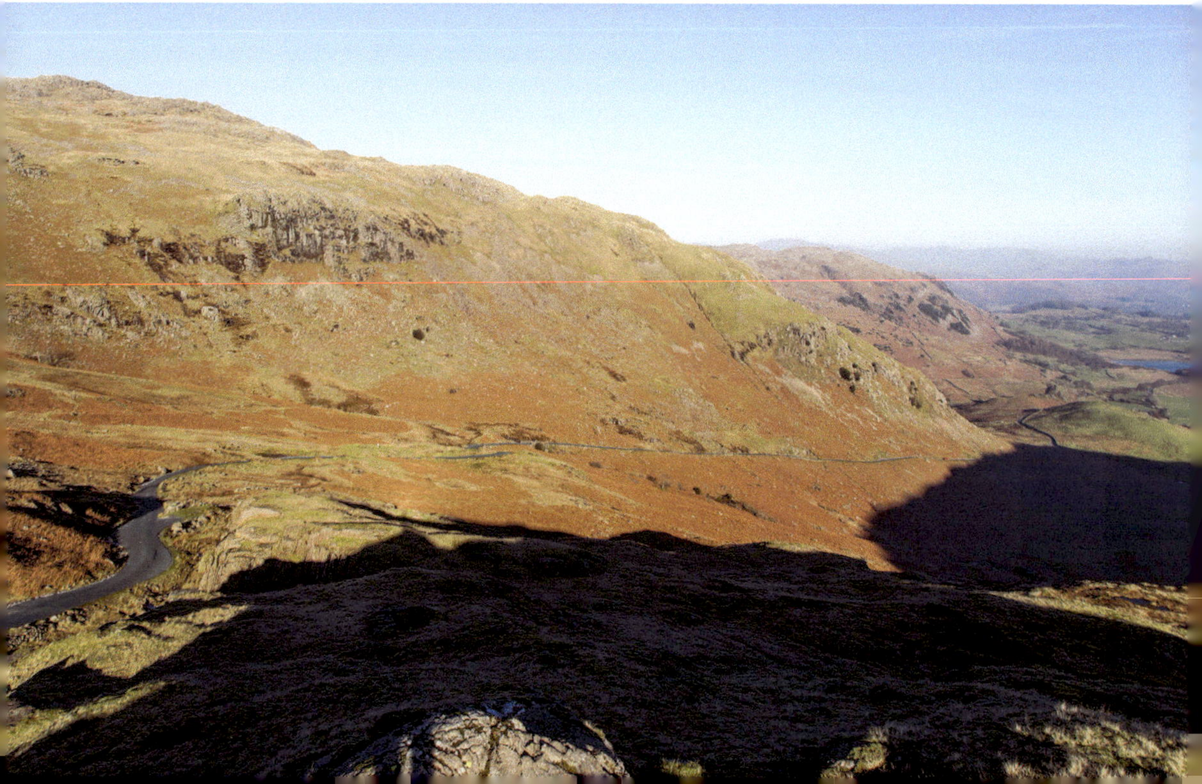

The stretch through Little Langdale was wonderfully peaceful and it's always been a quiet little valley with blissfully little mobile phone signal. Telephones first reached the valley in 1923 but a year or two later all the lines were brought down with snow; the reports from that time all focus on the problems of the wires all across the road with no mention made of the inconvenience of having no phones.

The route was also popular with Victorian visitors on charabanc tours who would journey up and over past Blea Tarn to the Old Dungeon Ghyll for lunch. The driver of the charabanc would stop at the top of the pass and blow his horn to let the inn know they were coming, with the number of blasts informing staff as to how many passengers to expect. The inn has always been popular with those drawn to the outdoors with many famous rock climbers staying there over the years, but surely the most intriguing guest was the future emperor of Japan, who stayed there as a prince and enjoyed a little rock climbing in September 1915.

At the end of the valley, just before the road climbs up to Wrynose Pass, there's small mound in a field behind the farm. This is the Ting Mound, thought to have been the site of an ancient Viking assembly and situated here to take advantage of the road already put in place by the Romans. There's not a lot to see there today but it was clearly a site of some importance in the past.

The iconic Three Shires Stone at the top of Wrynose Pass was sadly missing when we visited, having been knocked over and damaged, possibly deliberately, in August 2017. It marked the historic point where the boundaries of Cumberland, Westmorland and Lancashire met and was made from limestone quarried near Cartmel. The National Trust is repairing it and hopefully it will soon be back where it belongs.

The route along Wrynose Bottom has an other-worldly feel of isolation and loneliness, despite the ever-present cars. It's a remote valley, high in the fells, and I wonder what the Romans made of it when they arrived for the first time. During the Roman occupation there was an era of climate warming known as the Roman Warm Period, so temperatures may have been a little warmer than today and less of a shock to those more familiar with a sunnier climate. Having waded through the surrounding fields, it seems appropriate that Hardknott Fort was known to the Romans as Mediobogdum.

Ting Mound.

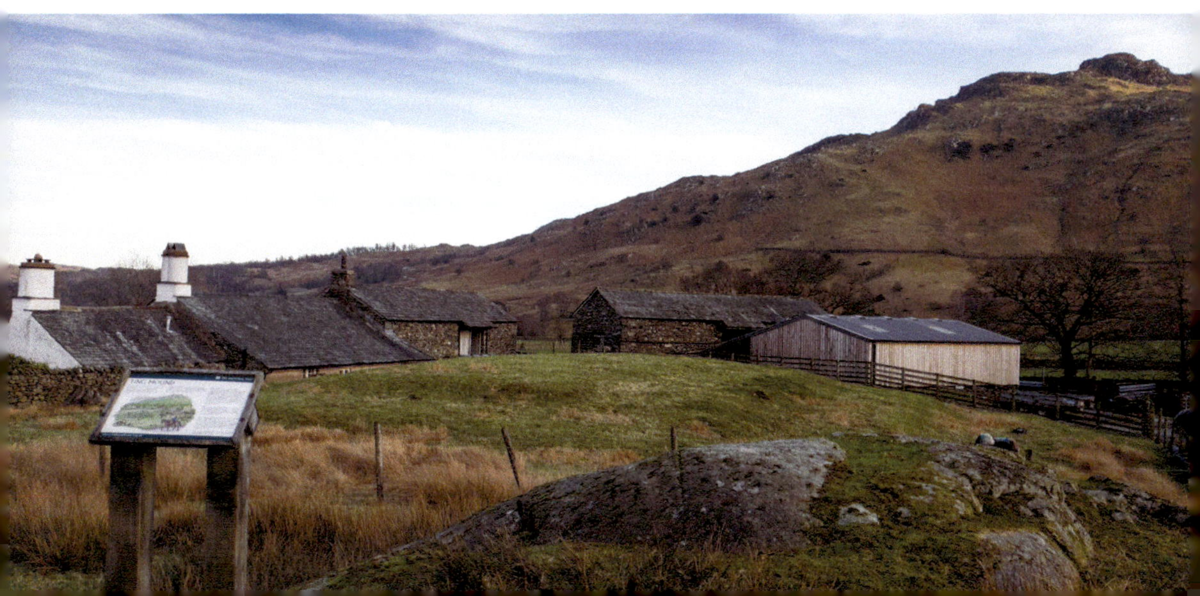

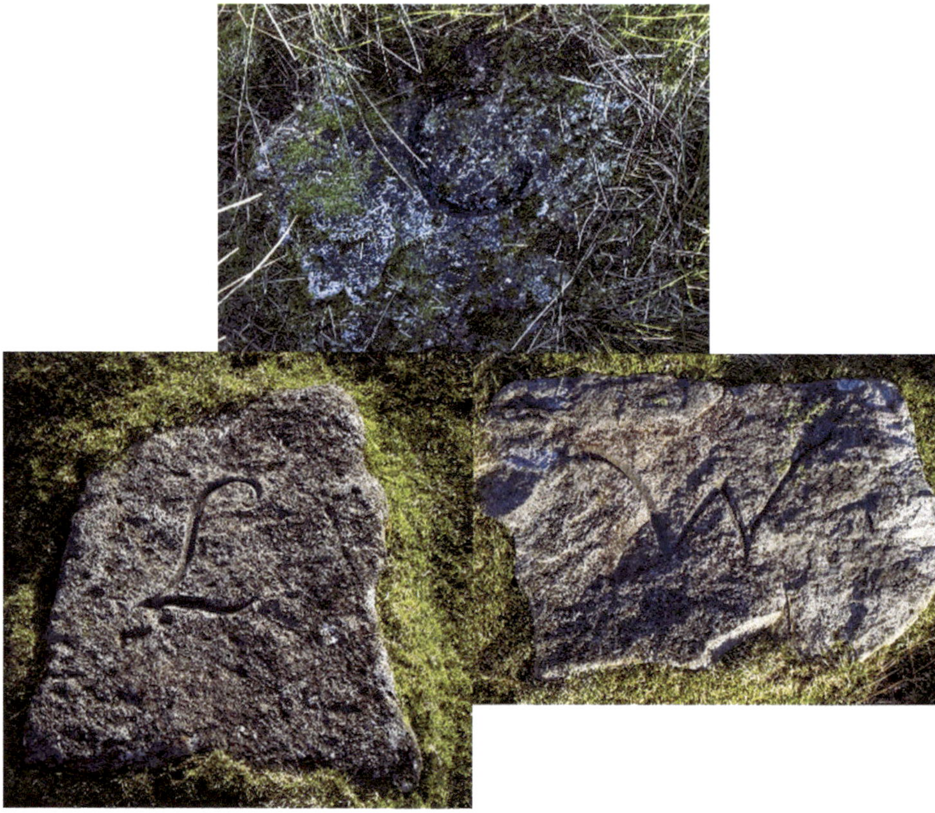

Remains of Three Shires Stone.

The current road route over Hardknott Pass deviates from the original Roman road, which stayed on the valley floor past Black Hall before climbing up the fell. We noticed this as a common feature when following the old routes; they often stay lower longer before shooting up and over the fells, whereas modern roads follow a more gentle gradient. I'll be honest, I haven't found any data on why this is, but I'm guessing it's to do with the fact that the valley floors were less exposed to the weather so time 'on top' was kept to a minimum.

The fort there is magnificent. The day we visited for the walk, the weather was foul but we've been lucky to be there completely alone on a warm, sunny evening and the views are immense. It was built in the second century during the reign of Hadrian and housed a cohort of 500 men. The layout of the fort is still very easy to see including the commanding officer's house, the granaries and the nearby parade ground.

Dropping down through the Eskdale Valley was an absolute treat, and although it's popular with visitors today, that wasn't always the case. In Maxwell Fraser's *Companion into Lakeland* he states, 'Those who avoid the Lake District because they fear it is overrun with tourists would do well to visit Eskdale.' In the 1959 journal of the Fell and Rock Climbing Club one report reads that 'Eskdale has never had much attraction for rock climbers', adding 'If you fancy climbing somewhere new, on unscratched routes, relatively free from vegetation ... Eskdale is the place for you.'

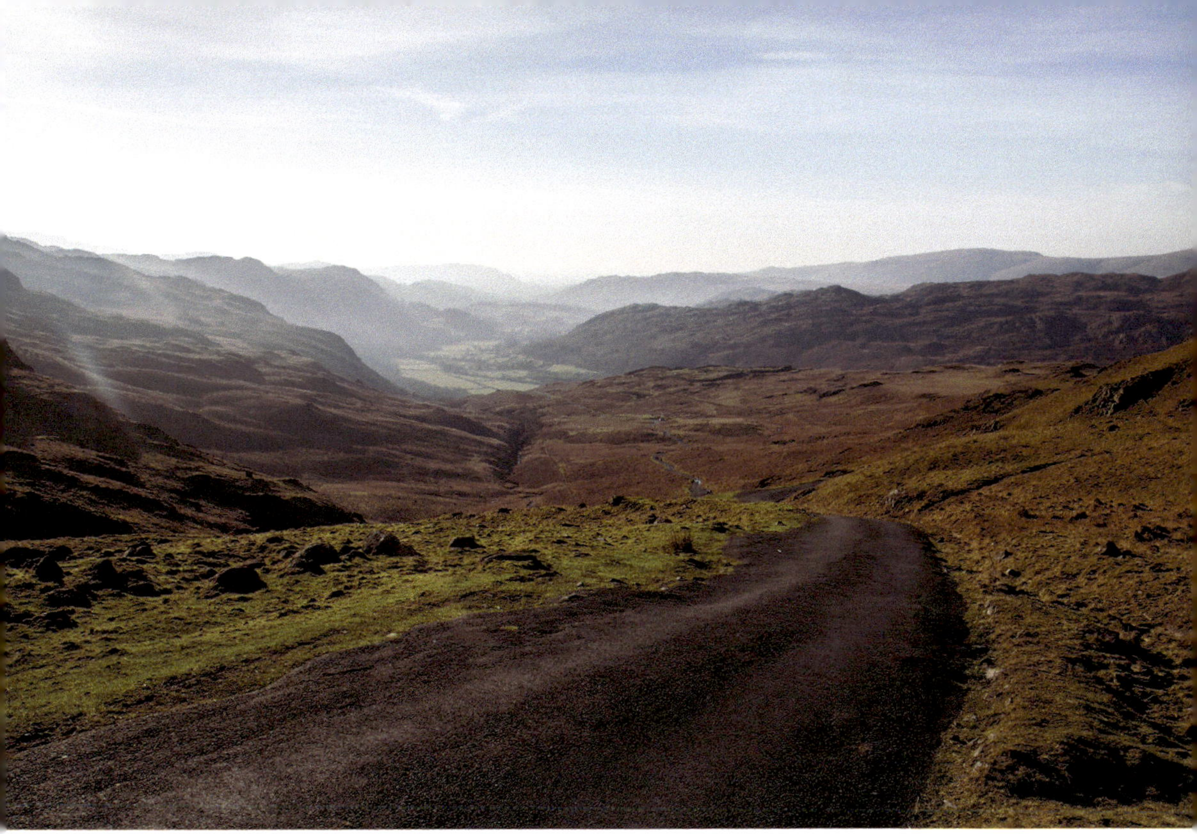

Above: Top of Hardknott Pass.

Below: Hardknott Roman Fort.

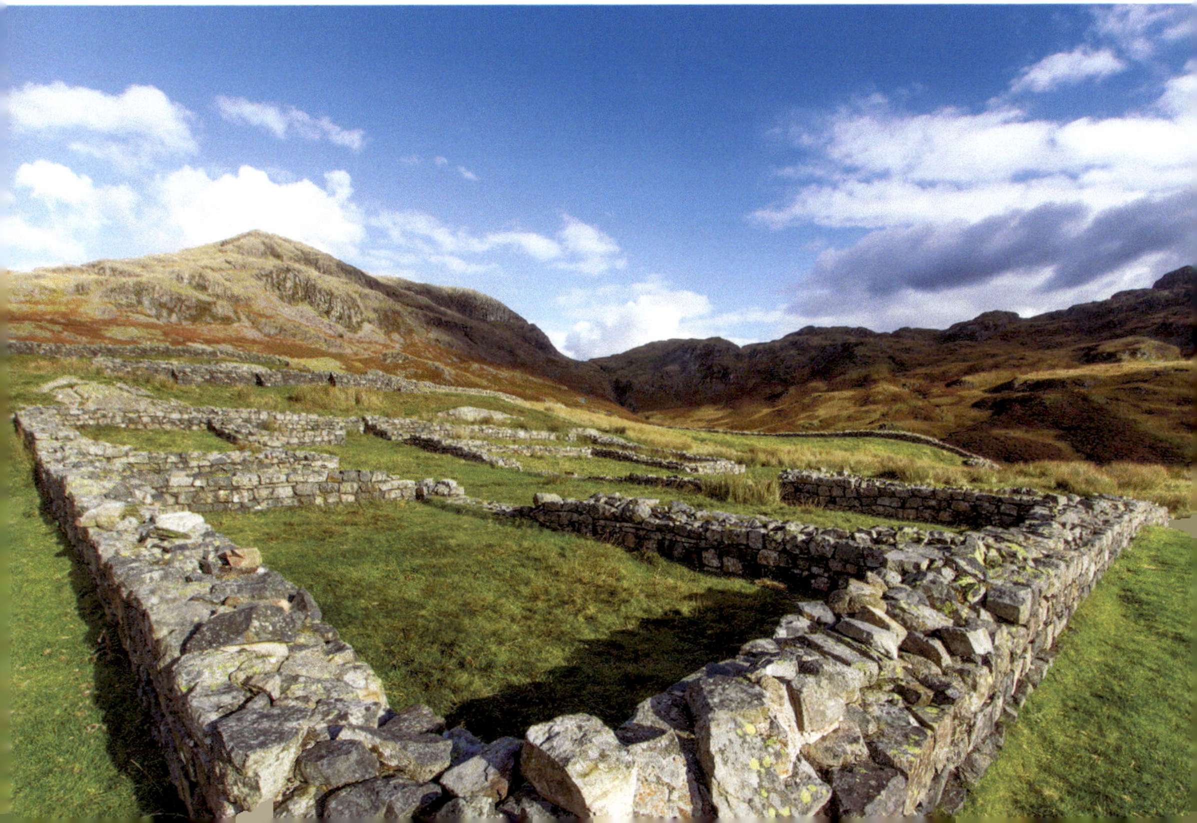

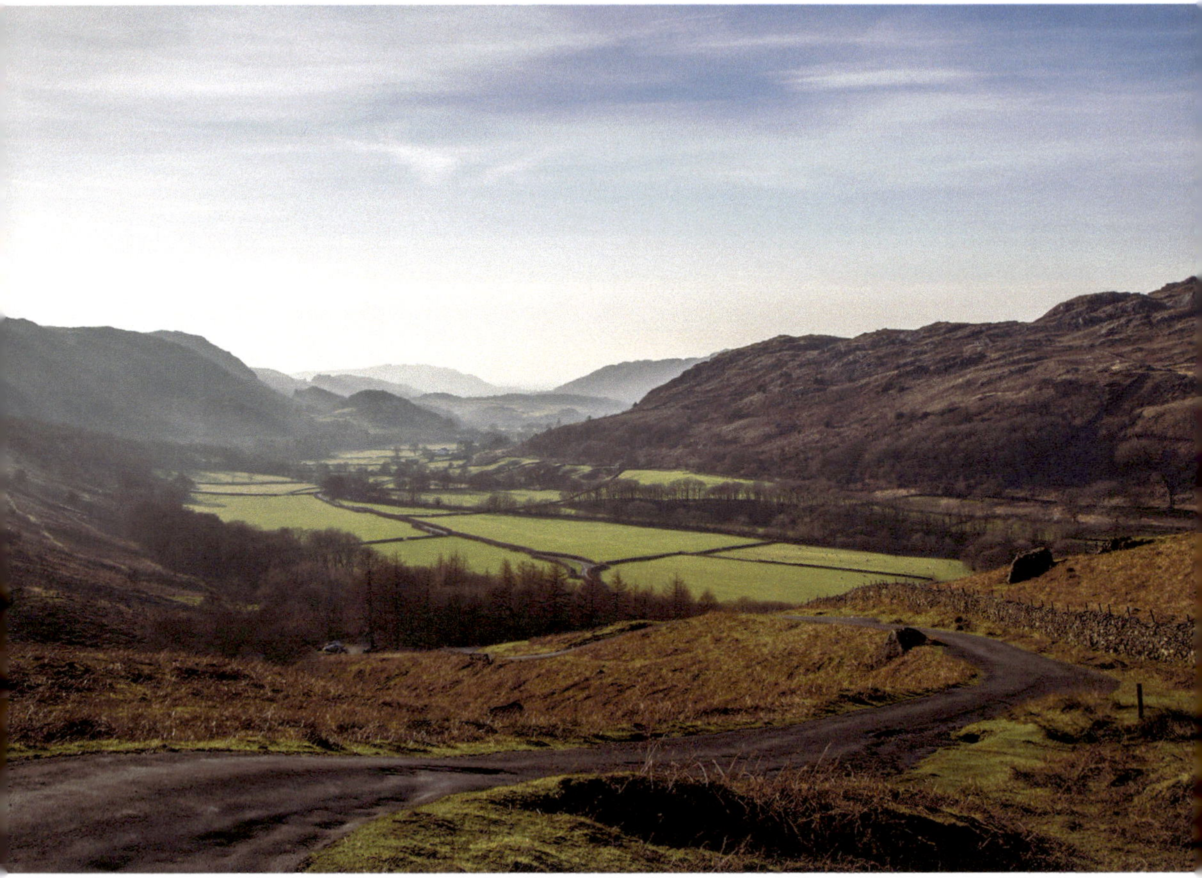

Eskdale Valley.

Of course in such a remote place there are a number of stories of hauntings and odd goings on. A long-deserted farmhouse in Eskdale Green is reputedly haunted by a man who posed as a gypsy woman to gain entry to the farmhouse where a woman lived alone with her baby. When she discovered the ruse, she waited until he fell asleep then poured boiling tallow down his throat and he still haunts the ruins. There's also the tale of a horse that ran away coming over the old corpse road with a dead body strapped to its back. It was never found and now still haunts the valley.

The most popular attraction in the valley these days is the Ravenglass & Eskdale Railway, known as La'al Ratty. The route dates back to 1873 but the present railway has been running since 1915, originally moving passengers and goods along the remote valley. Today it is a popular, and rather wonderful, visitor attraction with the journey from Ravenglass to Dalegarth, taking around forty minutes.

On the walk to Ravenglass you'll soon pass the King George Inn, which was originally named the King of Prussia Inn, before being retitled during the First World War. Further down, the route passes straight through the grounds of Muncaster Castle, which has been owned by the Pennington family for over 800 years and is home to a broad variety of events throughout the year.

The approach into Ravenglass passes the Roman Bath House, which was built alongside the fort that once occupied the field opposite. There are plenty of walls still left to admire at the bath house – in remarkable conditions considering they're over 2,000 years old – but nothing remains of the fort, although there have been many interesting pottery and jewellery finds over the years.

If this seems a convoluted way to approach Ravenglass then spare a thought for the folks who tried to get there via the coast road over the years. When John Wesley (one of the founders of Methodism) visited in 1759, it took him from 8 a.m. until midnight to travel from Bootle to Whitehaven, causing him to remark, 'I can advise no traveller to go this way, he may go round by Kendal and Keswick, often in less time, always with less expense and far less trial of his patience'.

In 1824 help was sought to improve the roads but ten years later there were still problems, highlighted by specific complaints about the inability of mail coaches to reach the area. When a new county road surveyor was appointed in the 1870s he said they were 'the worst kept roads I have yet examined', with problems of upkeep and flooding, especially around

Ravenglass Roman Bath House.

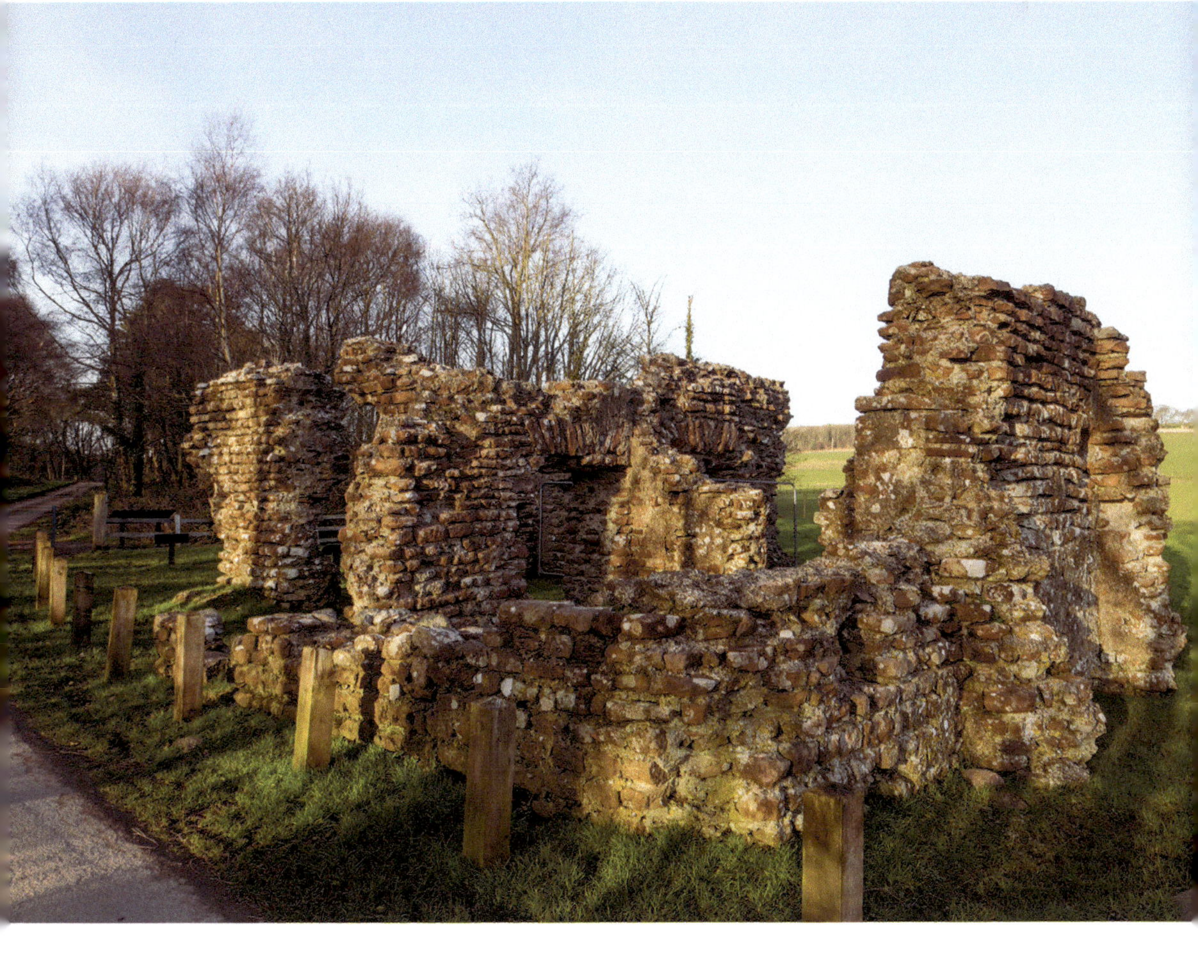

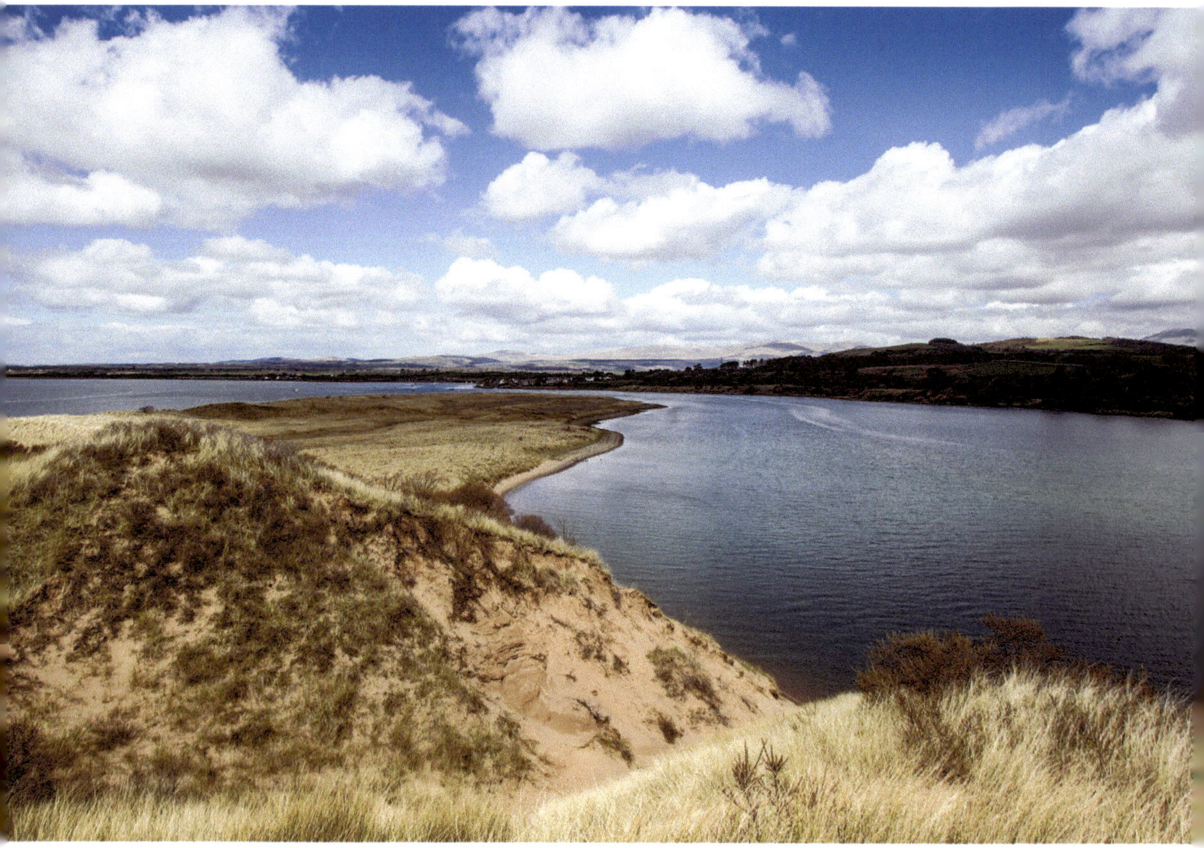

Eskmeals Dunes and Ravenglass.

Eskmeals Dunes. By the late 1800s the railways arrived and changed everything, reducing the cost of travel and improving travelling conditions.

Despite the challenges, Ravenglass was still a popular place to visit, having been granted a market by King John in 1208, although when the plague hit in the 1500s the advice was clear: 'It will not do to buy at the Ravenglass Fair as "the sickness" is rife in Walney and dealings with any man in Cumberland must be avoided'.

Thankfully that was all cleared up a long time ago and now Ravenglass is the perfect place to start, end, or stop off on any journey.

5. CARLISLE TO BOWNESS-ON-SOLWAY

Introduction

This is the last of our trilogy of Roman walks, and for a county so full of Roman history, it's impressive they only make up three of the routes explored in this book. Again, there's a lot more to the history of this region than the Romans, even if it does include Hadrian's Wall. Although it's low level throughout, this walk is exposed in many sections; when I read that in a book, I imagined the issue of the exposure will be the wind and the rain but, in this case, it was the sun. We undertook this walk during the very hot spell of June 2018 and even though we broke it into smaller sections we still struggled with the relentless heat.

The Route

This one's easy as we followed Hadrian's Wall Path from Carlisle through to Bowness-on-Solway. Starting on the banks of the River Eden, the path leaves the city and passes through a series of very pretty villages including Burgh-by Sands (which also has an excellent pub) and Drumburgh with its fascinating castle. (We found the very exposed stretch between these two by far the most challenging with no shade whatsoever.)

After looping inland slightly towards Drumburgh Moss the path returns to the coast, passing through the fascinating hamlet of Port Carlisle before ending in Bowness-on-Solway, where there are plenty of facilities to greet the weary walker.

Exposed route across salt marsh.

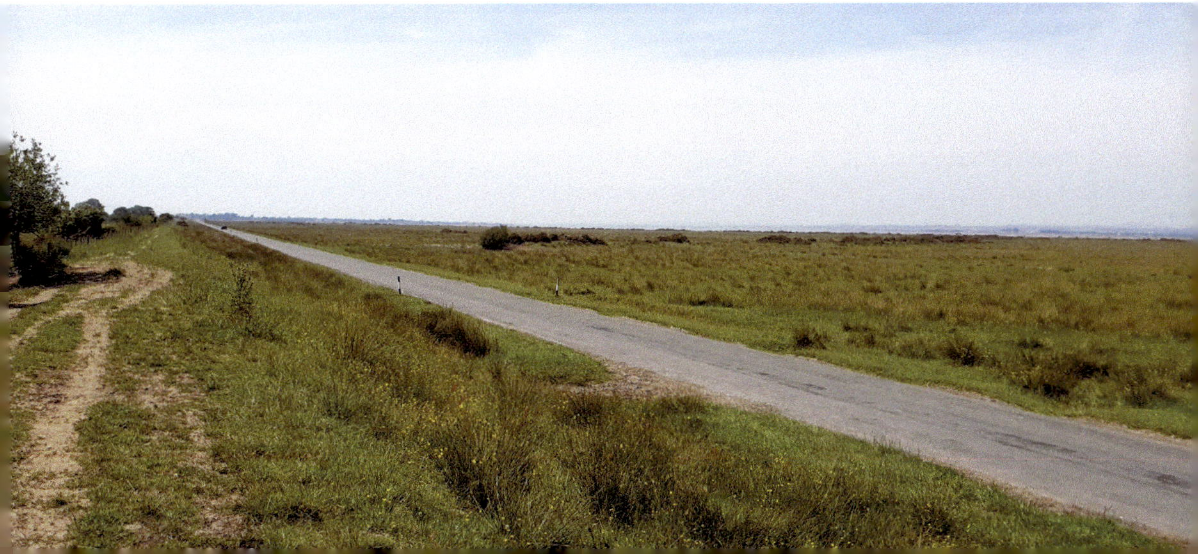

The History

Volumes of books have been written about Carlisle, and rightly so as the town is relentlessly interesting with glorious nuggets of history lurking around every corner. I would love to give you a potted history of Carlisle but even an abridged version would easily fill an entire book, so I will restrict myself to just the bits that relate to this route and strongly recommend that you visit the Tullie House Museum for a full history of the city. Tullie House is a fine Jacobean house built in 1689 and was a family home until the 1840s when it became a cloth warehouse. It was saved from demolition in the late 1800s and opened as a museum in 1893. You'll find everything you need to know about Carlisle in there, plus some fine cakes in the café too.

Clearly the Romans are famed for being in the city, although they were far from the first. There's evidence of land management in the region dating back to the Mesolithic Period (9600 BC–4000 BC) as well as Bronze Age and Iron Age finds. It's likely that when the Romans arrived they built on a pre-existing habitation as the region had a lot going for it; plentiful water supply surrounded by dense woodlands and right on a main thoroughfare to the north.

The first fort was built in AD 72, occupying a site roughly where the castle is today, with a later fort built at nearby Stanwix. The timber forts were demolished around AD 150 and replaced with a stone fort, which served throughout the rest of the Roman occupation. In Bitts Park near Stanwix you'll find the Sauceries where football has been played for at least 500 years; it's even said that Mary, Queen of Scots watched a game when she was ensconced in the castle.

Hadrian's Wall was built around AD 120 and ran for 80 Roman miles (73 imperial miles or 117 km) from Bowness-on-Solway to Wallsend on the River Tyne and was originally planned to be constructed of turf for the first 30 miles and stone for the rest. Prior to that the forts in the region had been linked by a road known as the Stanegate and when travelling along the road, if they were not staying at a fort, Roman soldiers would have camped under animal skin tents and dug defensive ditches each night as protection.

Rather like an ancient episode of Grand Designs the original plan for the wall was altered, with the Romans adding both a *vallum* (defensive ditch and mound) and another

Carlisle Castle.

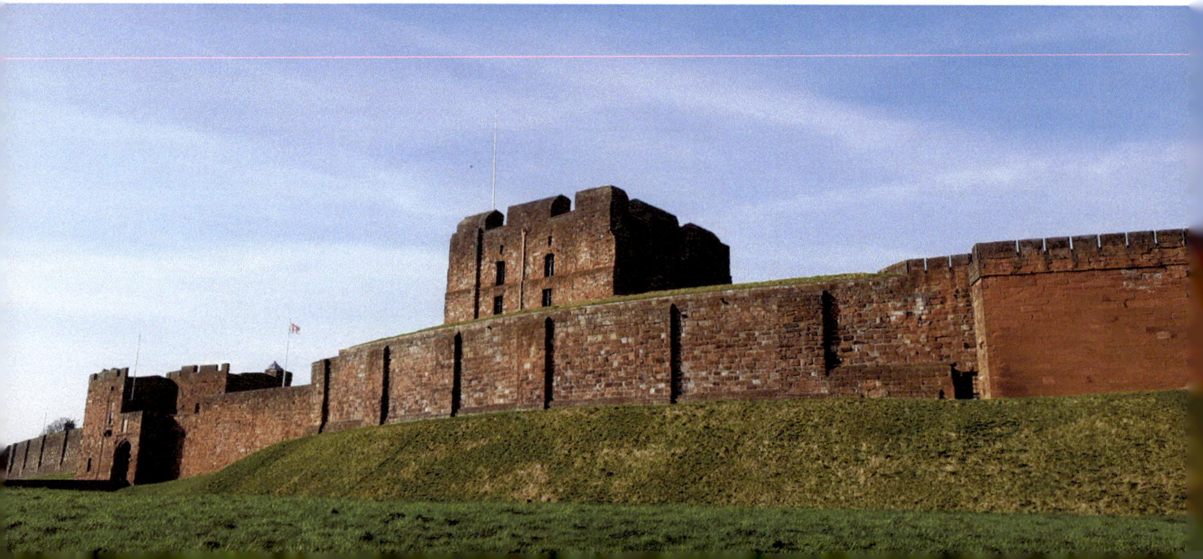

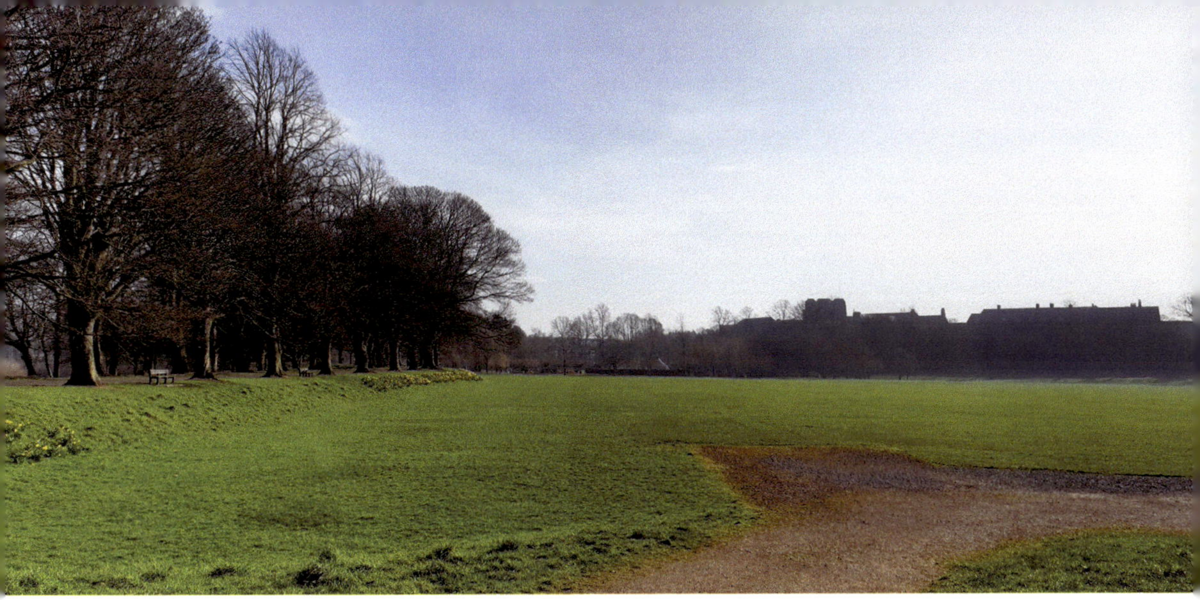

Carlisle Castle, with the route of Hadrian's Wall on the left and the Sauceries in the foreground.

road to the original plans as well as upgrading the entire wall to stone. Kevin McCloud would, no doubt, have been 'deeply worried' by how this would affect their budget.

A castle was first built in Carlisle in 1092 by King William Rufus. It was largely made of wood and built partly over the site of the old Roman fort. In 1122 Henry I of England ordered the fortification of the castle and, although ownership regularly changed hands, over the following century successive kings continued fortifying the structure. The castle has seen plenty of action, with invasions, battles, five sieges and the imprisonment of Mary, Queen of Scots. In the nineteenth century, things calmed down and today the castle is managed by English Heritage and houses an interesting military museum.

Carlisle has long been a vital transportation hub and during the late 1700s, eight mail coaches and seven stagecoaches entered and left the city every day, with eighty horses stabled in the city to support them. During the nineteenth century, steps were taken to turn Carlisle into a port and the plan was to create a canal from a village called Fisher's Cove along the coast to move people and goods into the city from the coast. From 1819 to 1823 a canal was cut at a cost of over £90,000 (the equivalent of over £7.5 million in today's terms) and the village renamed Port Carlisle.

This may seem extreme but travel by sea was far cheaper than coach travel back then. For example, to travel from Whitehaven to Liverpool by sea was 15*s* for first class and 10*s* 6*d* for second, whereas the coach fare for the same journey was 24*s* for 'inside' and 17*s* for 'outside'. To take advantage of this, in 1826 a company was set up to establish a steamship route from the newly named Port Carlisle to Liverpool.

Sadly, despite all of this, the canal never managed to pay its way. The Liverpool steamer service was diverted to Silloth and the canal was eventually filled in and, ironically, turned into a railway. To convert the canal the locks were removed and the bridges raised before the track was laid on the drained canal bed. Between Drumburgh and Port Carlisle the 'trains' were horse-drawn coaches with converted wheels known as 'Horse Drawn Dandys', which ran until 14 April 1914; after that steam took over and the line remained open until 1932.

Carlisle's population boomed during the early nineteenth century, rising from 10,221 in 1801 to 29,417 in 1861, thanks to this improved access and growing industries. In 1847, a large gasworks was built and by 1851 it had eleven spinning mills, but in my opinion

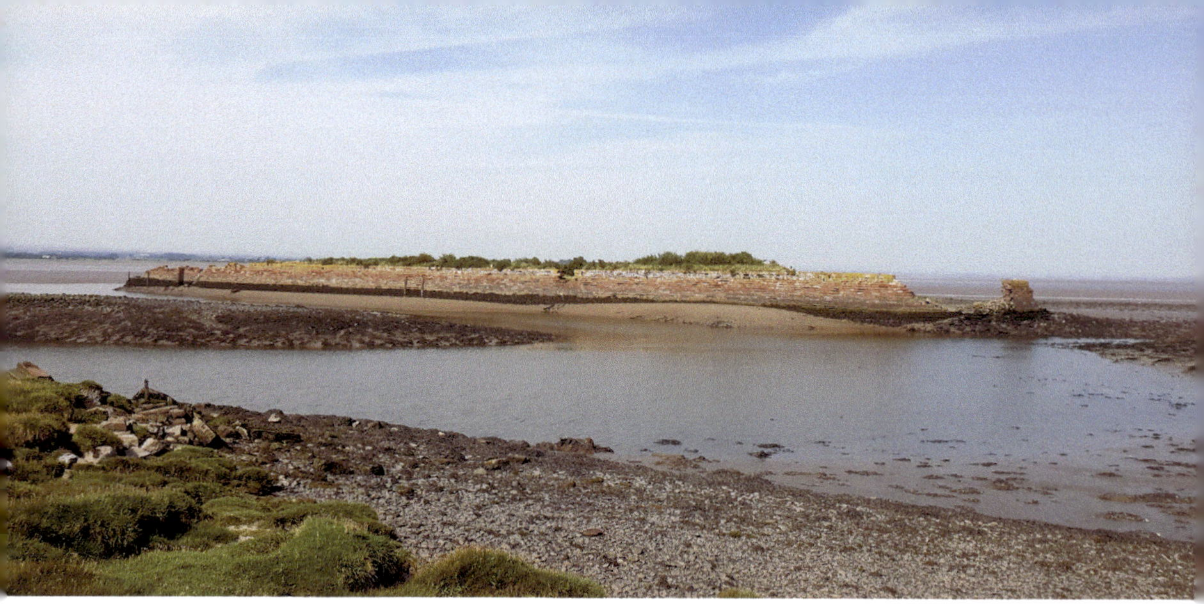

Above: Port Carlisle.

Below: St Mary's Church, Beaumont.

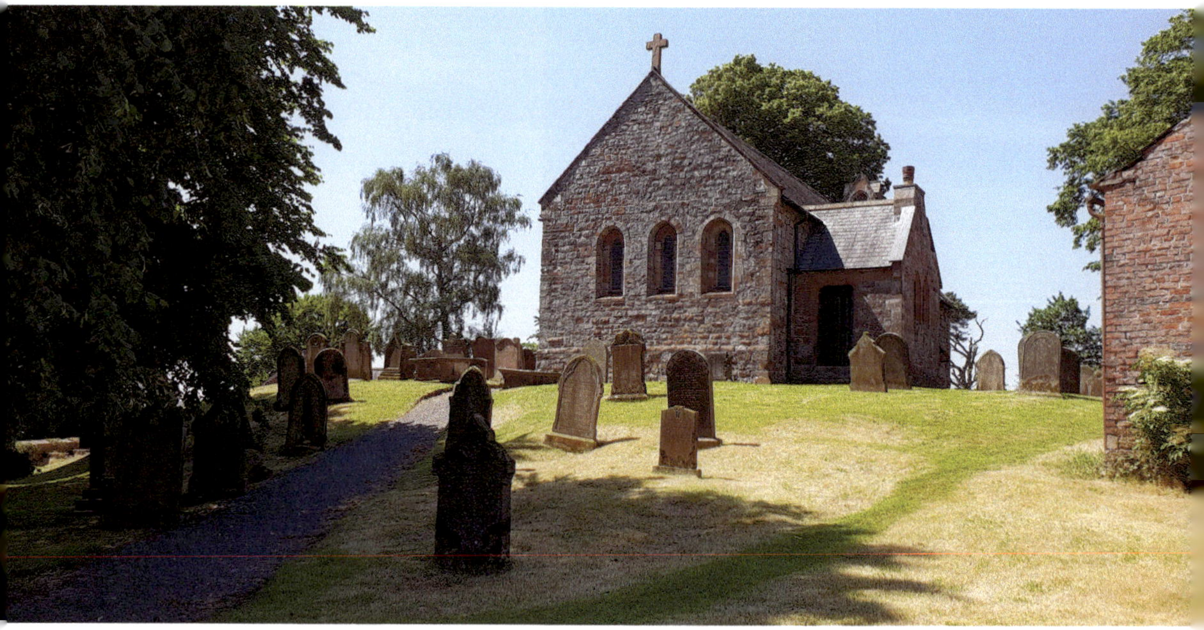

the most important development was the opening of the Carr's Biscuit Factory in 1831. In the 1840s, it was the biggest biscuit manufacturer in Britain on account of the fact that dry biscuits stayed fresh for longer and so could be transported further. Now owned by McVitie's, the site still produces many of our favourites. The nation held its breath when the factory was flooded following Storm Desmond in December 2015 but thankfully by April 2016 our beloved Bourbon Creams were back on the shelves again!

The Solway coast is a magical place full of fascinating history and folklore. Although our route follows Hadrian's Wall, the wall itself is not visible, at least not in wall form, as the stones have been robbed out and used in the creation of other buildings. Many of the buildings we now see are a result of the activities of the monks at Holme Cultram Abbey, who managed the land during the twelfth and thirteenth centuries.

Even if you are not of a religious nature, there are three fine churches to explore along the route: St Mary's Church in Beaumont, St Michael's Church in Burgh-by-Sands and St Michael's Church in Bowness-on-Solway. St Mary's is the only church built directly on the line of Hadrian's Wall and stands on the site of an old Roman fort and subsequent Norman motte. The small hill it stands on was known as Beau Mont, or 'Beautiful Hill', and gave the village its name.

St Michael's Church, Burgh-by-Sands.

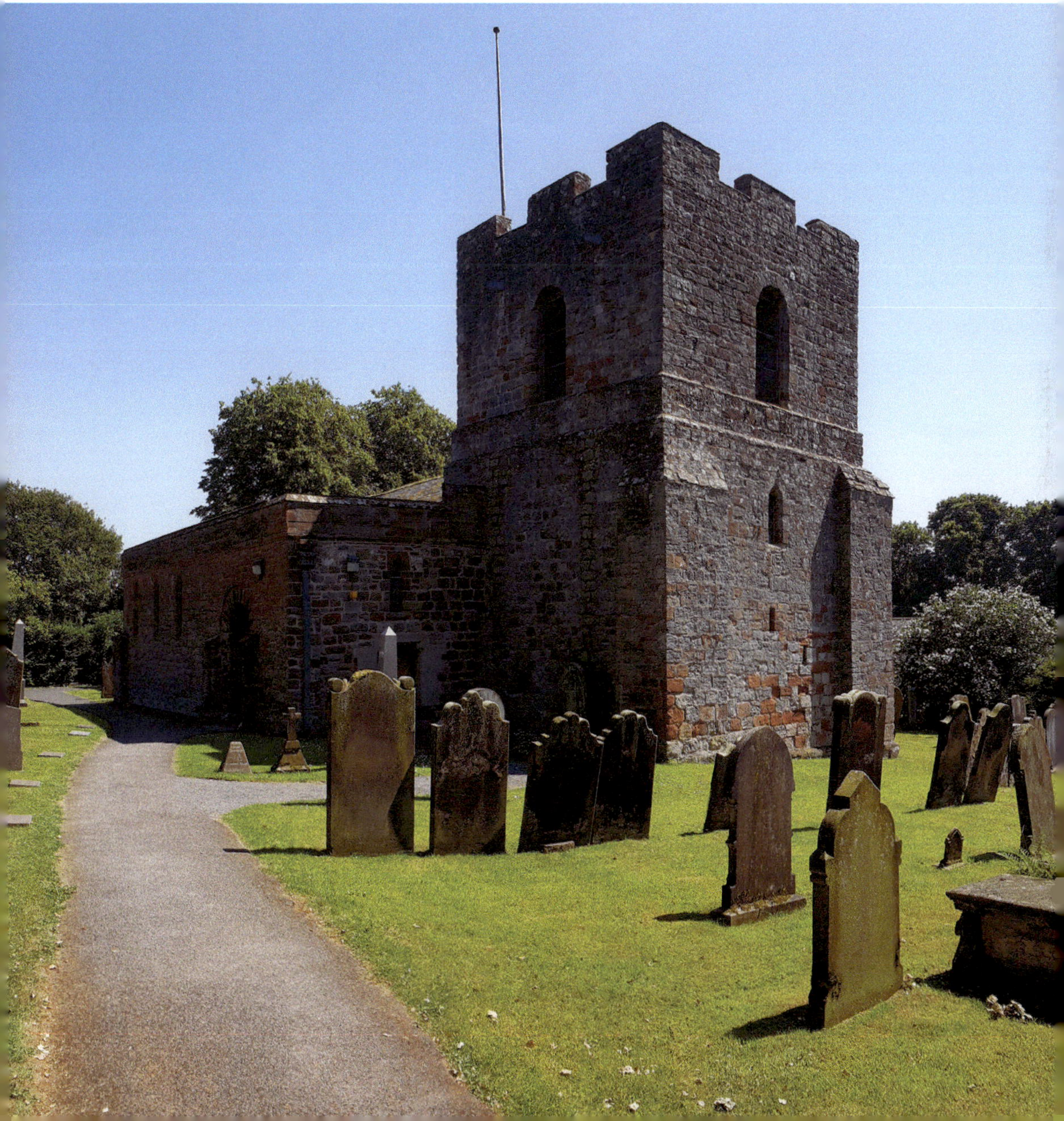

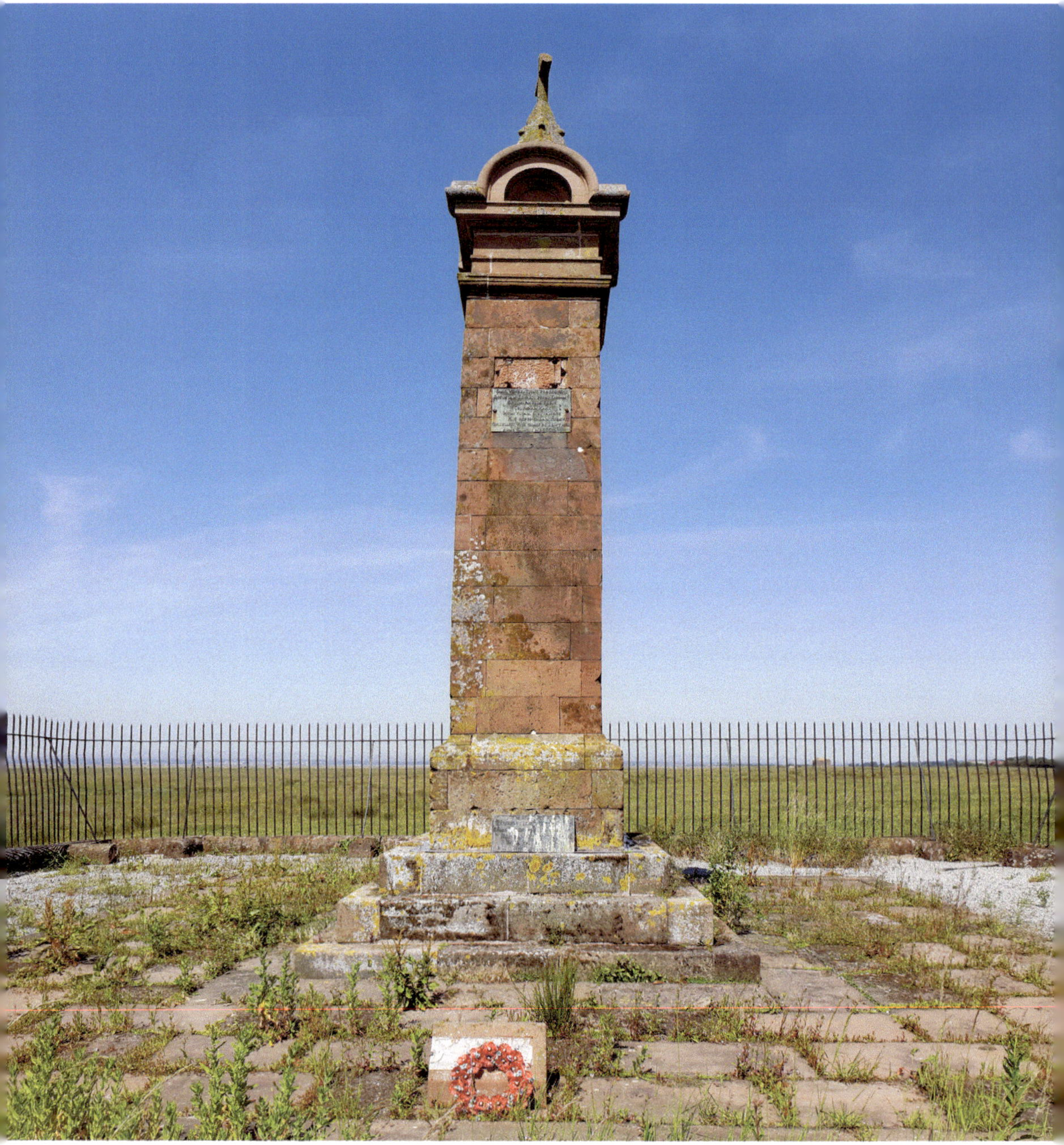

King Edward I Monument.

St Michael's in Burgh-by-Sands was built with stones from the wall and houses a wonderful array of mythological creatures carved into the stonework, probably of Anglo-Saxon origin. In 1307, Edward I visited the church on his way to tackle Robert the Bruce but died out on the marshes and his monument out on the sands (and clearly marked on the OS map) is certainly worth a visit. His body was brought back to the church to lie in state before being transported back to London for burial. The unusual church tower doubled up as a place of refuge from the regular Scots raids, hence its squat shape and barred gated entry.

In the middle of Drumburgh stands Drumburgh Castle, though it's a lot less castle-like than you might expect. Originally built as a defensive pele tower in 1307 and constructed with stones from Hadrian's Wall, the site fell into decay before being restored during the sixteenth century by Lord Tomas Dacre. Over the following centuries it passed through a number of hands and in the 1970s the castle was fully restored and became a private home.

Many of the other more humble homes in this region were built as 'clay dabbin cottages'. Materials could not be brought in from great distances so inhabitants had to make the

Drumburgh Castle.

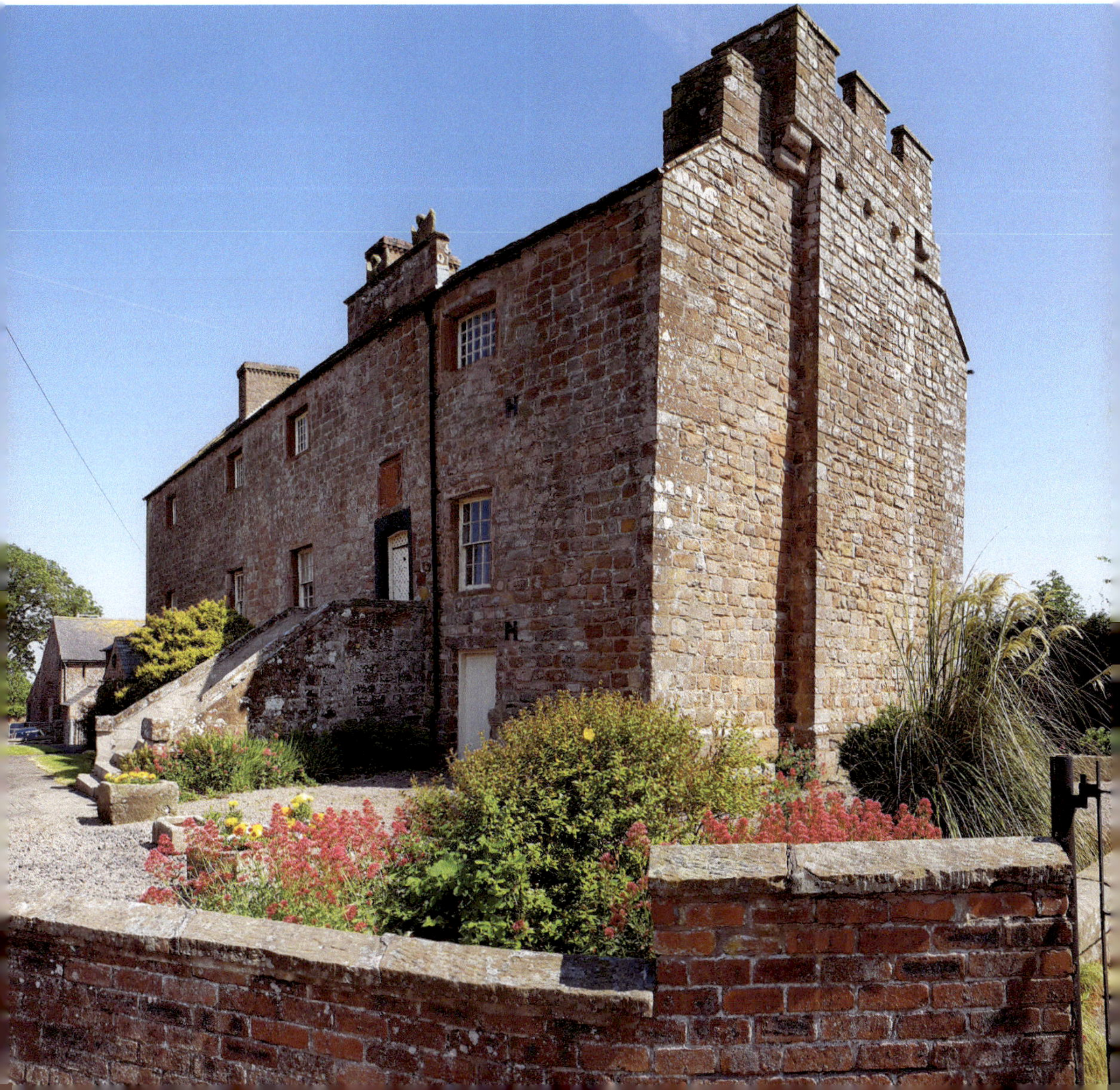

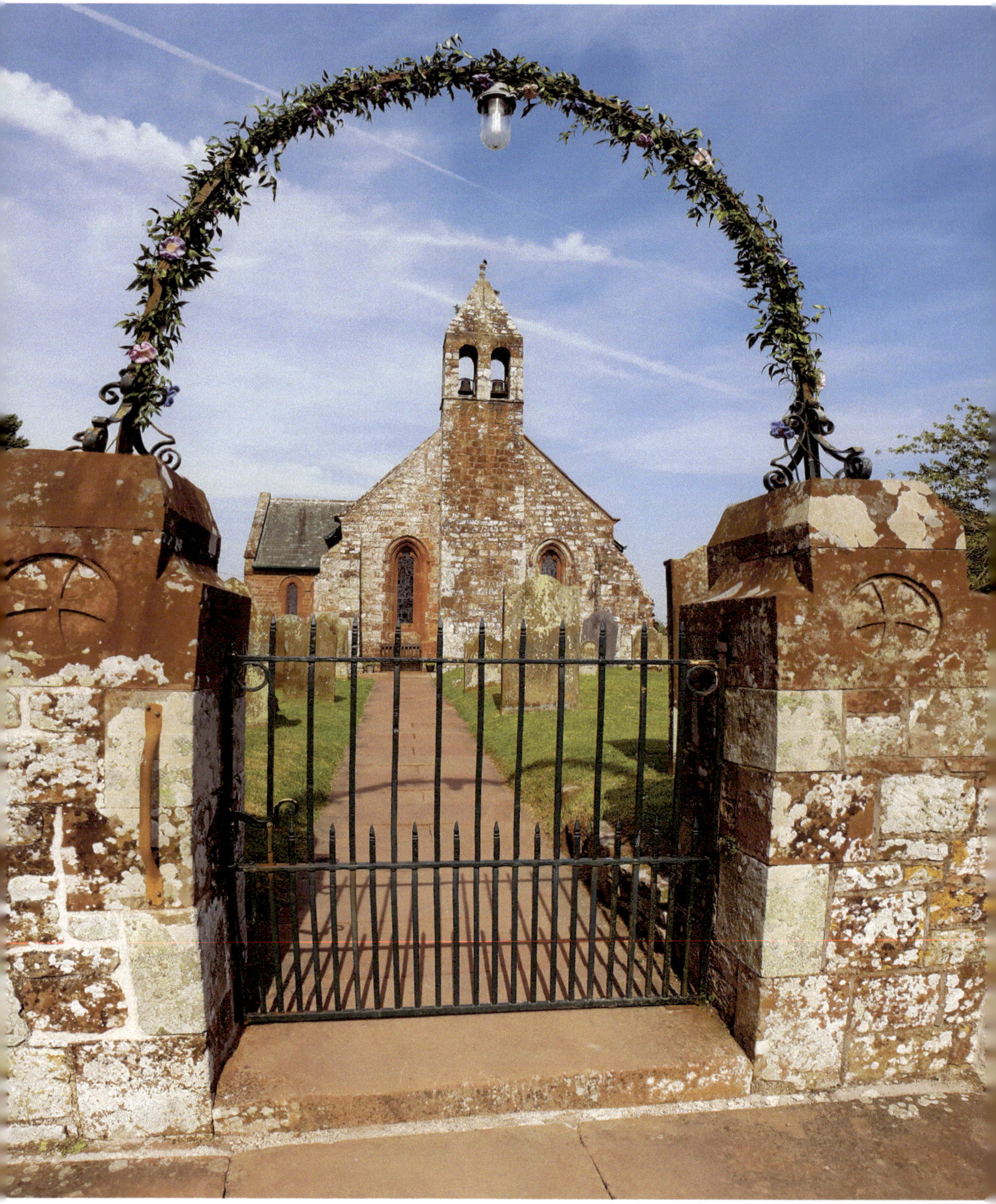

St Michael's Church, Bowness-on-Solway.

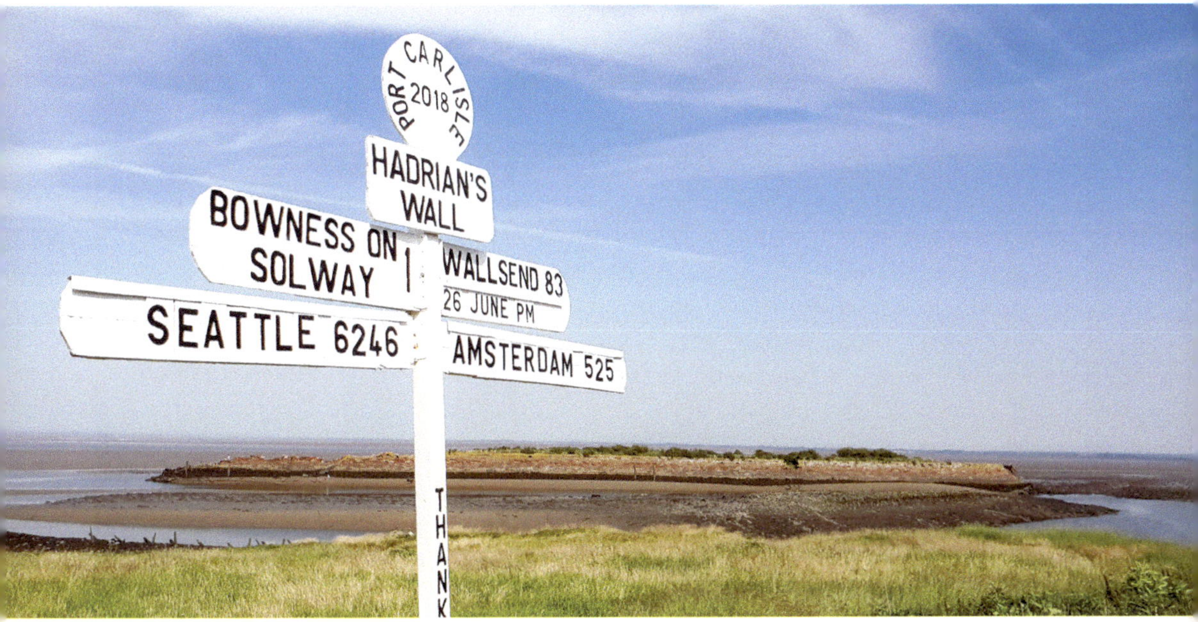

Hadrian's Wall Path.

most of what they had around them, in this case clay, cobbles and boulders for the walls, wood for the roof frame and turf, reeds, straw and bracken for the roof itself. At the turn of the twentieth century, there were over 1,300 'dabbins' in the area but today there are fewer than 300.

St Michael's Church in Bowness-on-Solway stands at the end of one of the ancient crossing points of the Solway Firth and is also built with stones from Hadrian's Wall. The original church bells were stolen by Scots raiders from Annan in 1626 but, as they were escaping, they dumped them into the Solway in attempt to lighten their load and the bells were lost forever in the sands. In retaliation a group of local men mounted a raid into Scotland and stole bells from churches in Dornock and Middlebie. Tradition has it that each time the parish of Annan (which includes Dornock and Middlebie) receives a new vicar, they request the return of the bells from Bowness but, for four centuries, all these requests have been ignored and the bells still sit at the back of St Michael's.

6. MARTINDALE AND PATTERDALE

Introduction

Ullswater is regularly voted as one of the prettiest lakes in the Lake District, and I'm not going to disagree; it is absolutely stunning. Perhaps because of that it is very popular with visitors throughout the year and many of the homes in the region are now holiday homes rather than permanent dwellings, but obviously that wasn't always the case. Before the advent of modern roads and technology, if people wanted (or needed) to visit each other there was only one way to do it – on foot and up over the fell. What we now see today as a rather lovely circular walking route from Patterdale was once a vital link between remote communities.

The Route

This really is a lovely route and even sitting here writing about it makes me want to grab my walking boots and head back out there. The directions are simple: from Patterdale

View over Patterdale and Glenridding.

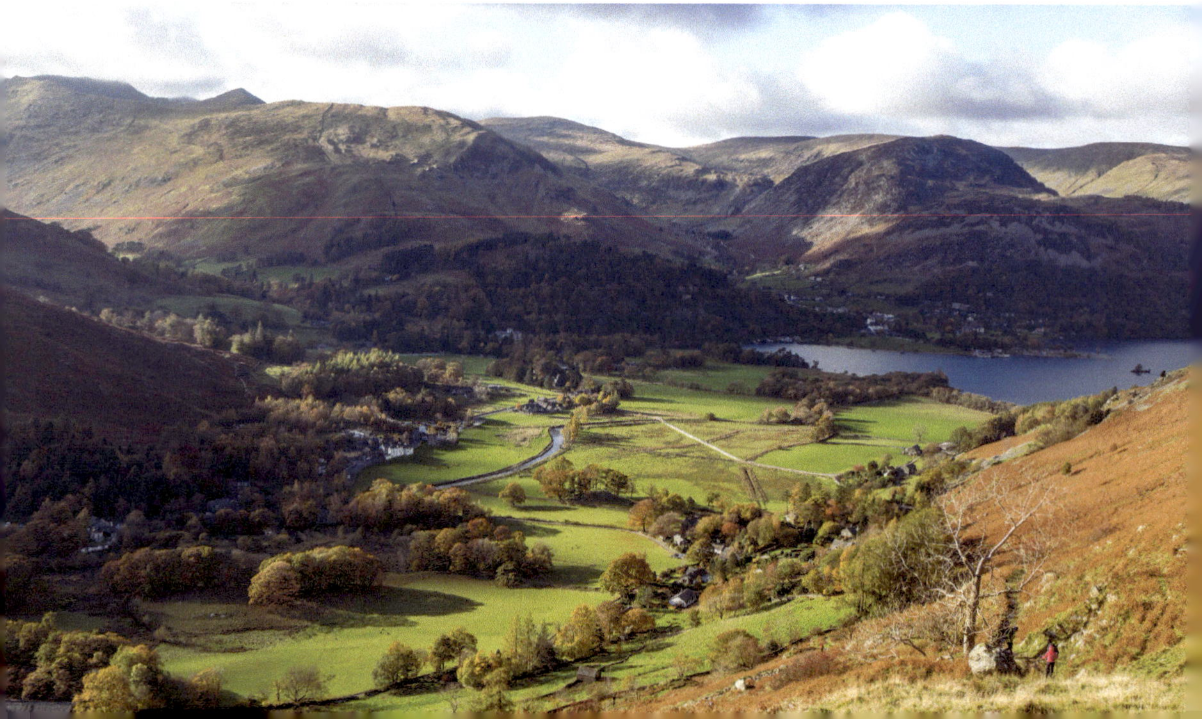

head up to Chapel-in-the-Hause then drop down along Boredale and back along the Howe Grain valley. There's a sharp climb at the start and a long gentle ascent back to the Hause at the end.

We've wandered around here many times and if you want to add on a little extra or try something different the top of Place Fell is a short(ish) sharp climb that will reward you with a spectacular panorama of the Lake District fells. Alternatively you could explore the top of Beda Fell, which is less of a climb and also has wonderful views.

The History

The starting point, Patterdale, takes its name from St Patrick's Church in the valley (St Patrick's Dale becoming Patterdale) and the saint is said to have visited the valley around AD 450. There's been a church on the site since the fourteenth century but the one we see today dates back to 1853 and was designed by Anthony Salvin who, when he wasn't designing churches, specialised in restoring collapsing castles; during his illustrious career, he worked on Norwich, Newark, Carisbrooke, Caernarvon, Warwick and even Windsor Castle.

St Patrick's Well is a little closer to the lake but, according to an account from 1797, it was once the site of some impressive St Patrick's Day celebrations: 'There is annually a ceremony observed here on St Patrick's Day of drinking a bottle of rum over the spring and on that day dancing and all sorts of merriment go on with great spirit' (*A Tour in the Lakes*, William Gell).

St Patrick's Church, Patterdale.

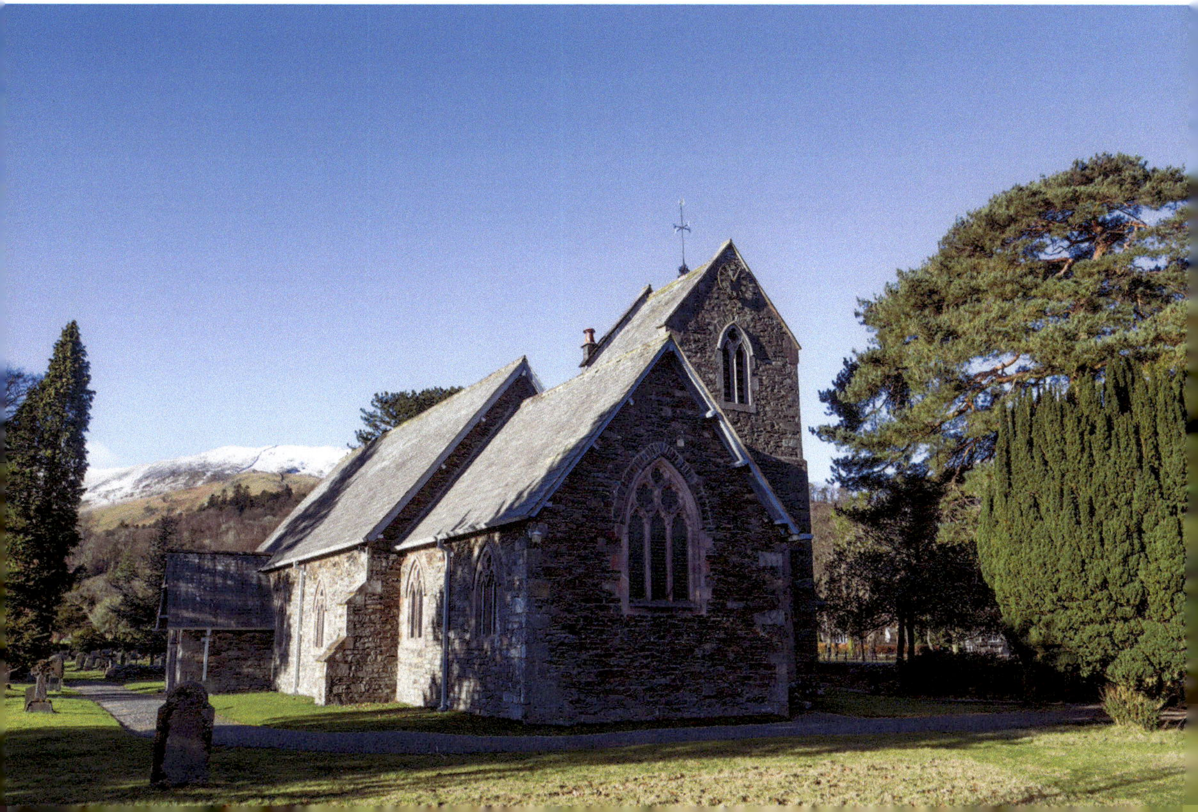

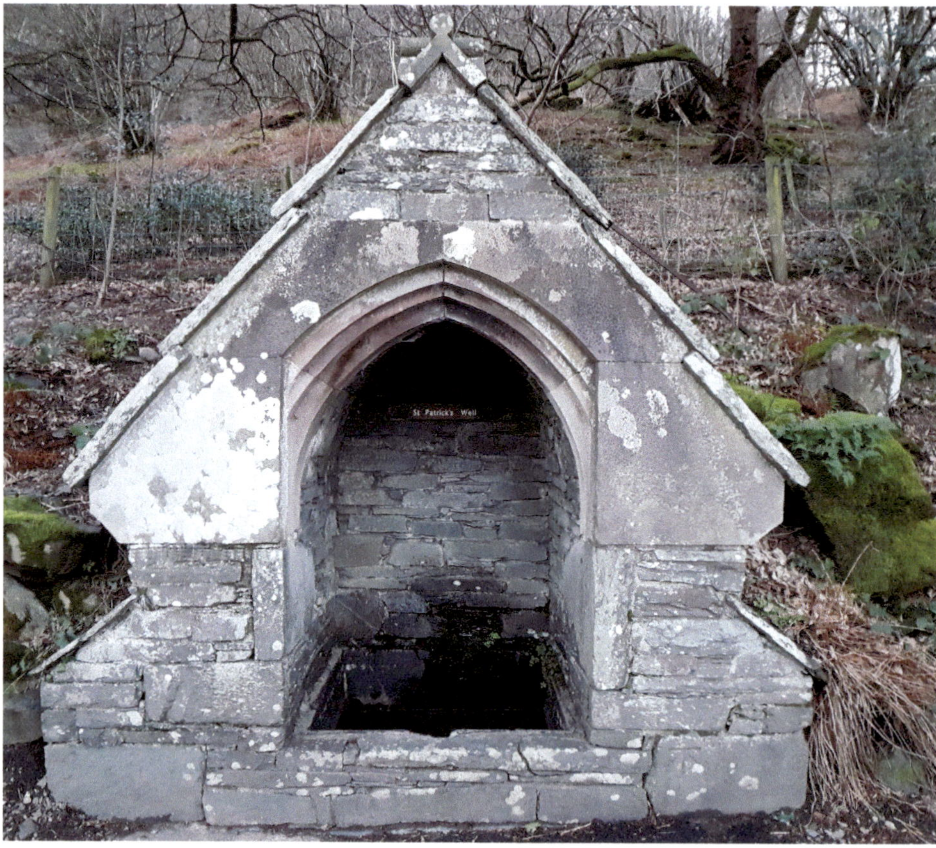

St Patrick's Well.

What we now see as a rural farming community was, until around 1960, a nationally renowned mining area. The Greenside Lead Mine just along the valley from Glenridding originally began production in the late eighteenth century and was famous for its production of lead and silver – the communion plate in the church is made of silver from the mine. These mines made an indelible mark on the landscape in several ways. Apart from the still visible mine fifty-two cottages were built in the area to house mine workers, and when the mine closed and the workers left many of these became the holiday homes we see today.

However, it wasn't just the housing that the mines affected, it was also the transportation routes; the ore from the mines needed to be shipped away and was sent by cart over to Carlisle where it could be moved more swiftly initially by canal and later by rail. This meant that the road route from Patterdale to Carlisle was much improved compared to other 'less important' routes.

Patterdale also gave its name to the Patterdale Terrier, a hardy short-haired terrier descended from Fell Terriers. Such dogs were regularly used to control the local vermin. The Fell Terriers were renowned for their toughness and persistence as this story from 1779 illustrates. A farmer went out at 2 p.m. on a Saturday afternoon and his dog took off after a fox. The dog was not seen again until the following evening when it returned, still

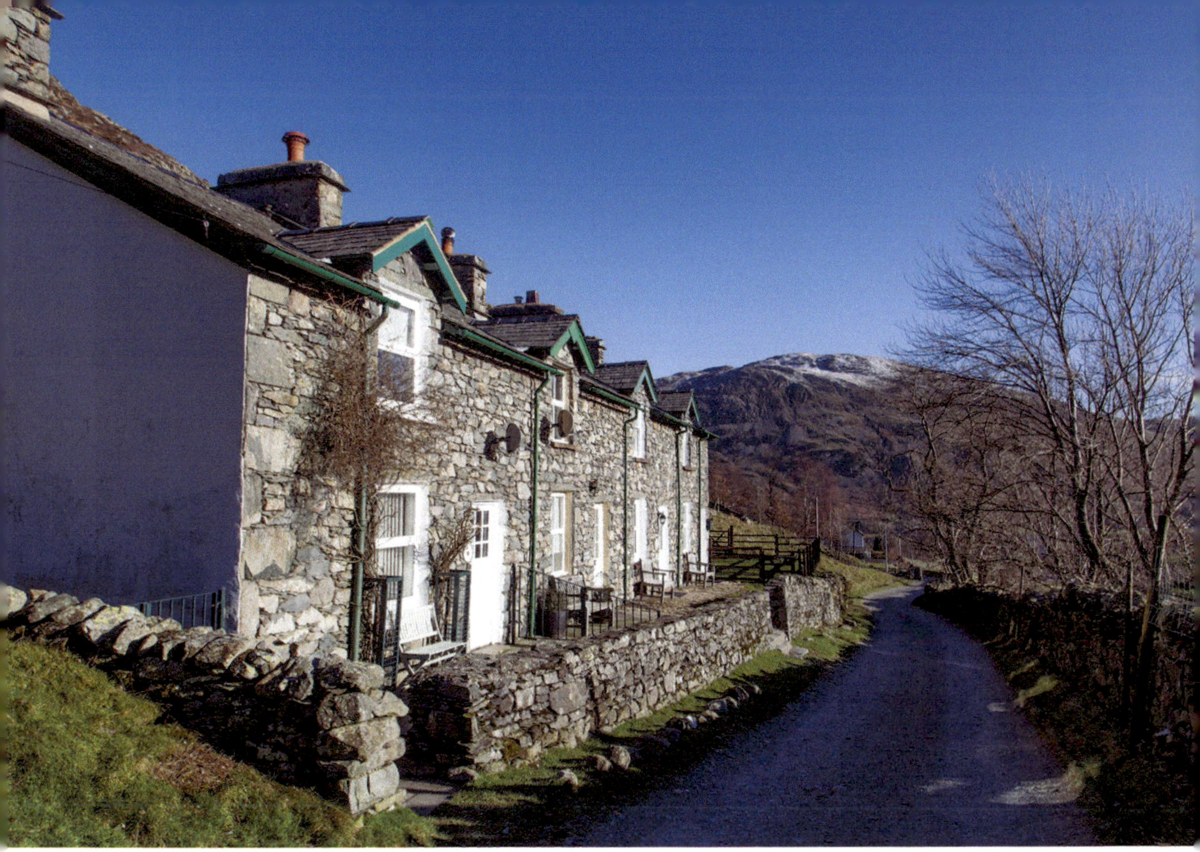

Old mine cottages.

in pursuit of the fox. Apparently both animals were so exhausted that they collapsed and lay down together under a gooseberry bush. After making enquiries, the farmer discovered that the dog had been seen chasing the fox in Wythburn (9 miles away) and Legberthwaite (13 miles away)!

From Patterdale, the path climbs to Chapel-in-the-Hause and the remains of what is reputed to have been a chapel. In his book Wainwright confidently states that the route 'also served as an approach to a chapel on the top of the pass', but having done a lot of digging around, I can't find any definite confirmation that the ruins there were ever an actual church. Trust me, I've investigated the records of the Anglicans, the Methodists and the Quakers, but there's no hard evidence.

The word 'hause' (or 'hawse') most likely comes from our Viking ancestors and means 'mountain pass', although interestingly what is now known as Hause Crag is listed as Horse Crag on the 1863 OS map. Differing snippets of folklore say that the chapel was either built by St Patrick himself in the fifth century or built later and dedicated to St Martin of Tours (*see* later), but there is no evidence for either of these. In Baddeley's thorough guide to the Lake District in the late 1800s, he clearly marks a shelter at that point, so perhaps there were more of the ruins left back then.

The first map I could find that mentioned 'Chapel in the Hause' was from 1863 but a map of the region from 1760 by Bowles, Sayer and Bowles clearly marks Martindale Chapel in Martindale and St Patrick's Well in Patterdale, but makes no mention at all of a chapel on the pass so, whatever it was, either didn't exist then or wasn't important enough to merit inclusion.

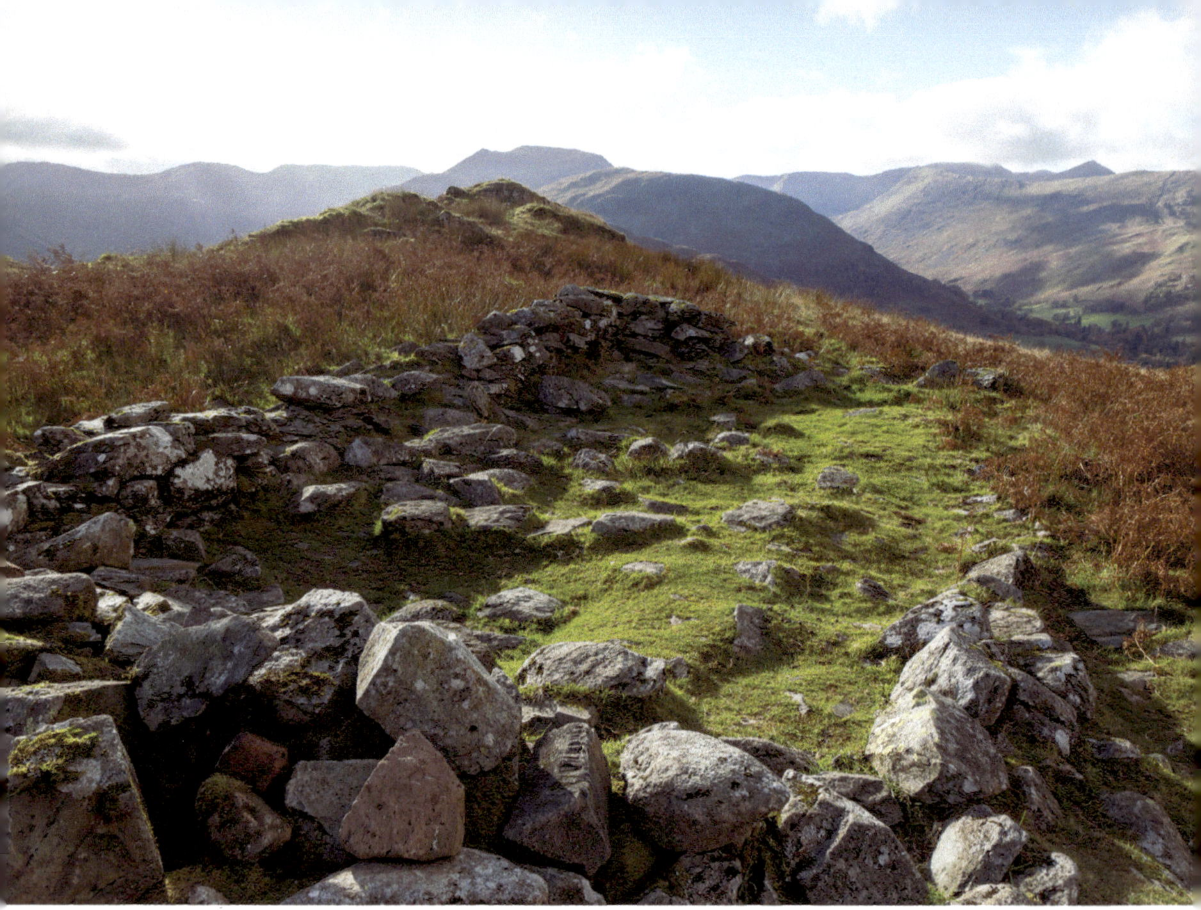

Chapel-in-the-Hause.

If you do decide to take the detour up onto Place Fell (historically known as Martindale Fell) then take heed of these words from 1778 when Thomas West described it as 'the most romantic, pleasing and terrible situation upon the lake, especially if the wind blows'. On one particularly parky visit we were lucky enough to find a series of frozen tarns full of frozen bubbles. I'd never seen anything quite like it before and it really was rather beautiful.

The route then follows Boredale Valley, which has also undergone a name transformation over the years from Boardale. You're unlikely to bump into any boars along there these days but, if you're quiet and don't have a dog with you, there's a great chance of spotting the red deer who have roamed these valleys for over 300 years. There's also a fantastic selection of birdlife to watch out for and buzzards and skylarks will accompany you on most summer walks.

Down in Martindale, there are another two churches to explore. The 'new' church of St Peter is on the top of Martindale Hause, was built in the 1880s and has a glorious collection of stained-glass windows designed by modern stained-glass artist Jane Gray, who also worked on the magnificent windows in the nave of the new Coventry Cathedral.

The 'old' church of St Martin of Tours is next to the road along Howe Grain. Records show that there has been a church on the site of over 700 years but there's also a yew tree near the church that is over 1,300 years old. Yew trees have long been associated with churches so it's possible there was some sort of place of worship here as far back as the

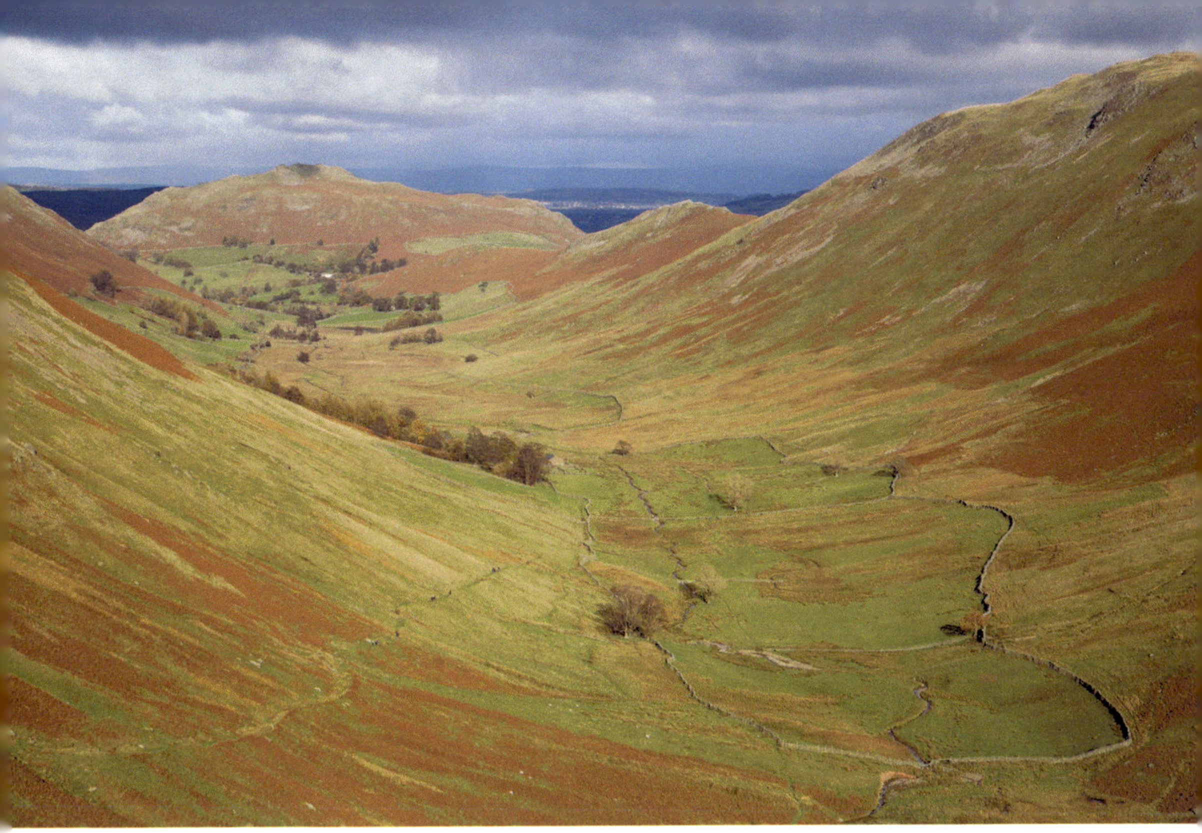

Above: Boredale Valley.

Below: Martindale 'old' Church.

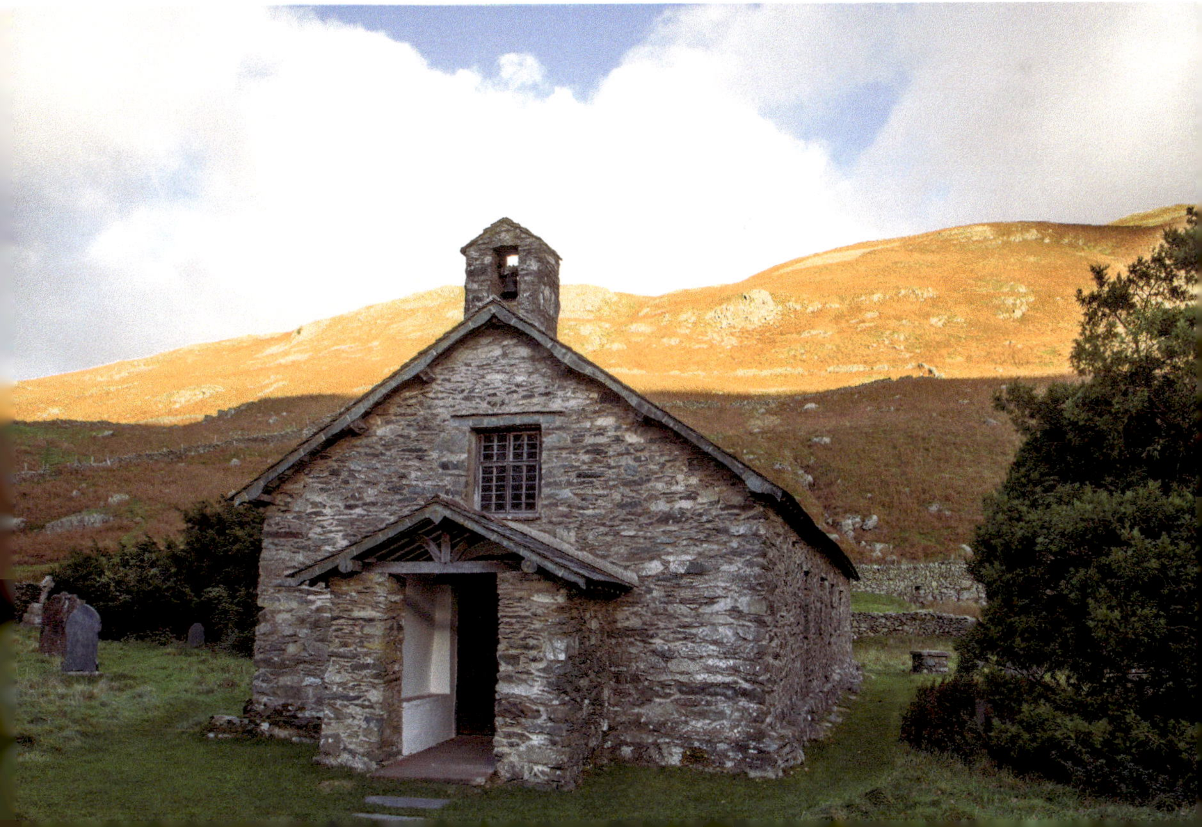

ninth century. The present church was built during the sixteenth century and was visited by William and Dorothy Wordsworth. William used his visit to the church as inspiration for his second book, *The Excursion* (1814):

Till, chancing by yon lofty ridge to pass
A heap of ruin, almost without walls
And wholly without roof (in ancient time
It was a Chapel, a small Edifice
In which the Peasants of these lonely Dells
For worship met upon that central height).

In his guide to the Lake District, written *c.* 1880, Baddeley states that 'Martindale parish church stands on How Grain about 1,000 feet about sea level and is one of the most remote and inaccessible churches in Britain'. His accompanying map, however, shows the two churches in Martindale, both well below 1,000 feet and no church marked up on Boredale Hause (for the record Martindale Parish Church is 636 feet (190 metres) above sea level and Chapel-in-the-Hause is 1259.9 feet (384 metres) above sea level).

While the parish church is in a remote valley, it is along the main village road and couldn't be described as inaccessible. According to the 1881 census there were thirty-four families living in the village at that time. Baddeley's guides were the go-to guides for the period and were incredibly popular, so much so that following his death a clock tower was built in his honour along the road from Bowness-on-Windermere to Windermere where it still stands today marking the boundary between the two parishes.

View of Chapel-in-the-Hause.

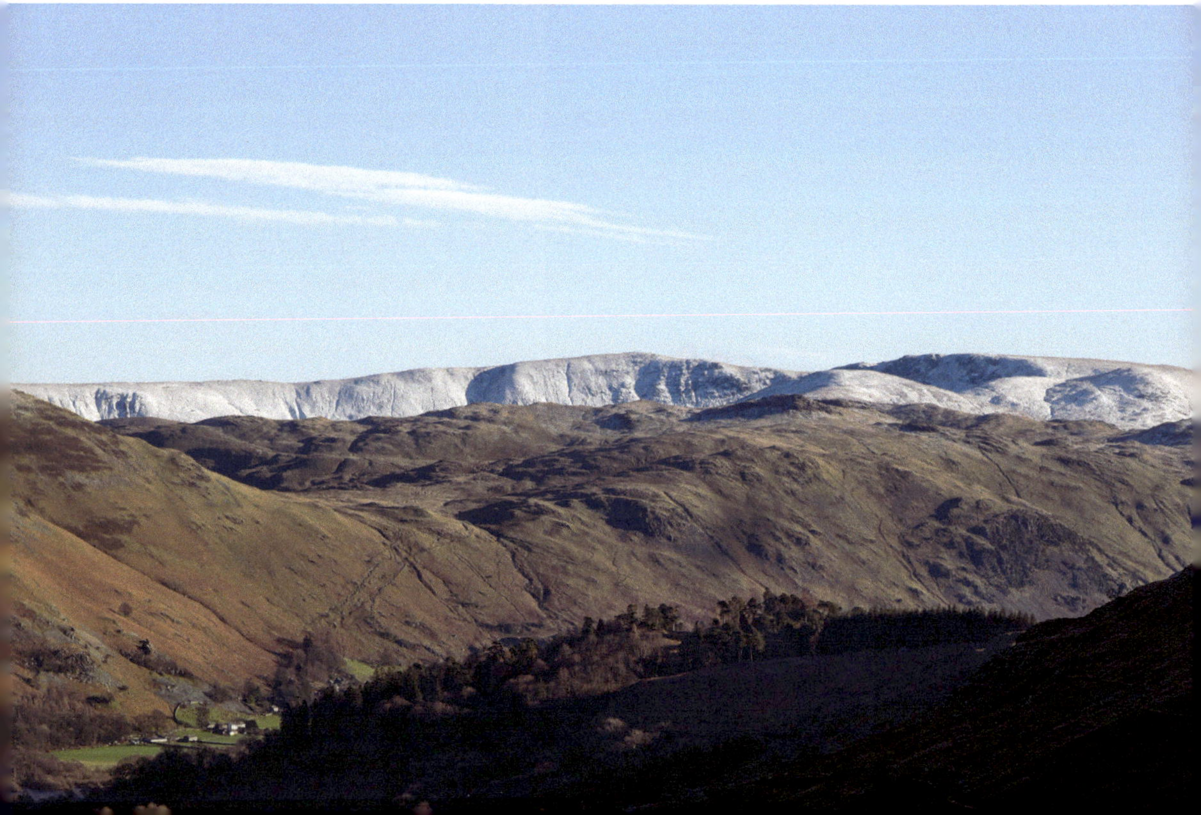

The parish church of St Martin fell into disrepair and would have been roofless when Wordsworth and Baddeley made their separate visits (the church was restored and reroofed in 1882). Our ancestors were a practical bunch and wouldn't have ventured up onto a fell top to attend chapel unless there was a very good reason for it. In the absence of hard evidence either way my theory is that the building referred to as the 'chapel' on Boredale Hause was a temporary solution that functioned as a church while the valleys either side were without a place of worship, and once the churches in the Martindale and Patterdale were restored, the chapel on the hause was no longer required.

Before I leave the subject alone once and for all, it's also worth adding that it was St Martin who gave us the word 'chapel' in the first place. Before he was a saint, Martin was a Roman soldier stationed in France. One day he found a shivering beggar so tore his cloak in half, giving the other half to the beggar. Following his death, St Martin's half of the cloak, known as '*cappa Saincti Martini*', was preserved and watched over by priests known as 'cappellani', which evolved into 'chaplain'. The small churches built to house the cloak were called 'capella', which then evolved into 'chapel'.

Heading back along the valley towards Dale Head, the red roof of 'The Bungalow' is very easy to spot away in the distance. These days it's a luxurious holiday villa but it was originally built in 1910 by the Earl of Lonsdale as a hunting lodge for a visit by Kaiser Wilhelm II who, despite having a very anti-British stance, was grandson of Queen Victoria and remained very close to much of the royal family. The kaiser also took a ride on the Ullswater steamer *Raven*, whose decks were painted yellow for the occasion (yellow being the Earl of Lonsdale's favourite colour).

'The Bungalow'.

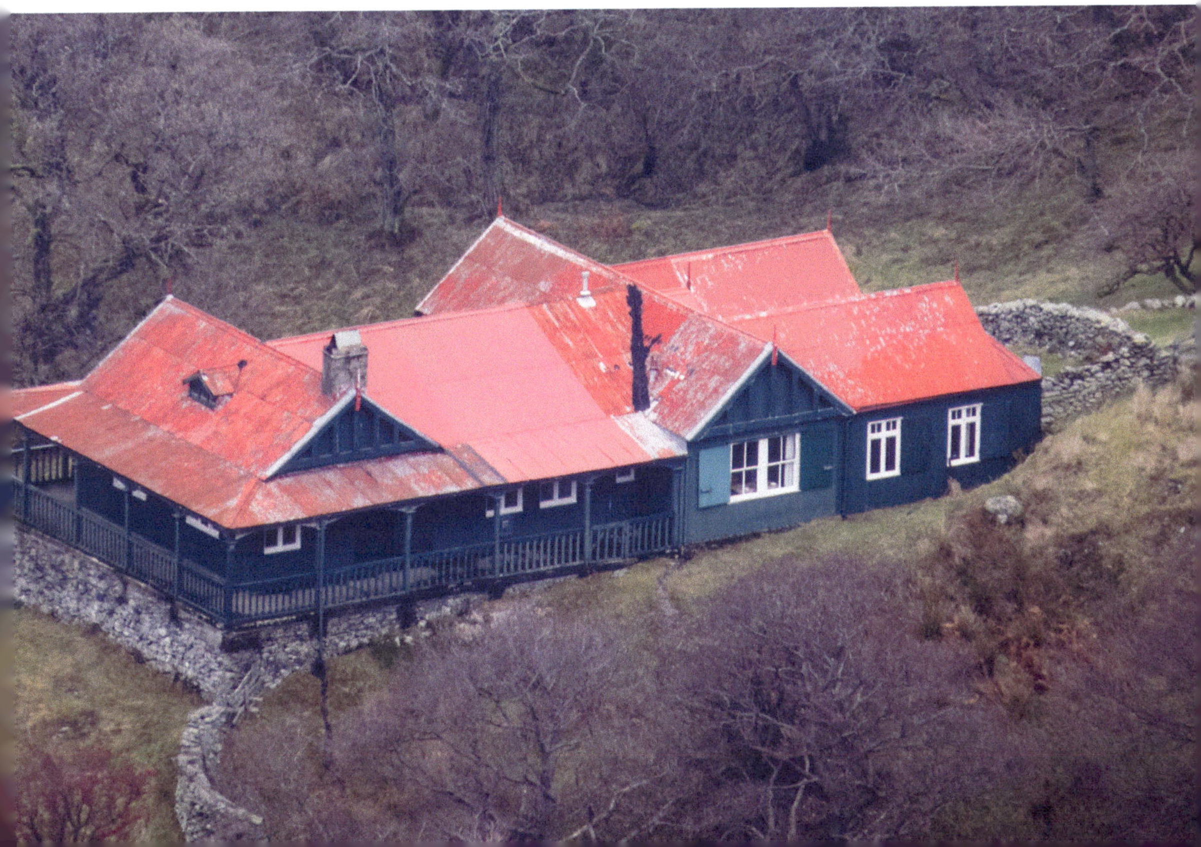

While we're on the subject of the lake, Donald Campbell set a water speed record there on 23 July 1955. The average speed of the two runs (and official record) was 202.32 mph (325.6 kph) but on the first leg he reached 215.08 mph (343.13 kph). These days most of us prefer to explore the lake at a rather more sedate pace, thanks to the Ullswater Steam Navigation Company, which was formed in 1855 to offer pleasure cruises along the lake. Prior to that it was reported that 'the navigators of this lake find much amusement by discharging guns or small cannon' (*A Guide to the Lakes*, Timothy West, 1778). Good job they didn't try that when the kaiser was around.

Red stag.

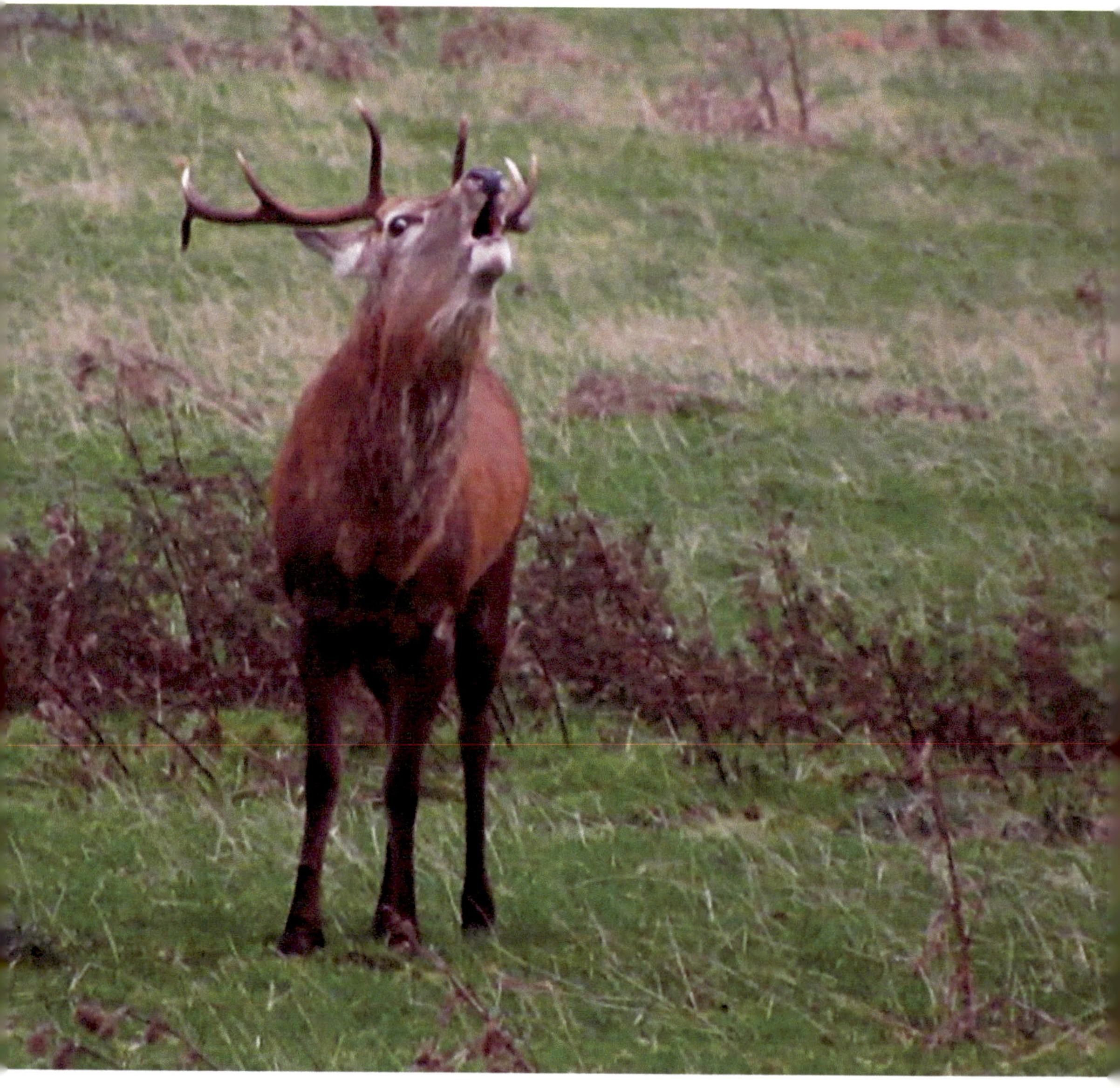

7. KENTMERE AND LONGSLEDDALE

Introduction

The final four routes all interlink around a cluster of eastern fells and are clear evidence that what we now see as quiet, dead-end valleys were once busy thoroughfares carrying people and goods. Today it's a 29-mile (47-km) drive from Sadgill in Longsleddale around via the A6 to the head of Haweswater, but it's only 3 miles (5 km) up and over Gatescarth Pass. Similarly it's 14 miles (23 km) from Kentmere around to Sadgill but only 2 miles (4 km) up and over the fell. If you were on foot, which route would you choose?

The Route

Starting and ending at Kentmere church, this is a very lovely 6.6-mile (10.6-km) circular route. Please note that parking at the church is very limited and there is an honesty box there so please do make a contribution. Plenty of people still live in the village so please park considerately.

Longsleddale Valley.

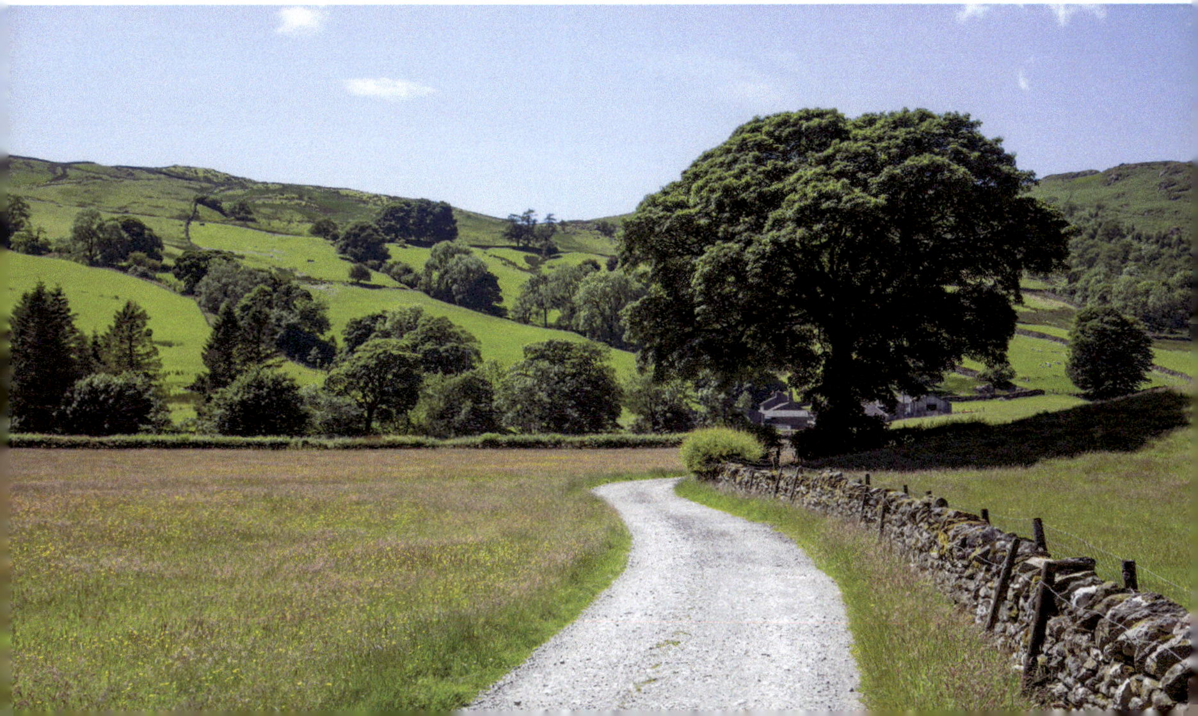

The easiest way round to walk it is to head out from Kentmere following the path that loops south towards Skeggles Water before returning back north towards Sadgill. This first part of the walk is less distinct probably because it was less used as it wasn't a direct path. The return journey up and over the bridleway is very clear and easy to follow.

The History

One of the most obvious landmarks in the village is St Cuthbert's Church. The church is named in honour of St Cuthbert, who lived on Lindisfarne and was originally buried there before the Danes invaded in AD 875 and local monks removed his body for safety and took it on a tour of the north of England. Kentmere lies on what was once an important route between Shap Abbey and Furness Abbey so, although there is no evidence, it is possible that St Cuthbert's body may have rested in the village.

Despite its size and the considerable cost involved in its construction, very little is known about its origins. It is thought that it was built during the sixteenth century and recent renovation works have identified that it was built well, with very little settling or other movement occurring over the centuries. Dendrochronology tests on the roof beams confirmed that the trees used were felled around 1514 and once supported a lead roof. Much more of its history was uncovered during the renovation work and it's well worth visiting the Kentmere.org website for more detailed information.

A lovely insight into life in the valley comes from a curious old book: *The Annals of a Quiet Valley*, edited by John Watson. It is purported to be the edited diary of a country parson from the eighteenth century and, although it may not quite be all that it seems, there

St Cuthbert's Church, Kentmere.

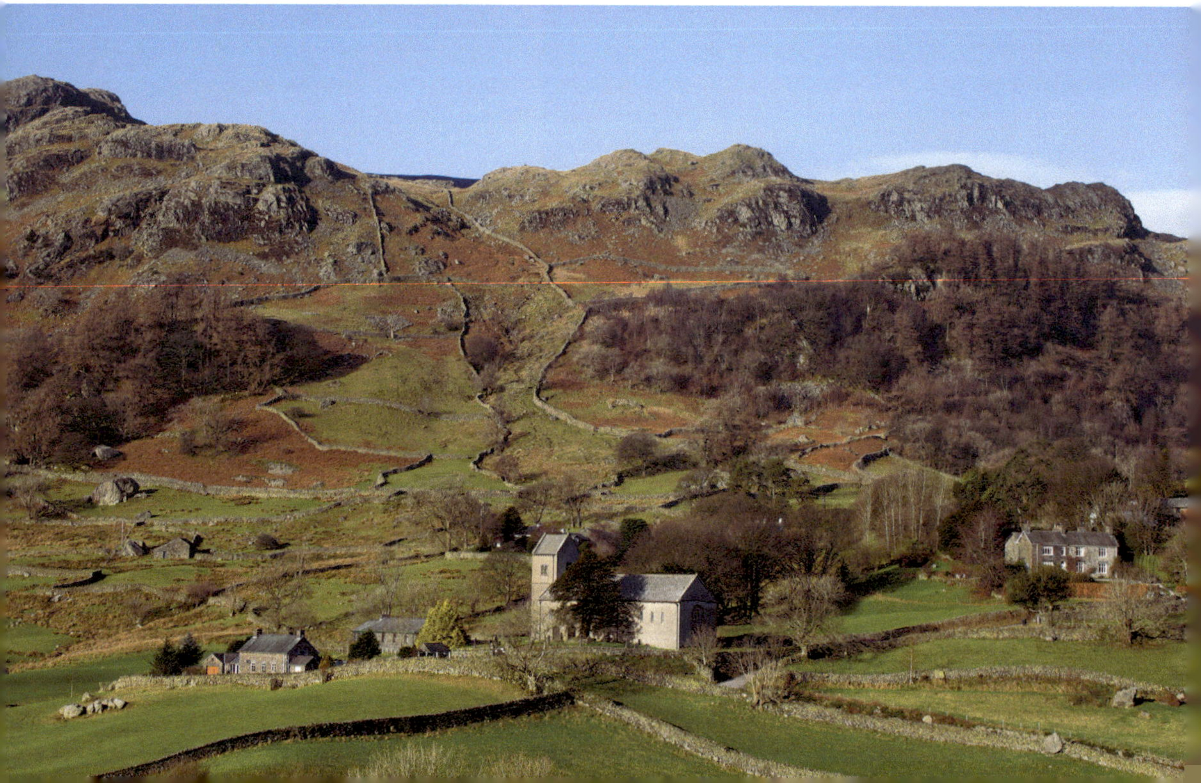

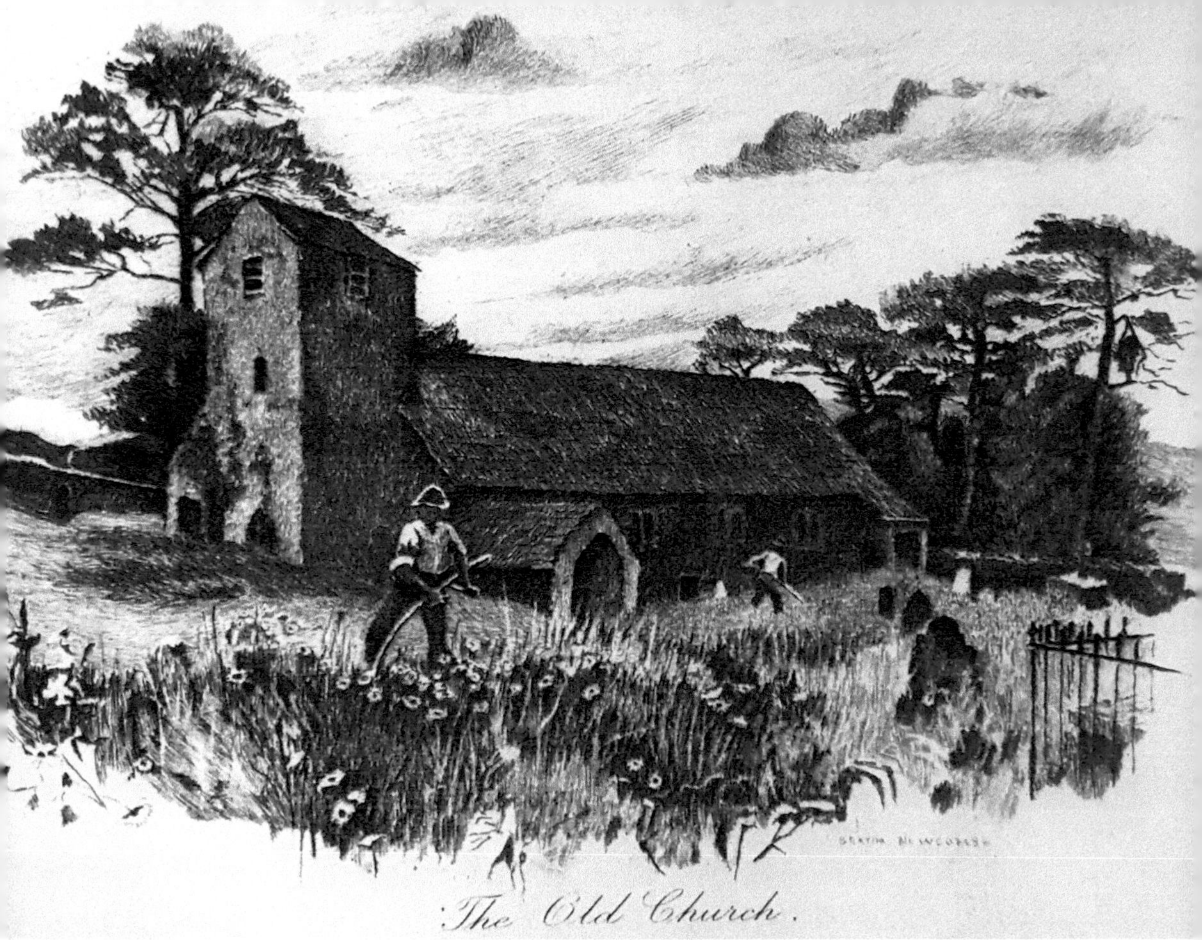

Drawing of St Cuthbert's from *Annals of a Quiet Valley*.

are plenty of interesting stories in there that give a feel for what life must have been like. He tells of shearing festivals when all the sheep were brought down from the fells for clipping. Everyone in the village would have been involved in one way or another and a shearing feast was laid on at the end by the farmer with 'tobacco, ale, spirits and a series of most inspiriting ballads'. There were also athletic events associated with it, with the best wrestler being rewarded with the finest fleece clipped. Then there was the Auld Wives' Hake, usually held on Christmas Eve and 'observed by matrons only', which appears to be an evening of tea drinking and gossiping.

My favourite of them all has to be 'Nut Monday', which occurred on the first Monday in September, when the whole village would go out 'nutting'. There are some wonderful old photos of dozens of people crammed into open horse-drawn coaches heading out in their 'nutting party' – obviously all dressed in their finest clothes. They were off to gather the hazelnuts along the valley, much to the dismay of the local squirrels. The hazel has long been thought of as having mystical powers, but from a purely pragmatic perspective, the nuts would have been an important source of food during the winter months.

In these remote valleys, fresh food through the winter was generally confined to eggs, poultry and geese, but thanks to the rivers, salmon was very popular; in fact it was so popular that local schools and employers often had to write into their contracts that fish would be served no more than three times a week. A pamphlet from 1827 ('Manners and

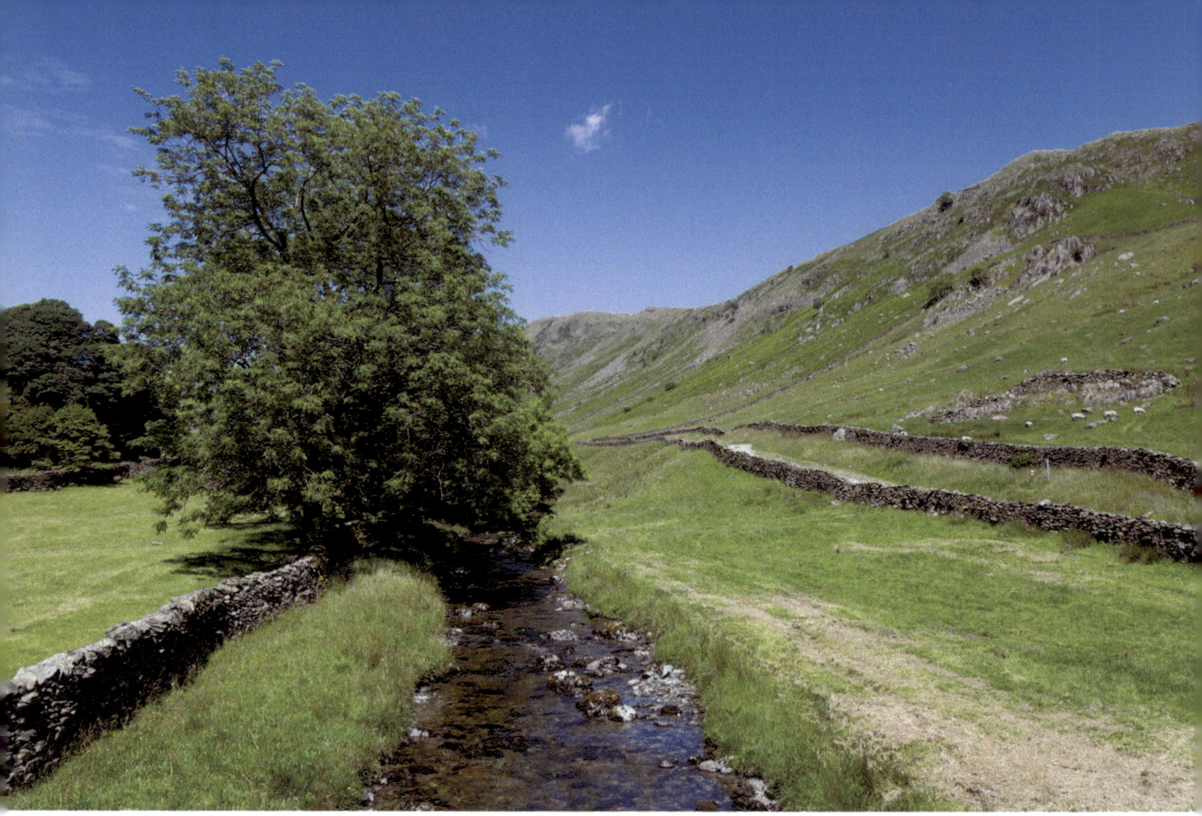

River Sprint.

Customs in Westmorland') describes the food as being primarily 'oaten bread, dressed barley and a few onions' and any animals killed were salted and smoked to preserve them with nothing wasted: 'The briny liquor in which the beef had been cooked, thickened with a little meal, was taken as broth, and this meal was helped down with pickled red cabbage'.

Potatoes weren't really eaten until around 1730 and even then there weren't many of them. Tea arrived at much the same time and was a popular drink with the ladies, but not everyone warmed to it. One elderly lady received a pound of tea from her son in London and proceeded to smoke it as she was under the impression it was tobacco. She complained that it wasn't as good as her usual Virginia!

For many years the church in Longsleddale was without a door and to prevent the cattle wandering in, a large thorn bush was dragged into the doorway. The responsibility for putting the thorn bush in place rested with the last person to leave but the parson would often have to intervene if someone had skipped their duties. In the winter months, the congregations would dwindle during periods of poor weather when people just couldn't get there, which meant there was more communion wine to go around and the clergyman was often heard to whisper 'drink gayley deep; there's not many o' us this morning'. There was also one notable occasion when the communion wine ran out and the vicar replaced it with rum thinking that no one would notice.

This part of the world is 'Herdy Central' and a walk around here simply would not be complete without the smiling face of a Herdwick sheep brightening up the day. They've been on the fells for hundreds of years and are so well adapted that they can be left on the high fells all-year round. During heavy snow, Herdies will generally not follow the other sheep and shelter alongside walls, where they are likely to get caught in drifts; instead they

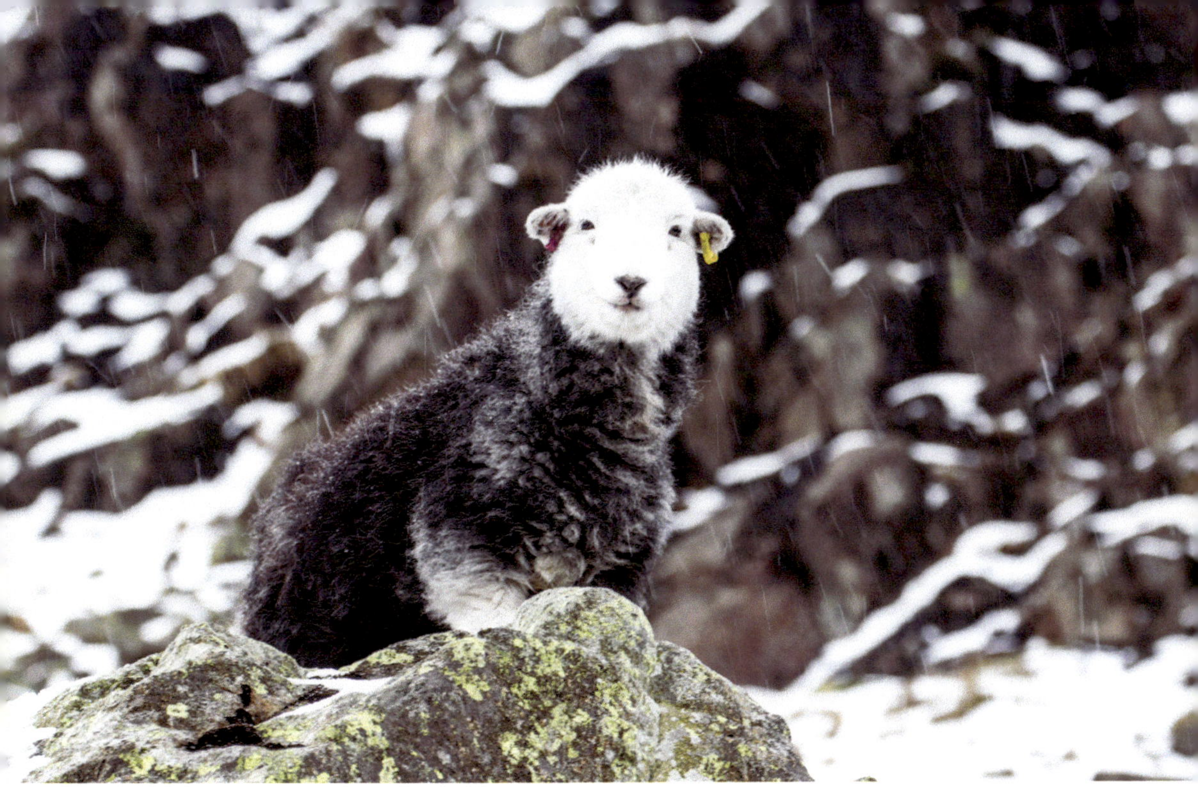

Herdwick sheep.

will instinctively make their way to higher, open areas to avoid getting buried. Even if they do get buried, they still don't give up and will eat their own fleeces to keep them going until the farmer comes to dig them out.

One of Kentmere's most famous residents was Bernard Gilpin (1517–83), whose many acts of kindness earned him the name 'The Apostle of the North'. As well as feeding and clothing the poor, he would also support poor boys in their education. Whenever he met one on the road he would chat to them and if they were intelligent, he would pay for them to attend university; one young boy went on to be provost of Queen's College, Oxford, and another became the Bishop of Chichester.

The main section of the route is part of an ancient road linking Shap to Barrow and is still very well used, although the presence of 4×4s on the route is contentious and often makes the local news as campaigners make their feelings known. Transport in the valley has long been an emotive issue and locals were amazed and horrified when the first horse-drawn chaise arrived in the valley. People had generally moved between the valleys on foot or horseback, with women riding pillion behind the men, and few people travelled further than they absolutely had to.

Even in the 1940s, a trip to Kendal was considered a big day out. In *School in the Fells*, Olwen Harris recounts how she left her home in Dudley in the West Midlands to spend fifteen months working as the schoolmistress of Longsleddale School from 1940. She describes the scene on a Saturday afternoon in Kendal when everyone was getting ready to board the bus back from town with the farmers' wives 'laden with their huge market baskets'. They had sold all their eggs and butter and the baskets were now filled with food, sewing materials and clothes, plus they had batteries for their wirelesses, which had been taken to town for charging.

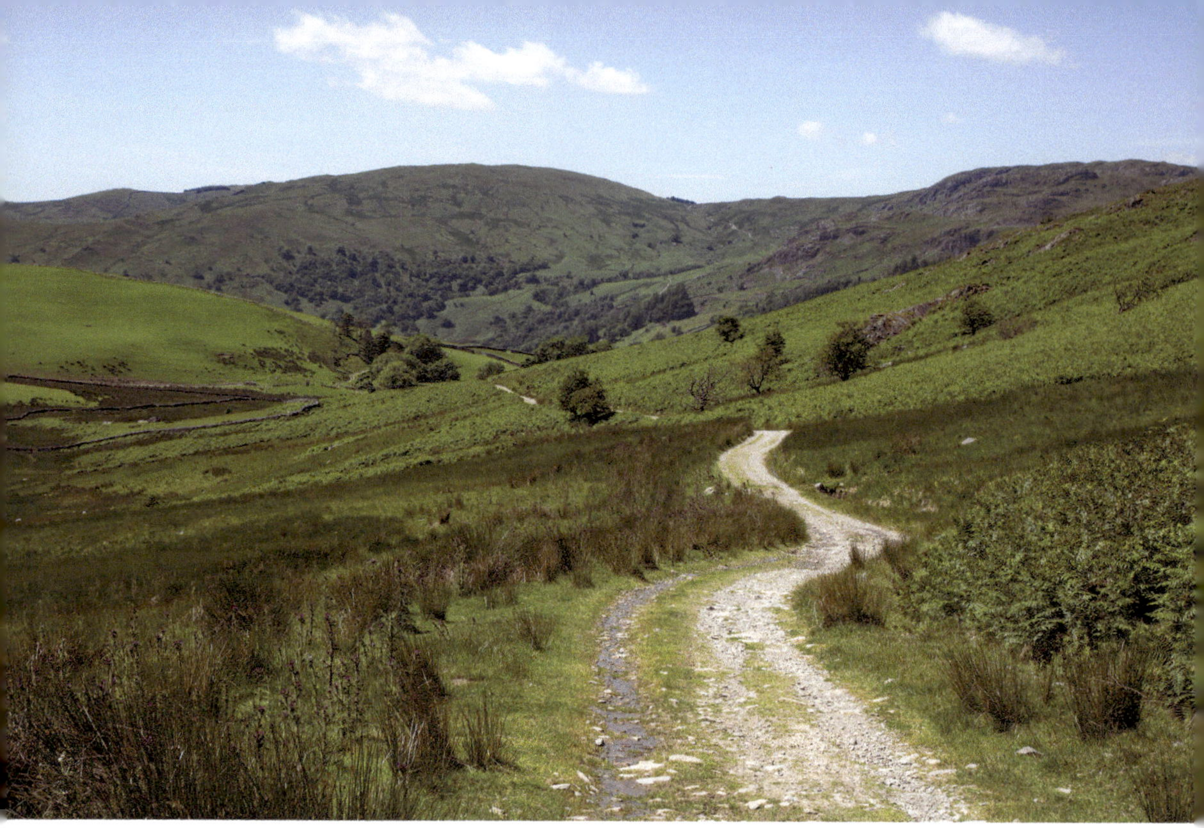

Above: Kentmere Valley and ancient linked routes.

Below: Cyclists in Kentmere.

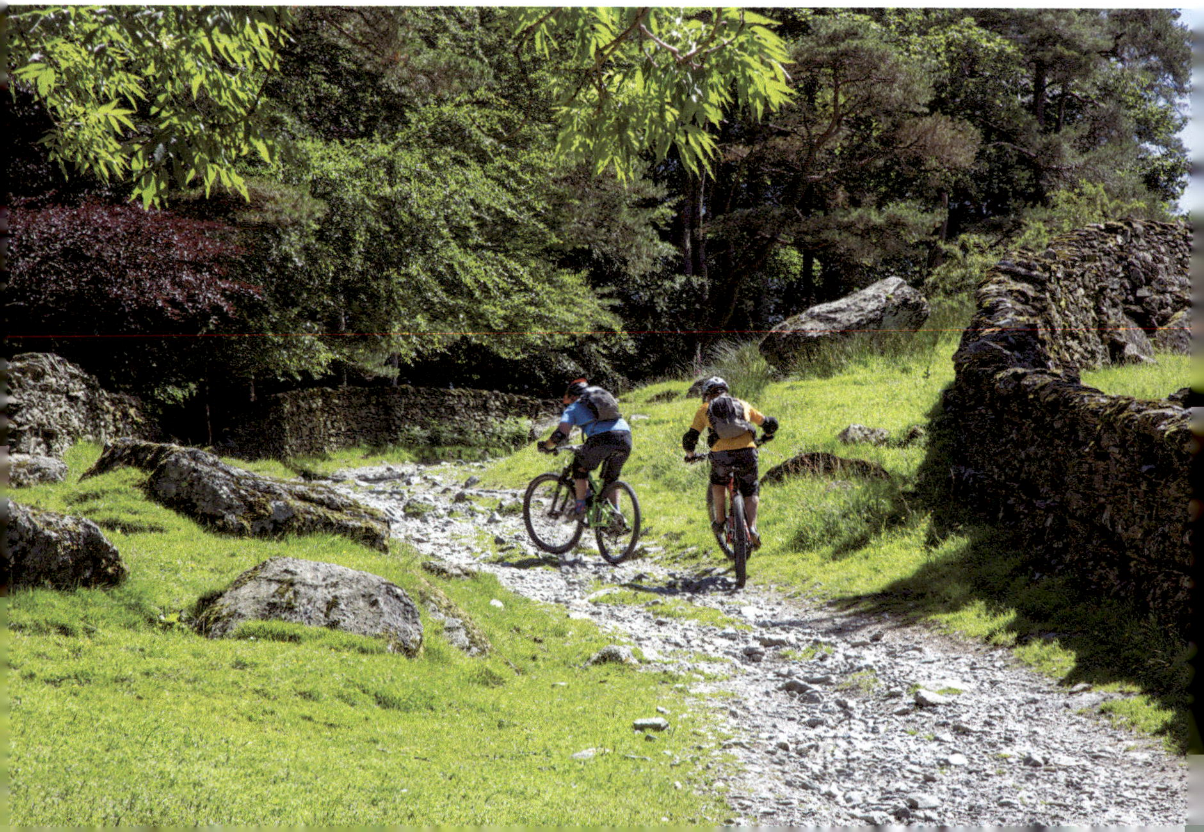

During her time in the valley, Ms Harris lodged at Beech Hill Farm, very near to the church and school. She describes an idyllic scene teaching eighteen pupils between the ages of five and fourteen, spending plenty of time in the outdoors and connecting with the nature around them. Books and other literature came from Kendal Education Office, and a box of books from the library would be delivered and collected by the local bus driver.

Many of the scenes she describes are still familiar today. She talks about trying to get the train back from the West Midlands and not being able to get a seat because of all the visitors coming up for their holidays or the day Mr Dixon was knocked off his bicycle by a lorry that didn't stop and she had to bandage him up. She also describes the deprivation of some of the children; how pencils and a penknife were quickly stolen from her desk and how her own family would regularly send gifts of toys for the children.

At least there was electricity in the 1940s. Prior to that winter evenings in the village would have been very long and very dark. People rose and slept with the sun and, in the winter, the only light would have come from candles made of rushes and mutton fat. Despite the lack of light, Longsleddale Valley still produced a famous botanist by the name of John Wilson. He started off as a shoemaker, then became a baker to make more money and turned to botany as he recuperated from severe asthma attacks. In 1744, he published a *Synopsis of British Plants in Mr Ray's Method*, which was the first systematic account of British plants in English (Carl Linnaeus had published his *Systema Naturae* in 1735 but that was in Latin).

Remote as they valleys were, and tough as life undoubtedly was, they still knew how to celebrate and weddings were a great excuse for the villagers to have fun. In the 1700s, the bride would have been decked in a brightly coloured home-made outfit decorated with

Signpost for all forms of transport.

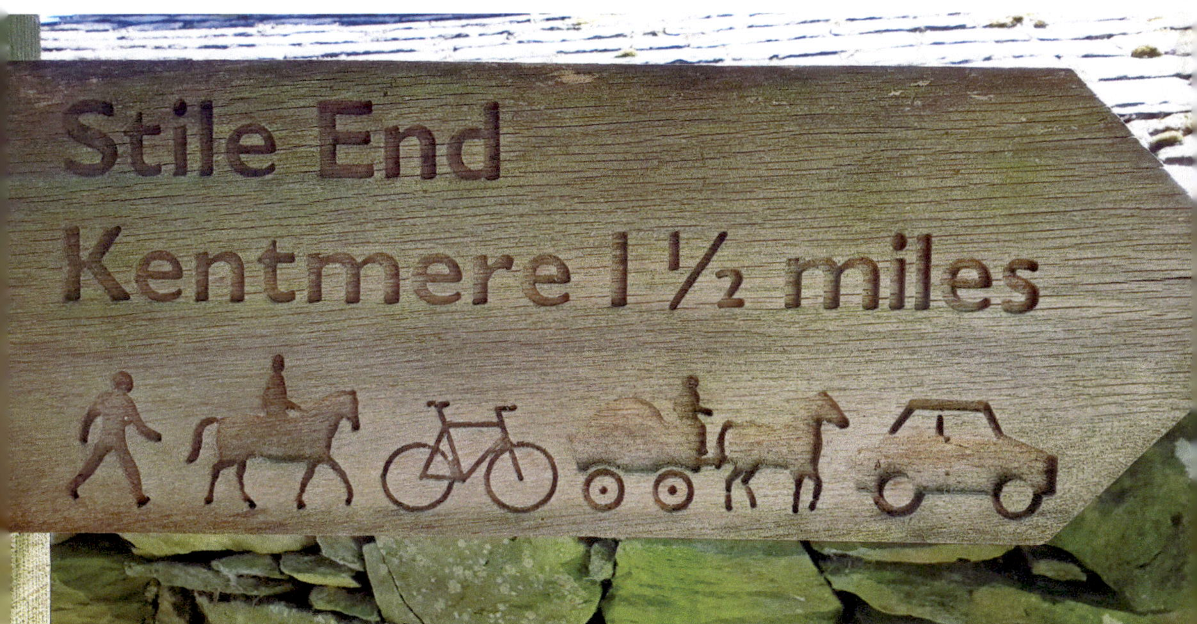

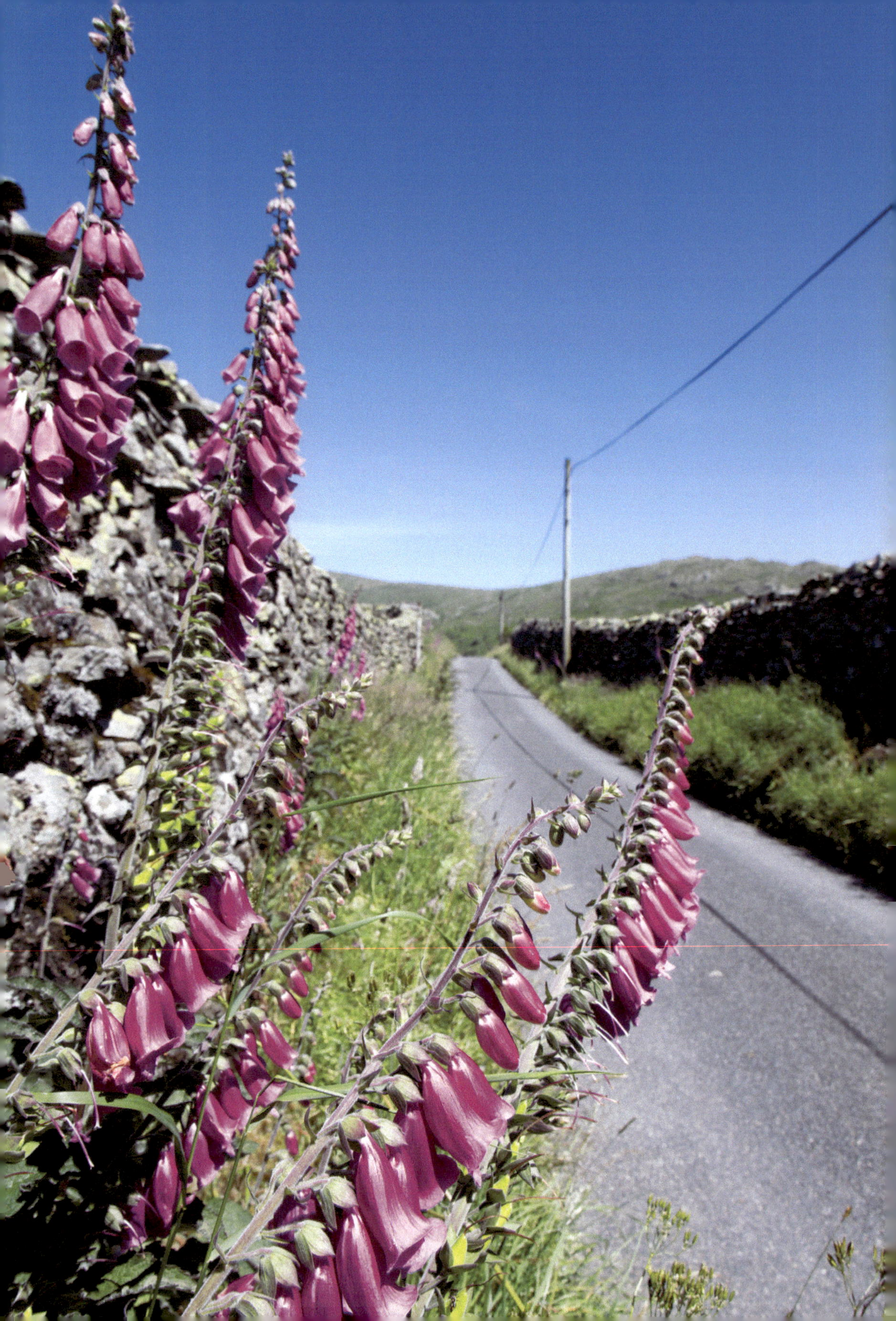

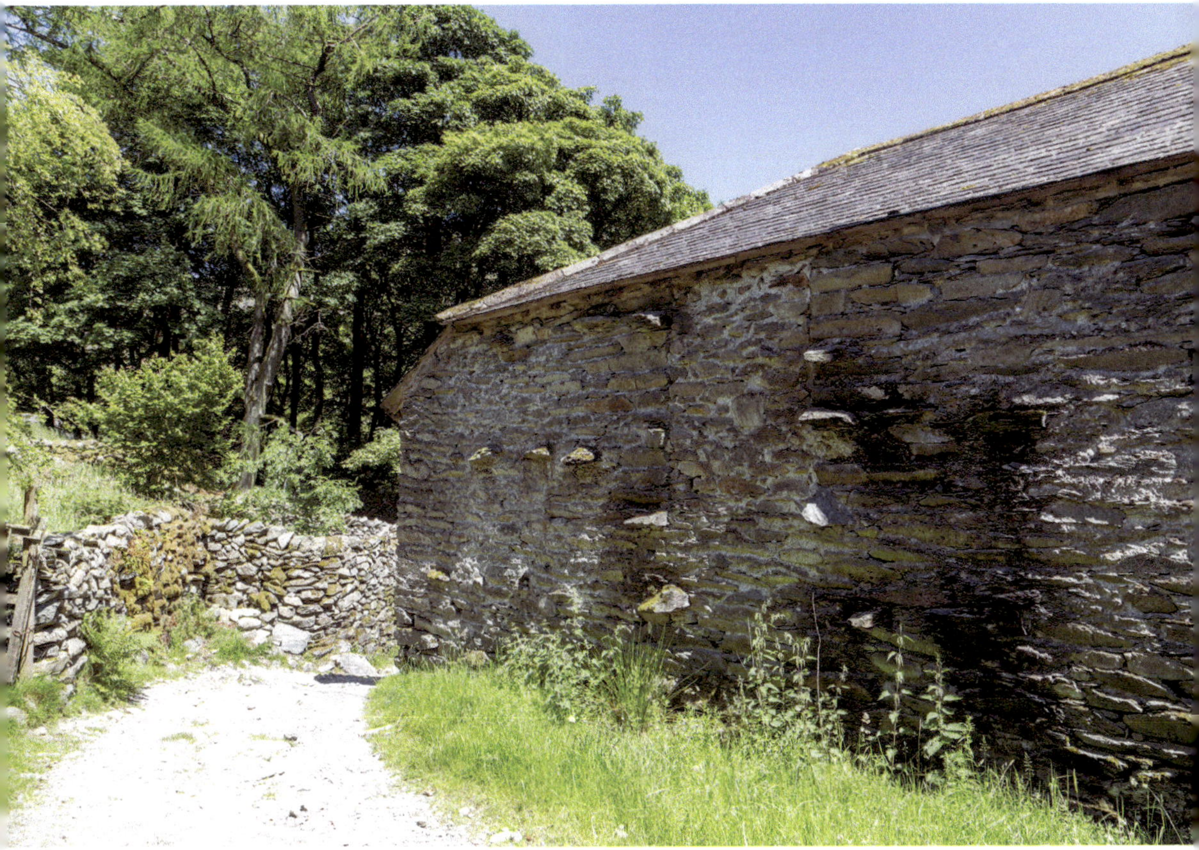

Above: Longsleddale Barn.

Opposite: Foxgloves.

large ribbons and following the ceremony an unusual custom took place. Once outside the church, the young men would pull off their shoes and stockings to show a ribbon wrapped around each leg. The bride would then start them off on the 'race of kisses' and they would run, barefoot, to her house and back with the winner being rewarded with a kiss and another ribbon from the bride. The parties generally lasted through the night with people finally dispersing as day broke. It was probably a good job the whole village was invited.

8. THE THREE PASSES – GARBURN, NAN BIELD AND GATESCARTH

Introduction

These are three of the most popular walking passes in the Lake District and connect remote valleys with busy trade routes. The scenery is magnificent, but if you're planning to do the Nan Bield to Haweswater then back via Gatescarth route then heed the words of Wainwright who warns 'This walk is rather too arduous to be done "there and back" by walkers of only average ability.' He does have a rather lovely solution to long linear walks though. He suggests making arrangements with another walking party, each parking at one end, and swapping car keys when you meet in the middle. Cheaper than a taxi but I feel sure the insurance companies would have something to say about it.

The Routes

Garburn Pass is still shown as Garburn Road on OS maps and starts down in Troutbeck as an offshoot of the old Roman High Street road. It's a long steady climb but the views of Troutbeck Valley provide a picturesque distraction as you gain height. Keep your eyes

Hikers on Garburn Pass.

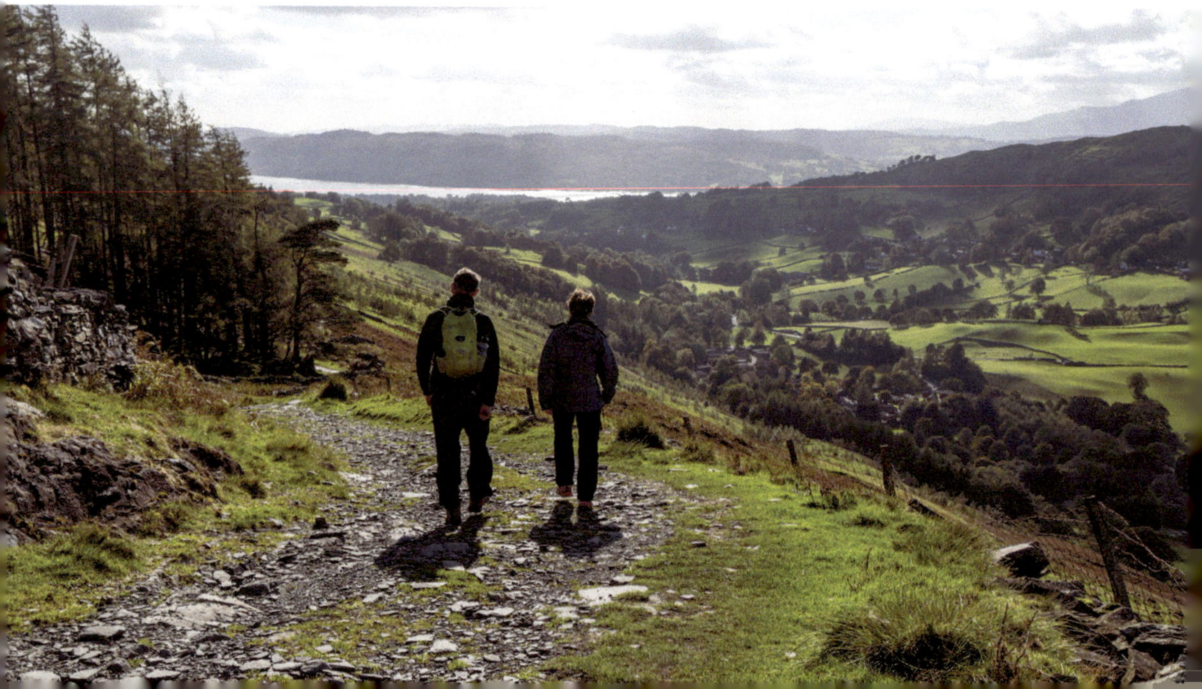

and ears open, as the route is very popular with mountain bikers but, since June 2011, it has been designated as a 'restricted byway' meaning it is now off limits for 4×4s and motorbikes. There was a proposal many years ago to fully upgrade it to a proper road, but this met with strong opposition and never came to fruition.

Nan Bield Pass is a little like Ravel's Bolero; it begins sedately with a long gently rising climb along the very pretty valley, but be ready for the final stretch, which is a very steep hairpin hike up onto the col between Mardale Ill Bell and Harter Fell. If you're doing the there and back route then this is where you have a choice: you can either drop down to Haweswater then climb back up Gatescarth Pass or nip up and over Harter Fell and enjoy magnificent views over Haweswater.

Gatescarth Pass also has a long steady lead in along the valley but the up isn't quite so sharp and nasty at the end. It's also a much broader and well-laid track but, again, you need to be aware of bikes and 4×4s, which also use the route.

The History

Garburn Pass – Maximum Height 447 metres (1,467 feet)

Troutbeck Valley, like many other parts of the Lake District, was once heavily wooded and Troutbeck Park was a popular place for pig farming, with the pigs happily snuffling around in the woodland undergrowth. Even back in the twelfth and thirteenth centuries, the woodlands were under threat and local lords were doing what they could to preserve them. 'Pannage' is the practice of allowing commoners to release pigs into woodlands to feast on the fallen nuts and in 1423 this was worth £6 15*s* to the Countess of Richmond

Troutbeck Church.

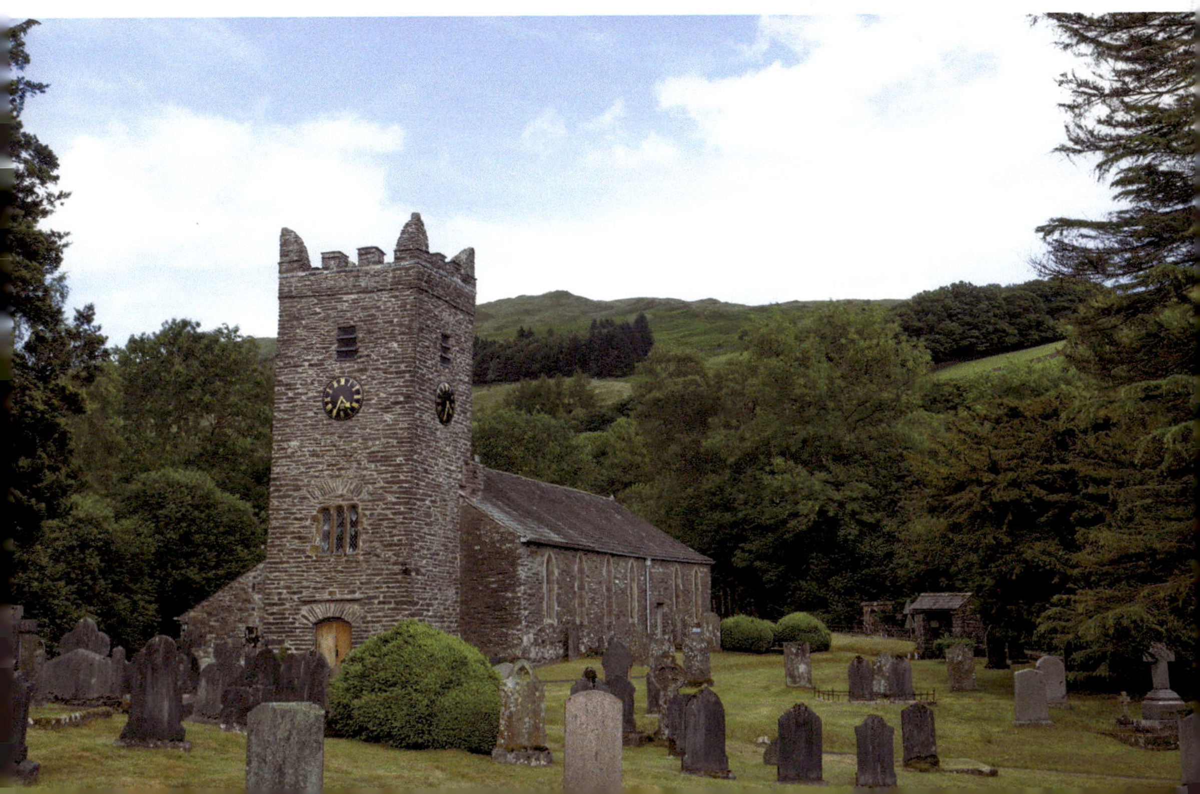

(who owned the land) but, almost ten years later, this value had dropped to *60s 10d*. By 1454 she was receiving nothing, most likely indicating that the woods, and the pigs, were no longer present.

By the late fifteenth century, woodlands were being damaged by cattle and sheep trampling or munching the saplings, and pig ownership was restricted to one per family, which had to be ringed and kept at the door and away from the woods.

The lords owned the woods but they were looked after by tenants who didn't always abide by the rules. The tenants were only allowed to take wood to meet the necessities – repairs, fencing, etc. – as well as being allowed to take dead wood for burning, but they often felled more trees than were required, and records show the manorial court regularly imposed fines on those overstepping the mark. The woods were also being depleted for making charcoal, which we mainly use today for relaxing summer barbeques, but back in the eighteenth century it was a highly valuable product much in demand from the various ironworks in the region and supplies were tightly guarded.

The route is very easy to follow and drops down into Kentmere just behind Kentmere Hall, a beautiful fourteenth-century pele tower. The tower, and farmhouse it now forms part of, were rebuilt during the sixteenth century, and it's said that the workmen were helped by a local lad named Hugh Hird (also referred to as Cork Lad of Kentmere or Hugh Gilpin in different texts) who was renowned for his strength and gigantic size. Allegedly he lifted a beam 'thirty feet in length and thirteen inches by twelve and a half in thickness' into place in the hall, without help from anyone else.

It is also said that he lived with his mother in Troutbeck Park, where they basically squatted in a house until the owner came to remove them. Hugh was then sent to London and, while he was there, took part in a wrestling competition attended by Edward VI.

Garburn Pass.

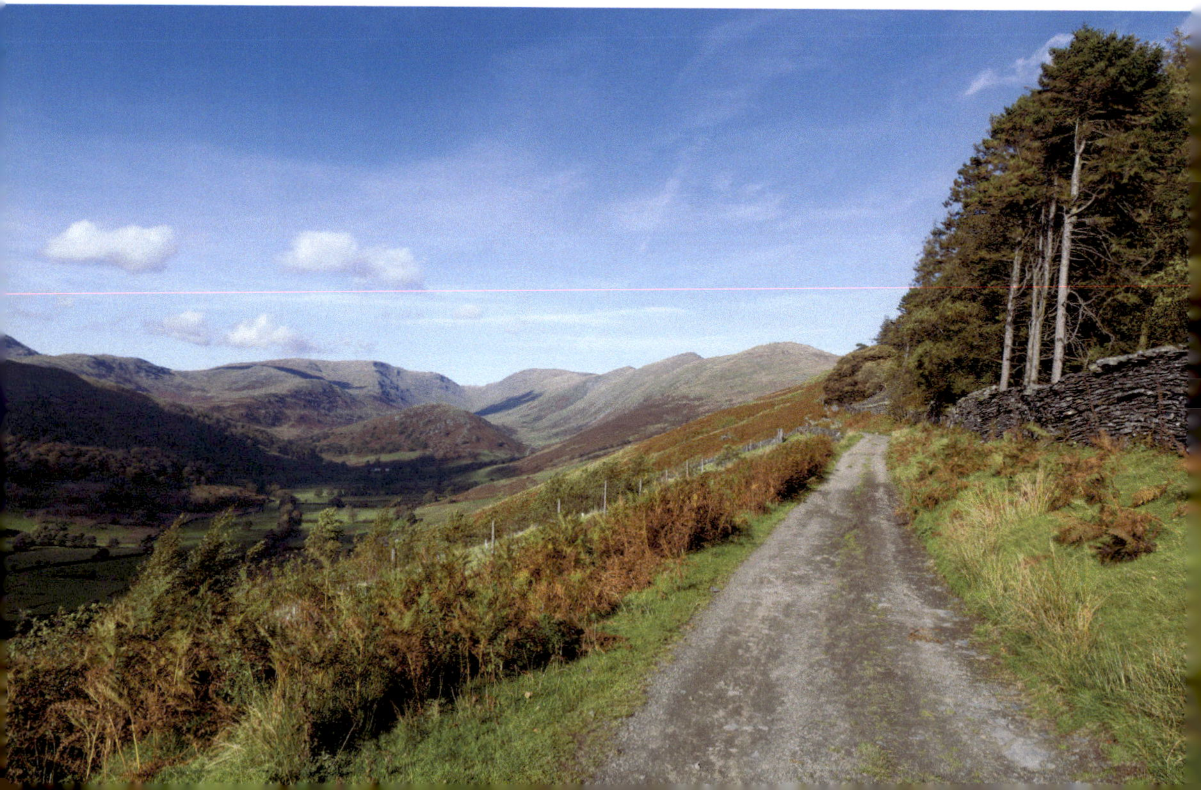

After winning the competition, the king asked what he would like as a prize and Hugh asked for the right to continue living in the house where they had squatted as well as modest rights to cut peat and wood. The king immediately granted this and Hugh returned to the house and lived there until he died pulling a tree up by its routes, aged forty-two.

Badger Rock or Brock Stone is an enormous boulder sitting in a field as you approach Kentmere church, most likely a huge glacial 'erratic' left behind when the ice sheets melted. These days it's a very popular with climbers and is well known among the bouldering community with thirty-two different logged routes to the summit.

Badger Rock.

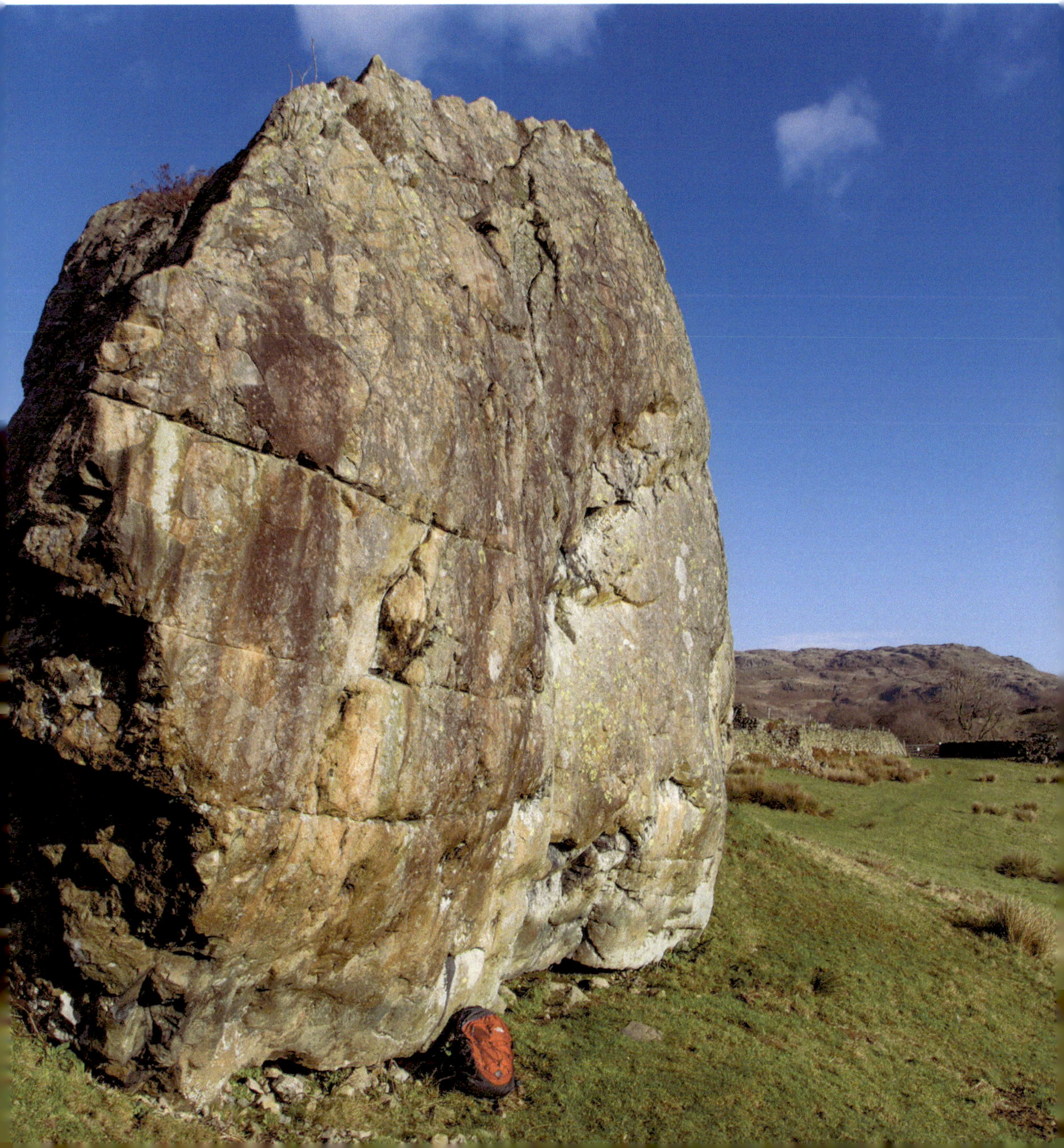

Nan Bield Pass – Maximum Height 640 metres (2,100 feet)

I'm always intrigued by unusual names and 'Nan Bield' is a curious name. The best I can come up with is that 'bield' means shelter and 'nan' is old English for 'none' so it could be that this was known as the pass with no shelter or shelters, although now there are a couple at the Haweswater end. When we tackled the route it was a surprisingly hot October day, which caught us out a little bit, and I can vouch for the fact that there was nowhere to shelter (and very few places to sit and have lunch) on the entire first section of the route.

What I sadly didn't discover until afterwards is that Toadhowe Well, which we splashed through on our way to the head of the valley, was once 'famed for being the best water in Westmorland' according to Harriet Martineau's guide from 1855. Harriet was a British novelist and journalist who, as well as travel guides, also wrote extensively on politics and religion. Born in Norwich, she moved to Ambleside in 1845, where she lived until her death, writing about her garden, her explorations of the area and her autobiography. I also love a tenuous link and it turns out that Harriet's great nephew, Francis Martineau Lupton, is the great-great-grandfather of Catherine, Duchess of Cambridge.

As the path climbs along Hallow Bank, look down into the valley and just below Tongue Scar you may spot the remains of a Romano-British settlement. This is an excellent example of these small farmsteads and consists of an enclosure containing the remains of ten stone huts, some of which are thought to be dwellings while others were most likely used for storage or as guards huts. The site is a Scheduled Ancient Monument so if you do decide to go down and pay it a visit, don't move anything.

Up above you on the right is the distinctive shape of Drygrove Gill, which, despite its name, is the source of a spring but its curious cigar shape had me reaching for my

Ullstone Gill.

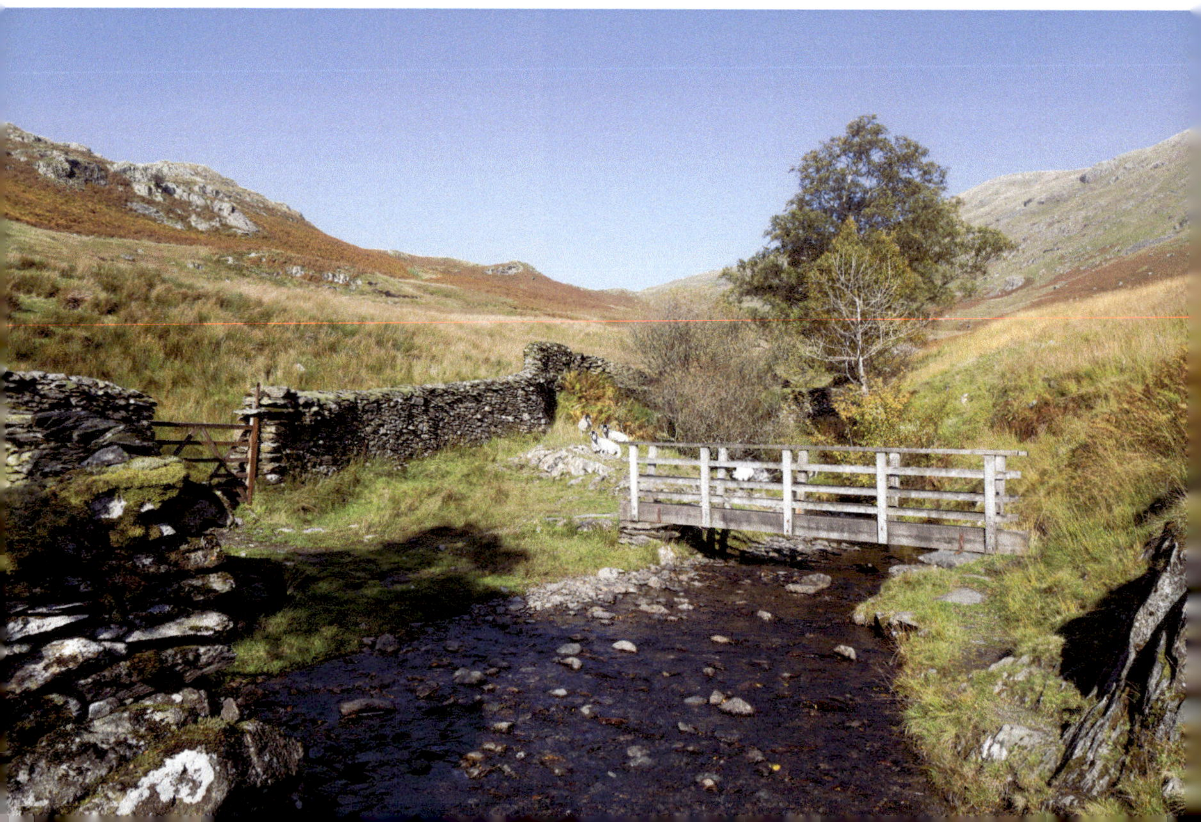

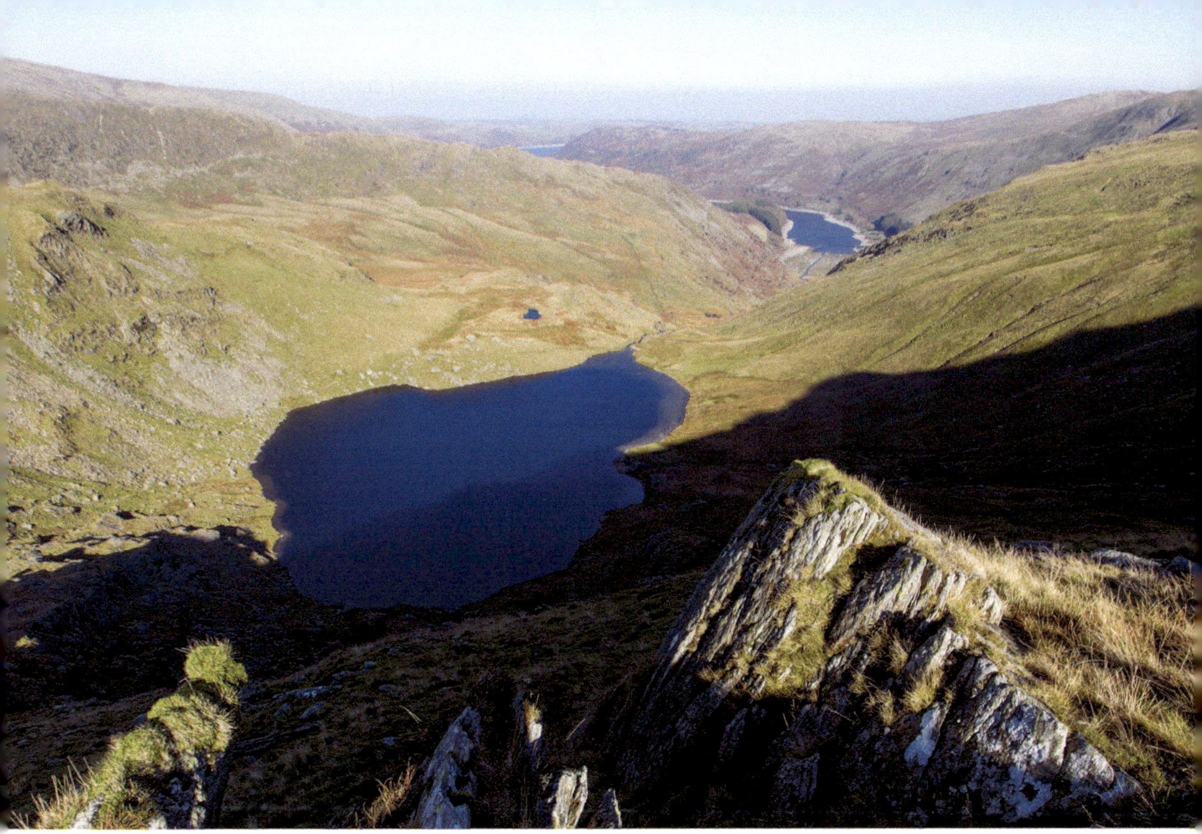

Above: Looking down Nan Bield Pass to Haweswater.

Below: Kentmere Reservoir and 'Gillespie Gill' on the far right.

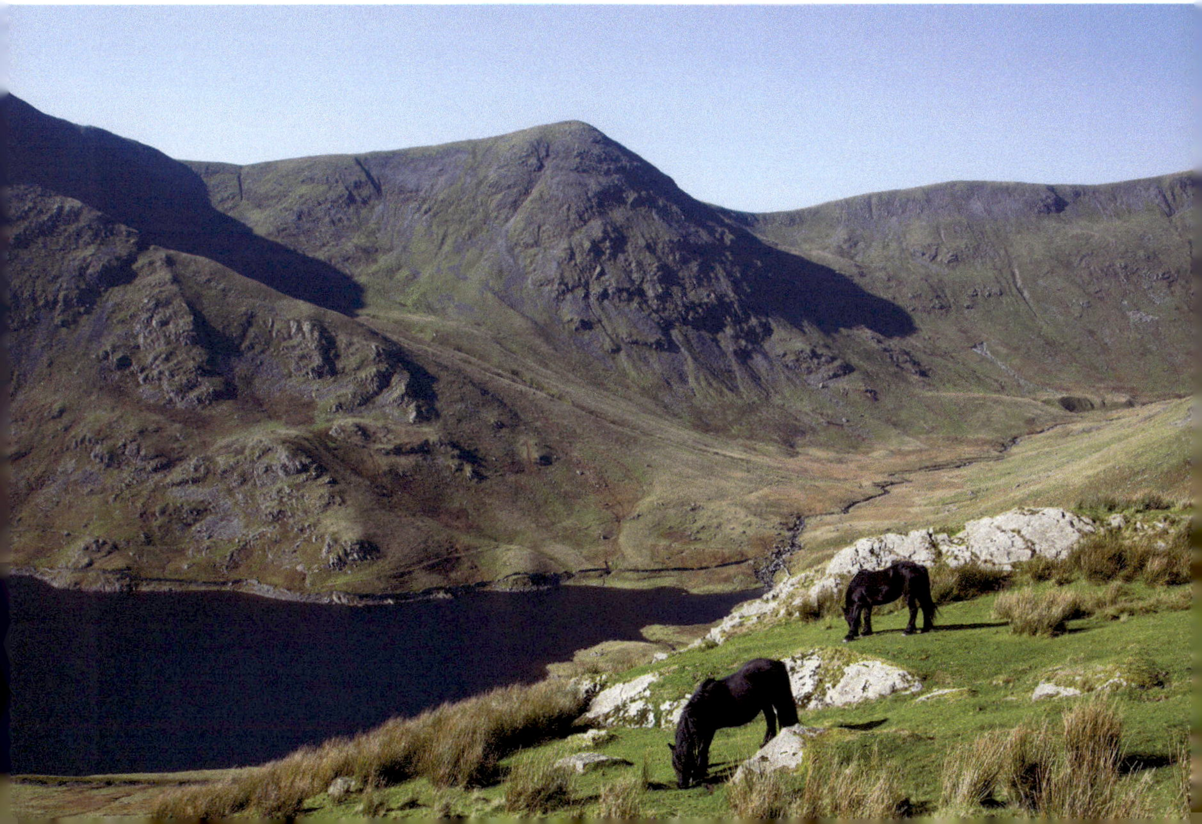

geology textbooks. All of the rocks on this section are Ordovician volcanic (around 461 million years old) but the rocks in Drygrove Gill are tuffs and therefore slightly softer than the surrounding andesite. In the short term this doesn't really matter but after 450 million years the differences will begin to show as the water erodes more quickly into the softer rocks.

Lastly for Nan Bield is a little bit of forgotten history, rediscovered thanks again to Harriet Martineau. In her book she mentions Gladgove Gill, which is the gill dropping down in between Wander Scar and Gavel Crag. She describes how it has recently changed name to Gillespie Gill in honour of a group of men who had recently died there. It turns out to be a very sad story from 1838 where two men, John Huddlestone and Thomas Gillespie, plus Thomas's fourteen-year-old son, perished on their return from a fishing trip to Hayes Water. The weather was 'very boisterous' and it is presumed they died of exhaustion and hunger.

Gatescarth Pass – Maximum Height 572 metres (1,877 feet)

The road to Gatescarth Pass starts at Sadgill Bridge, most famous for being 'the Postman Pat bridge'. John Cunliffe, who wrote the *Postman Pat* books, lived in Kendal and based

Sadgill Bridge with remnants of original bridge.

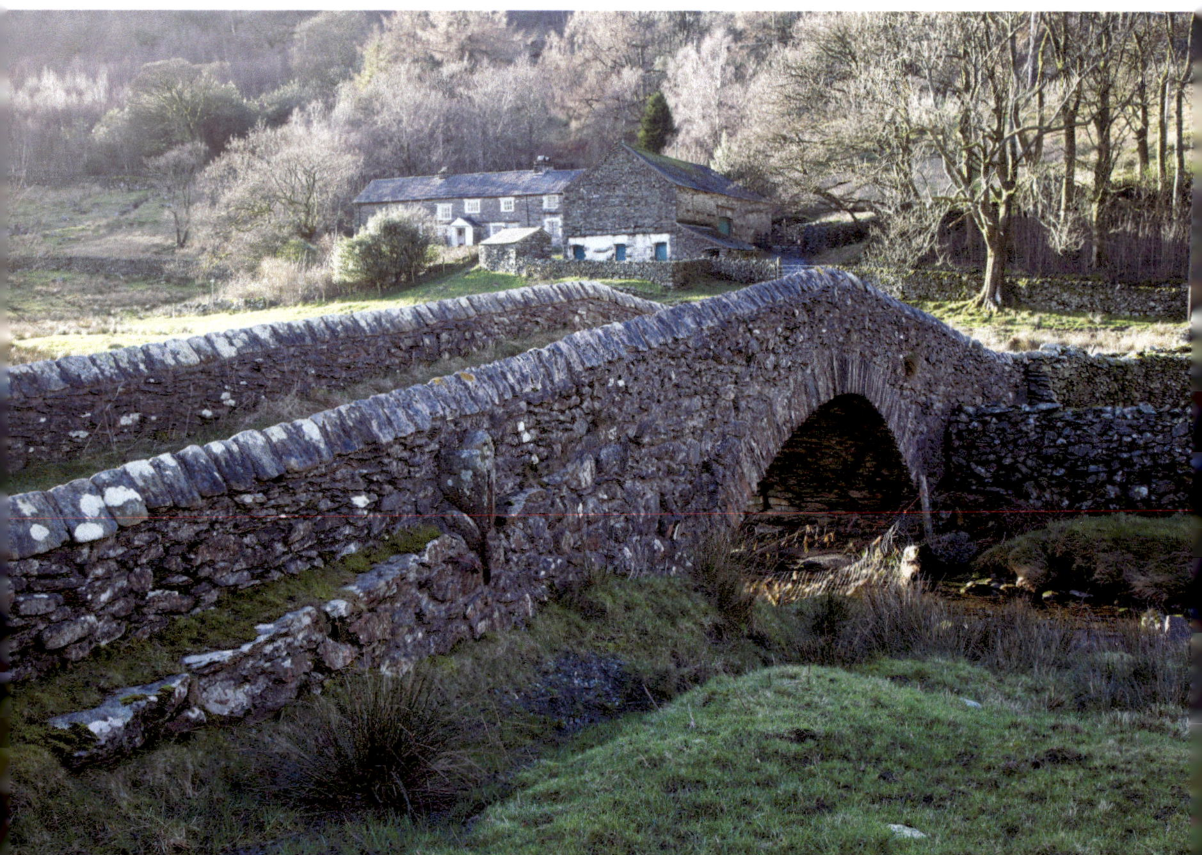

the village of Greendale in the books on Longsleddale and Sadgill Bridge is the bridge Pat drives over at the start of each episode. The local postmen must be famous as many visitors (us included!) have lain in wait to snap them as they drive over the bridge. The original bridge was built in 1717 and if you look closely at the sides of the bridge you can still see the remnants of the original, much lower, bridge.

Although the pass is open to 4×4s, they can only drive over there with a permit and usually only twenty to thirty permits are issued each year, so your chances of meeting one are fairly low. Plus they are restricted as far as Wrengill Quarry.

Deep under your feet as you make your way over the pass is the Haweswater Aqueduct. I am an unashamed geek of huge engineering projects, and have a very soft spot for both the Thirlmere and the Haweswater aqueducts. The survey posts from the building of the aqueduct can still be found on the fells in the area (marked as 'pillar' on the OS maps) and are the only indication of the lifeline running beneath them. The aqueduct carries over 570 million litres of water a day. It was completed in 1955 and in recent years current owners United Utilities conducted a thorough cleaning and upgrading of the pipes using specially designed vehicles and a team of 'aquanauts'.

Gatescarth Pass winding down to Haweswater.

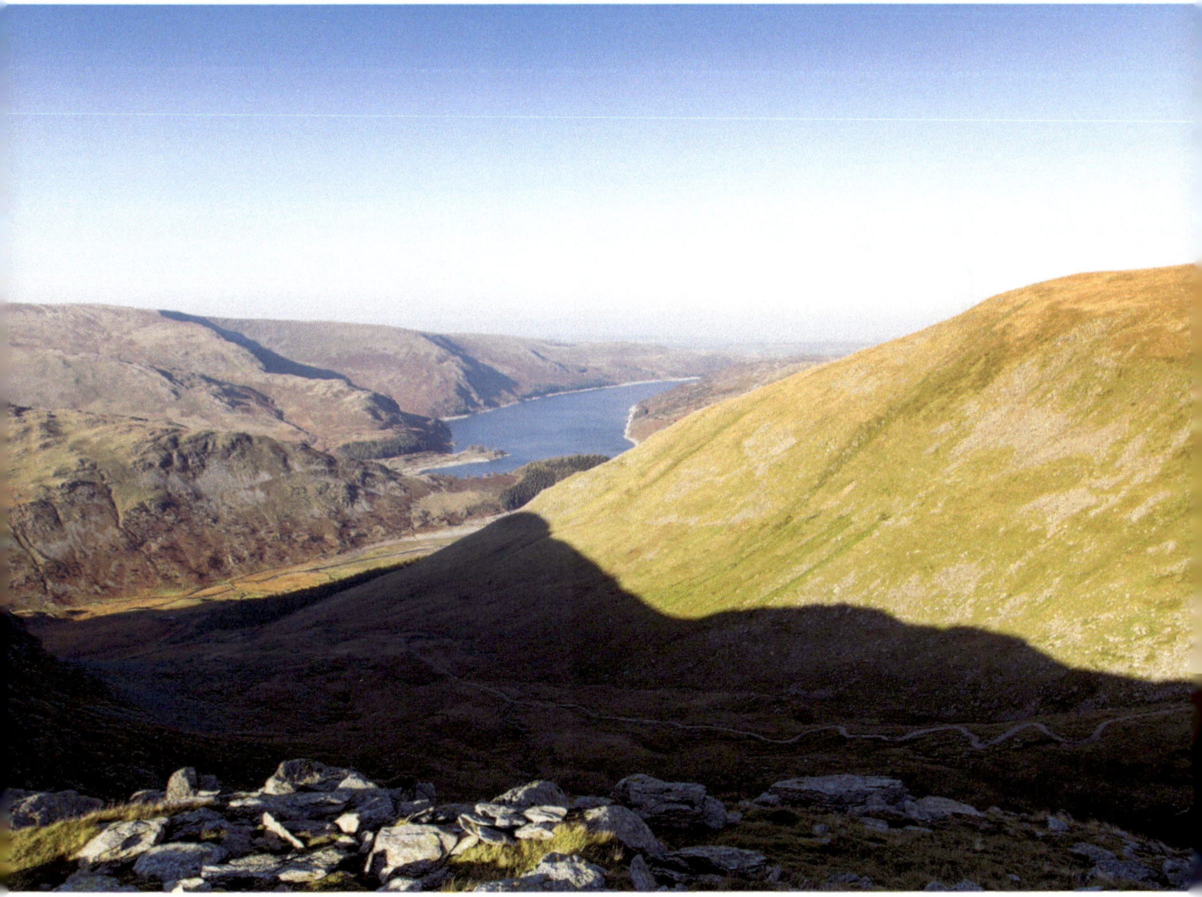

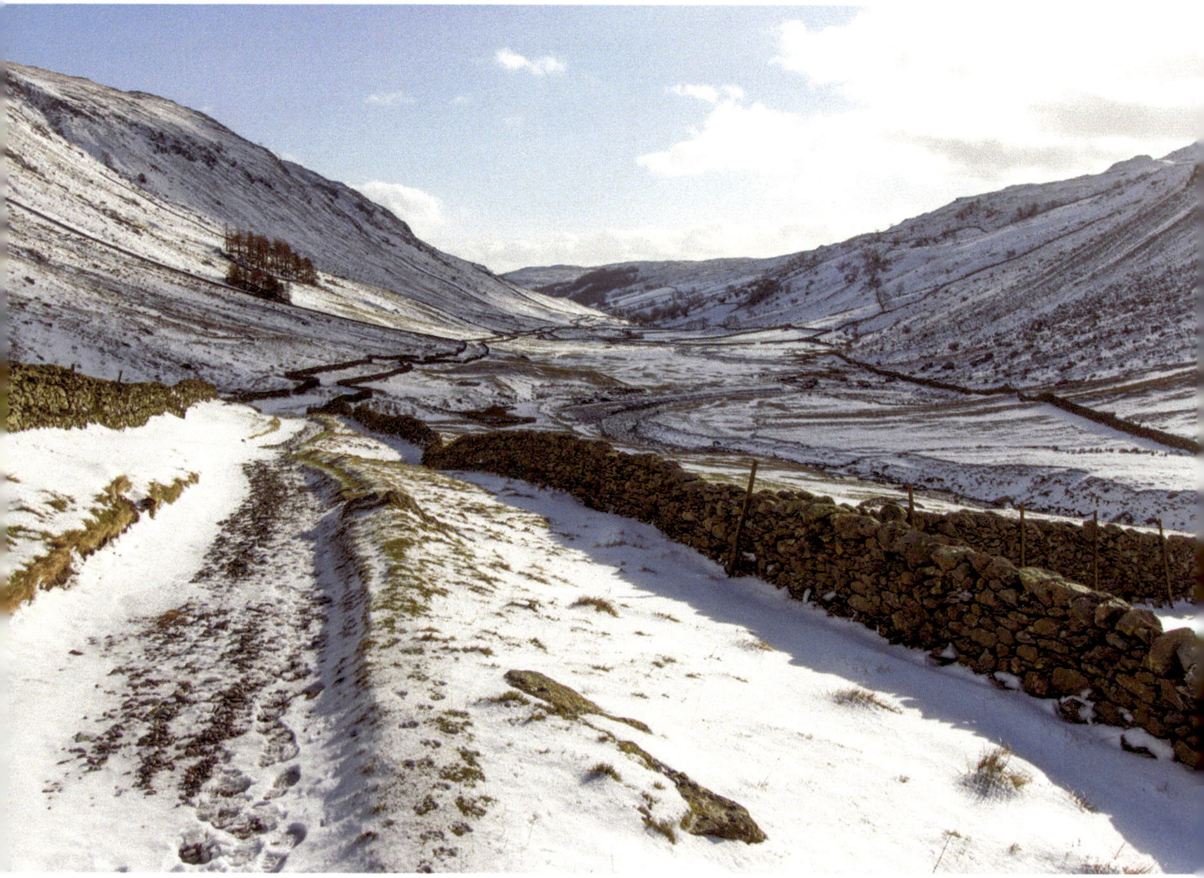

Gatescarth Pass in winter conditions.

Gatescarth Pass used to be famous for ending at the Dun Bull in Mardale Green but this is sadly no longer the case as the remains of the Dun Bull lie at the bottom of the Haweswater Reservoir along with the rest of the village. Instead the pass now ends at the car park at the head of the reservoir, which is very useful for parking but a decent pint would be nice...

9. HAWESWATER TO SHAP – OLD CORPSE ROAD

Introduction

We first walked this road in the middle of winter when there was snow on the frozen ground and the wind was stinging our faces and making our eyes water. Despite being well wrapped up in windproof down jackets with thick waterproof boots and socks, plus thermal woolly hats, we were still pleased to curtail the walk and get down to the Haweswater Hotel for a warming bowl of soup and a hot coffee in front of the fire. Imagine what it must have been like when none of those luxuries were available, and you had to transport your recently departed relative, strapped to a pony, over the unforgiving fells.

The Route

Obviously the Old Corpse Road used to start down in Mardale Green but, unless you have scuba gear, the starting point is now at the southern end of the lake opposite The Rigg.

Old Corpse Road sign.

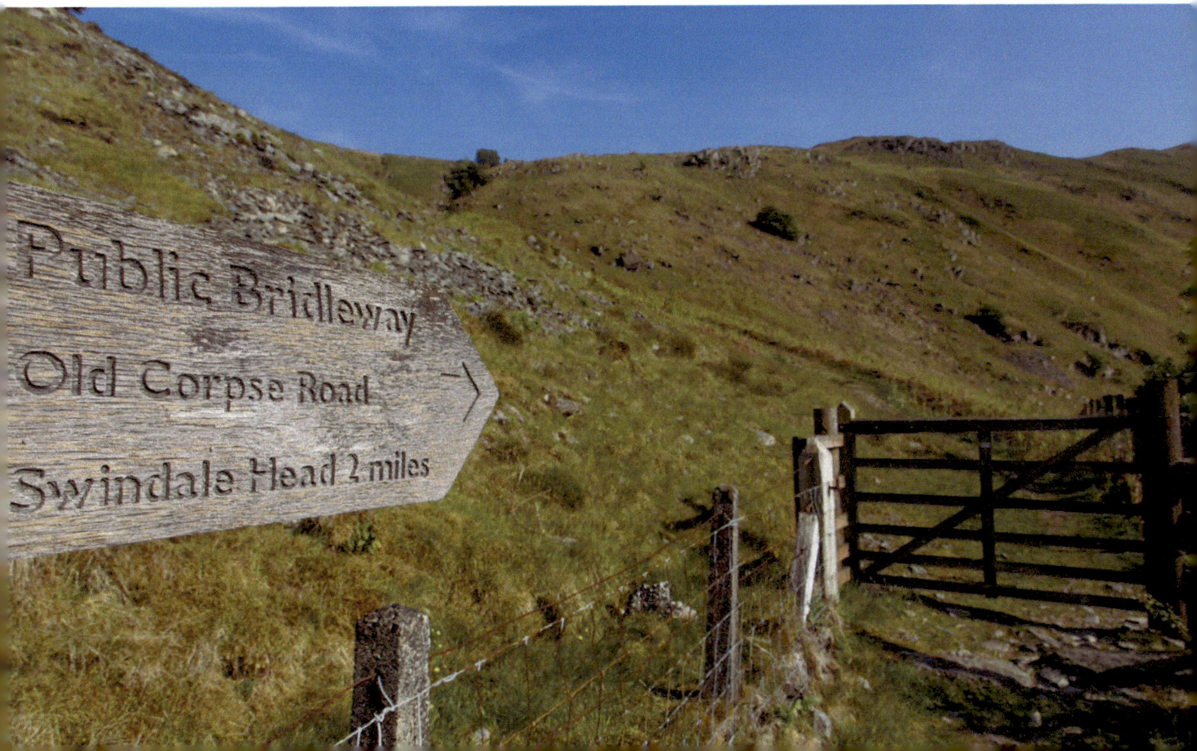

From there, it zigzags up and over Mardale Common, then down through Swindale. After following the road for a short way, cross the footbridge by the ford and follow the path as it skirts the lower edge of Ralfland Forest, then down through Keld and into Shap.

The History

Haweswater valley was very popular with visitors during the eighteenth and nineteenth centuries and is described in most of the guidebooks written at that time in the most glowing of terms: 'One of the loveliest of the lesser lakes and not nearly so well known as it deserves to be' (Martineau, 1876).

Where today we now see a large reservoir there was once a smaller lake. Although it's hard to picture what that lake would have looked like, Arthur Young's account from 1770 gives us some idea: 'The lake is a small one, about three miles long, half a mile over in some places; almost divided by a promontory of enclosures, joined only by a strait, so that it consists of two sheets of water.'

Thomas West (1778) tells us that at its narrowest part (below Sandhill Knotts) a man could throw a stone across it but he's not that impressed with Riggindale: 'Above the chapel all is hopeless waste and desolation. The little vale contracts into a glen, strewed with the precipitated ruins of mouldering mountains.'

There are numerous maps, images and accounts in existence which describe the village of Mardale Green, all of which help us to understand why there are so many important passes in the region, because what we see today as a dead-end valley was once a busy and important thoroughfare.

Haweswater Reservoir.

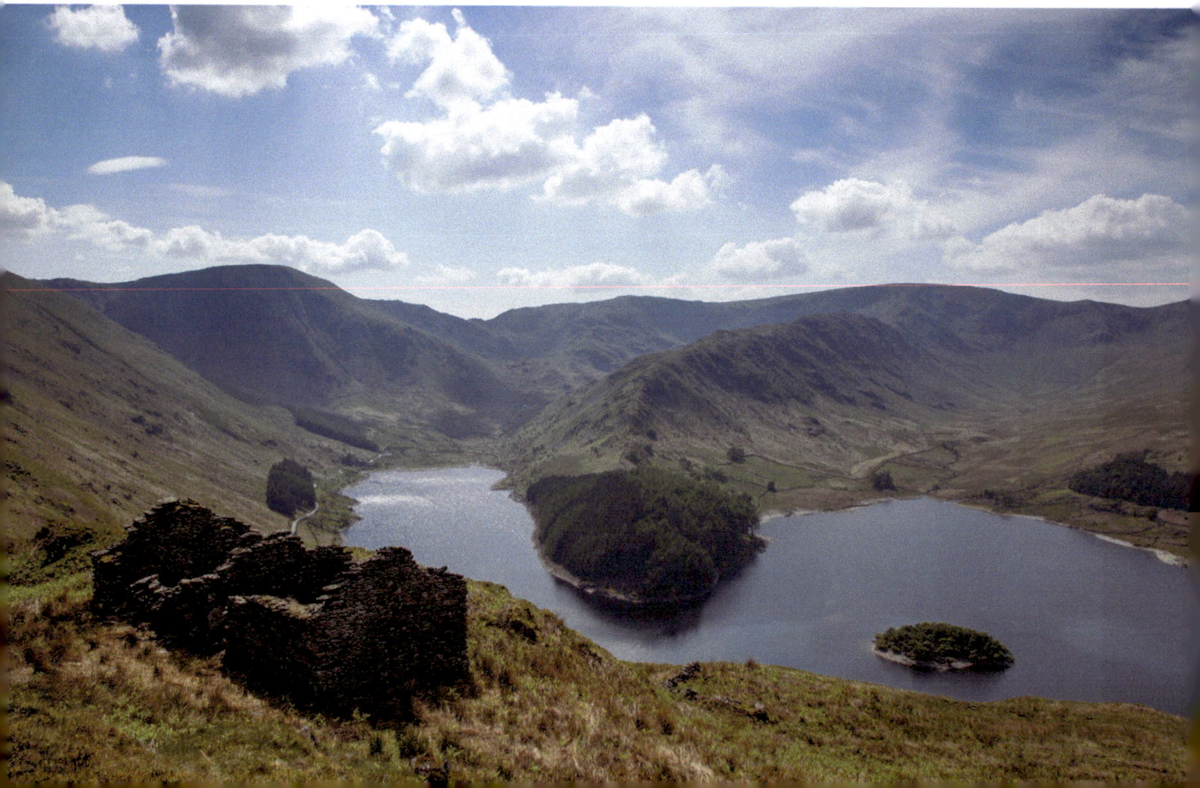

The dam to create the reservoir was built in the 1930s to provide water for the good people of Manchester, who were in desperate need of a clean, reliable water supply at that time. The settlement of Burnbanks was created at the northern end of the valley to house the workers but it was only ever intended to provide temporary accommodation. One guidebook of the time noted that the trees surrounding the village had been thoughtfully planted in order to hide the scars left once the temporary houses were dismantled. Although some houses were removed and the settlement fell into disrepair, it's still there today and makes for a very pretty and interesting stop on a walk around the lake.

The church in Mardale is believed to be medieval but the grounds weren't consecrated until 1729, so the dead had to be transported up and over the fell to be buried at Shap church. Post-1729 burials took place there but when the village was flooded for the reservoir these bodies were exhumed and reinterred in Shap.

As with all good coffin routes, there are a number of folklore and ghost stories associated with it. Hugh's Laithes Pike, just to the north, is said to be the final resting place of Jimmie Lowther, who apparently led 'a riotous life'. He died after falling from his horse while racing it when he was drunk. Because he died too suddenly to have time to repent, his ghost haunted the village so they reburied him on the top of the fell, safely out of the way.

The valley was a popular retreat for writers and artists, and a popular novelist of the time, Hall Caine (a vocal opponent of the reservoir), based his novel *Shadow of a Crime* around another piece of local folklore. A man from the village died and was being transported over the fell for burial but, unknown to the villagers, he had committed a serious crime (possibly

The Old Corpse Road, wild and remote.

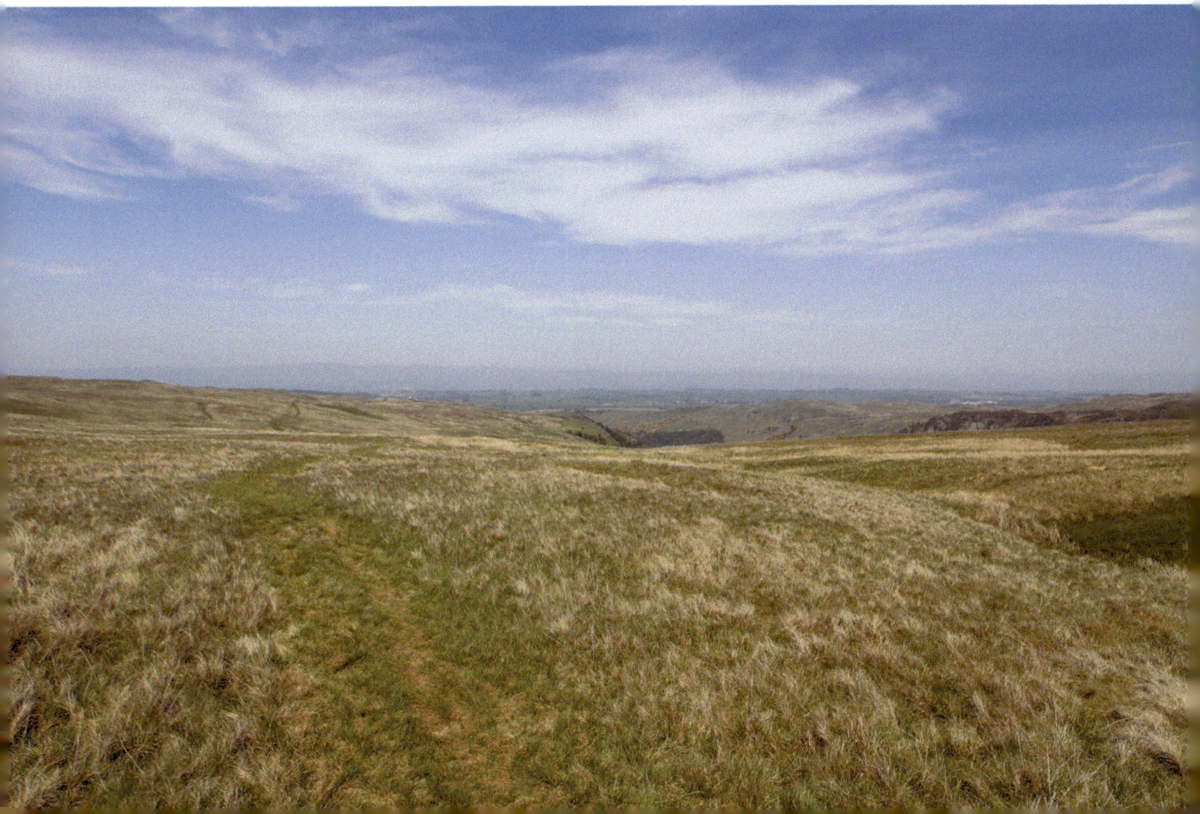

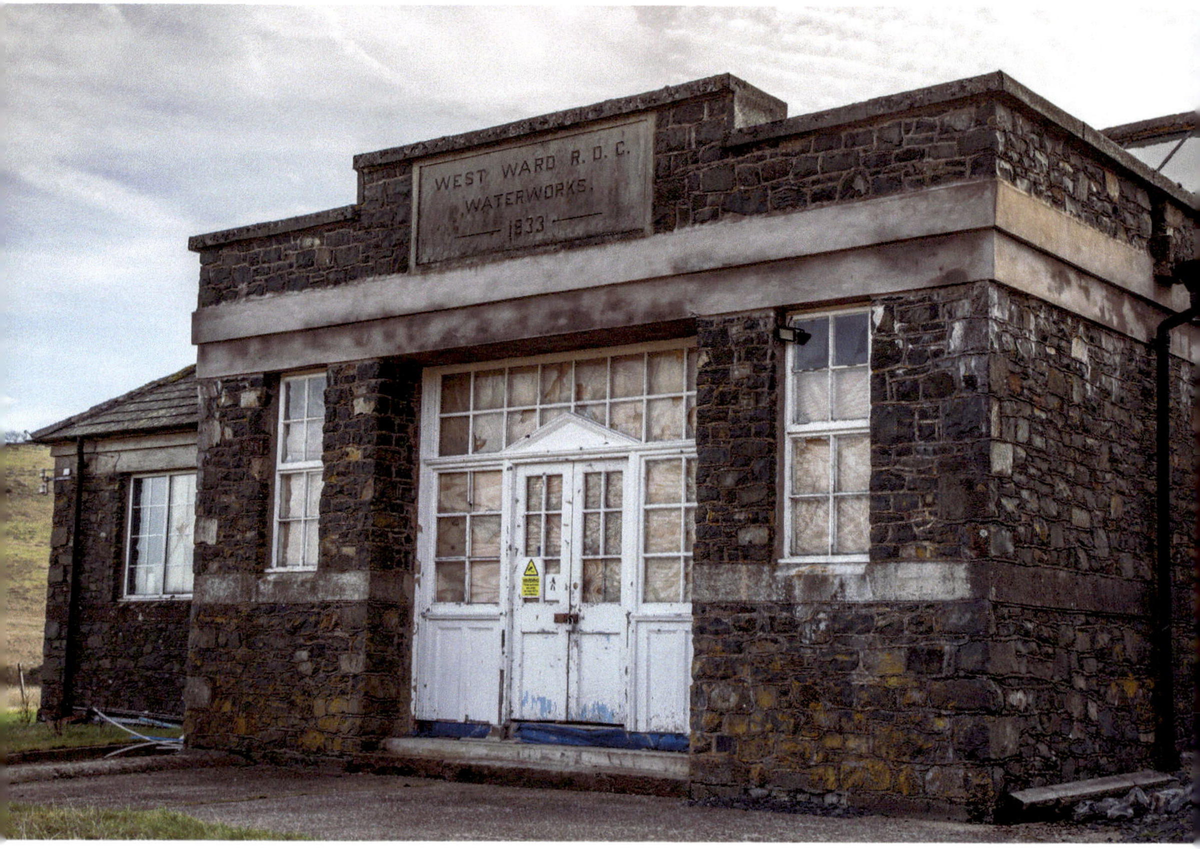

Old waterworks building.

murder). During the journey, there was a big storm and the horse carrying his body bolted, only returning three months later with the grisly remains of the body still attached. By now his crimes had been discovered, and the villagers deemed that this was a fitting punishment for his wicked doings.

The corpse road follows what would have been an old peat cutters track and drops down into the very pretty and very tiny village of Swindale, which Wainwright observes has been 'plundered unobtrusively for water'. The only evidence of this is a rather lovely old waterworks, dated 1833, at the edge of village, which, at the time of writing, is undergoing transformation into a self-catering holiday cottage.

What there is evidence of is a water intake structure, which at first sight sticks out like a sore thumb but on investigation was created for very good reason. During 2016, following extensive research, a project was undertaken to address flooding issues in the valley by 're-meandering' Swindale Beck. It had been artificially straightened over 160 years ago and had developed large levees along the banks as a result of generations of dredging. The result was that the river raced through the valley with no means of escape and, when it did overflow, the levees prevented this water from draining back into the beck.

By re-meandering the river and introducing gravel bars the flow has been slowed and, as a consequence, habitats for local wildlife have improved. Future plans include

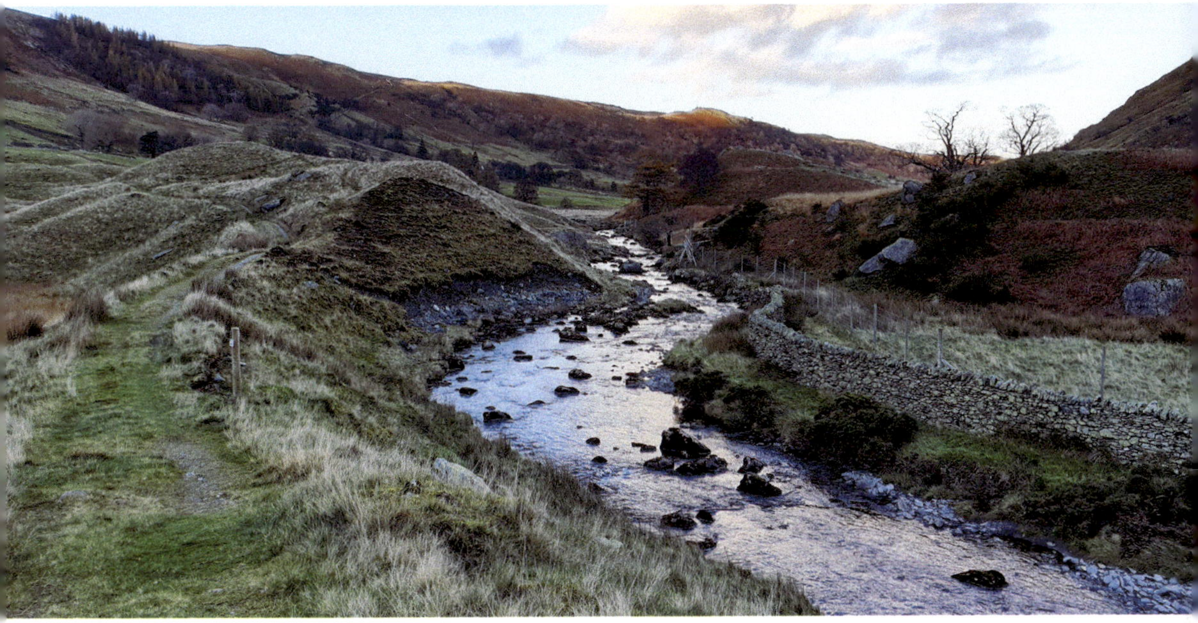

Swindale Beck.

further managing of the land, a controlled amount of replanting and introducing fencing along some sections of the channel, thus restoring it to how it would have been before it was straightened. The building around the water intake also allows for safe fish and eel migration.

The route from Swindale to Keld near Shap can be boggy and tricky to follow. It's a wonderfully remote valley missed by most visitors so the footpaths are not as well trodden as elsewhere in the county. On the approach to Keld, the Old Corpse Road is crossed by the more recent concrete road, which was built to link the A6 to Burnbanks and allow deliveries of the materials for the construction of the dam. Technically it's not open to traffic, but keep your wits about you, as it's still a popular cut through for locals.

Keld derives from the ancient Viking word 'kelda', which either means 'spring' or 'the still part of the water in a river' and the River Lowther does slow here as it navigates Keld Dub. Keld Chapel is a wonderful place to visit for a real step back in time. It's owned by the National Trust and although it is always locked, the key is kept on the doorpost of the house opposite and in a world of high-tech entry passes, it is a wonderfully huge, thick, 'proper' key.

Inside the chapel you'll find a series of reproduced letters exchanged in 1917 between Lord Lonsdale, his solicitor and Cardinal Rawnsley, where Lord Lonsdale argues that it was a barn not a chapel, and its location made it 'impossible for a full load of hay' to pass. He offered the cardinal £25 (equivalent to just over £1,600 today) to buy it so he could pull it down. Thankfully his offer was rejected and the chapel still stands.

It is thought (though it is not certain) that it may have originally been built as a chantry – a special chapel built for saying prayers for the dead – by the monks of nearby Shap Abbey. Sometime before 1698 it changed from a religious building to a private dwelling and

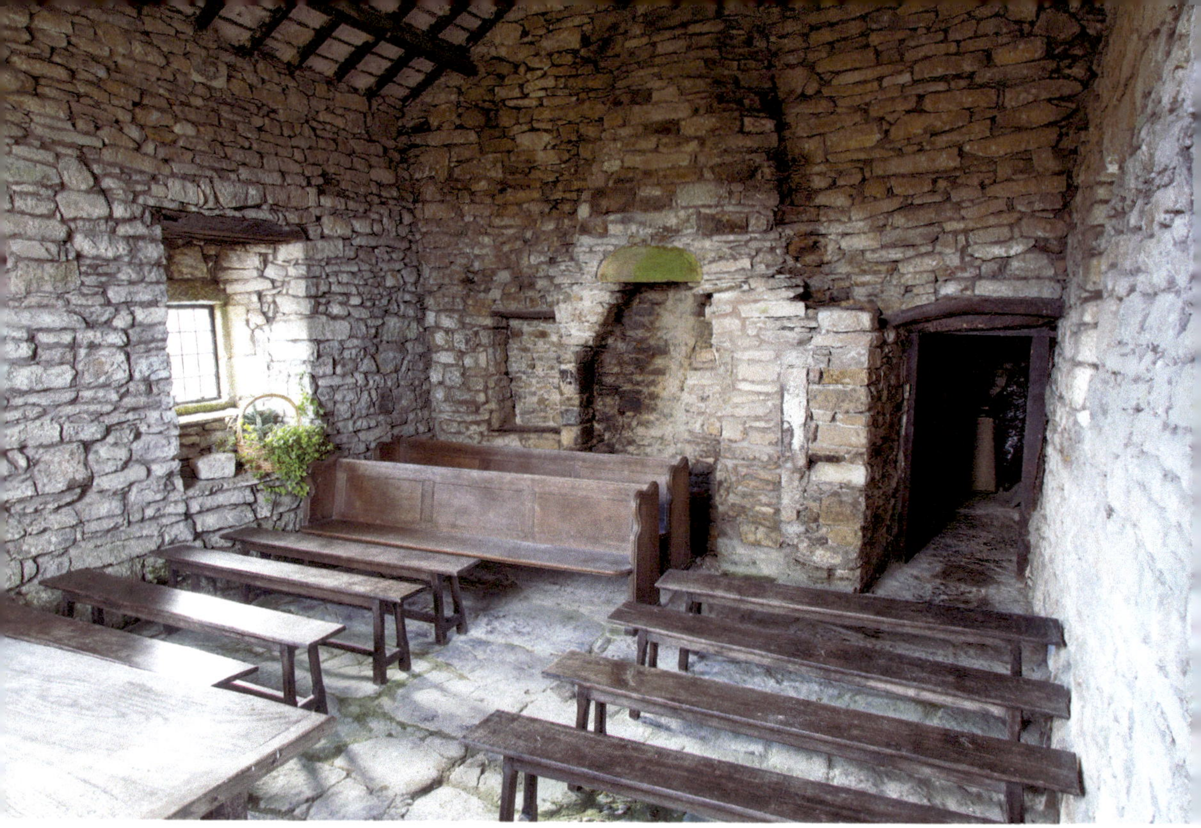

Above: Keld Chapel.

Below: Shap Abbey.

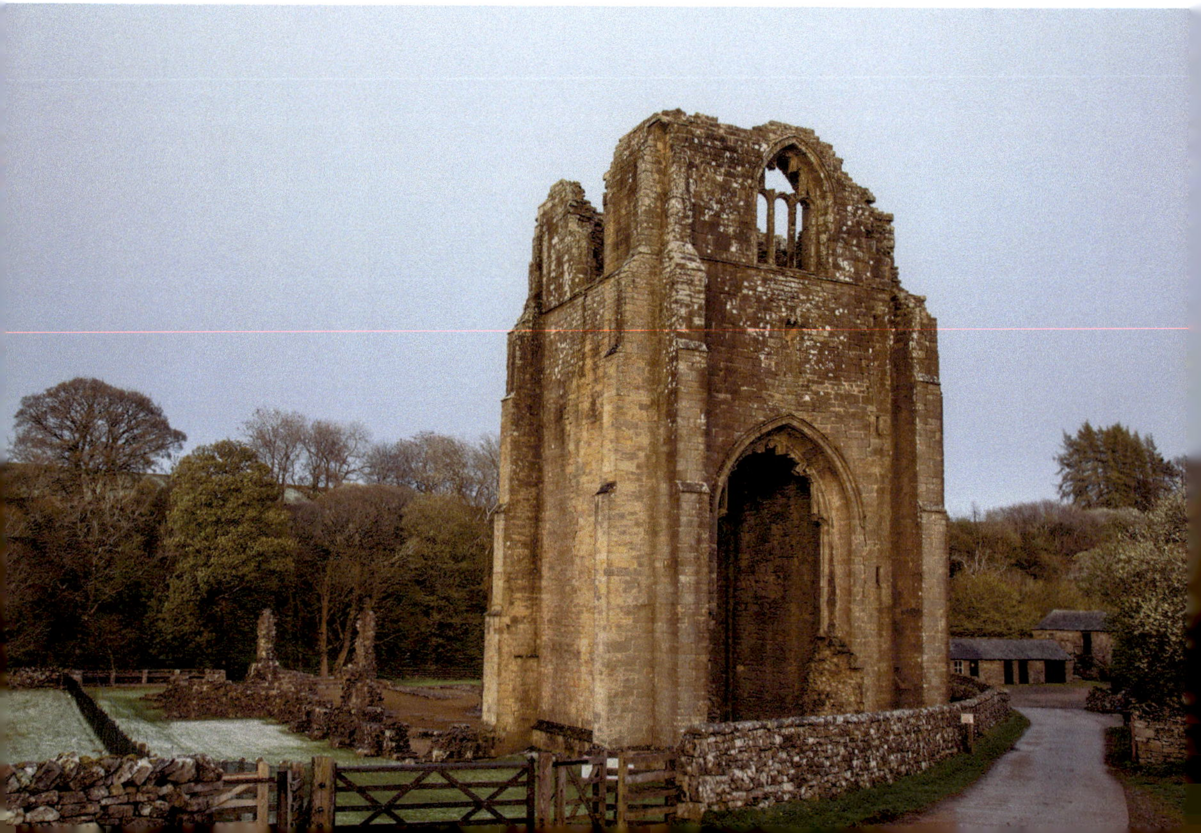

remained as such until the late nineteenth century when Revd J. Whiteside repaired the collapsed roof and reinstated it as a place of worship.

Shap Abbey is just a short diversion from the route, and although there's not much other than the church tower remaining, it's still an interesting site to explore. The abbey was founded in the twelfth century and holds the distinction of being the last abbey to fall during Henry VIII's Dissolution of the Monasteries, before it was finally dissolved on 14 January 1540.

The last point of interest on the route is Goggleby Stone, large and unmissable and adjacent to the footpath as you approach Shap. This is one of the final reminders of a once great and widely renowned 'Avenue of Stones' that existed here. It was described as being 'the Stonehenge or Avebury of the north of England' by Professor J. Y. Simpson MD (who, when he wasn't studying antiquities, introduced the use of both chloroform and forceps to the world of medicine). The avenue was nearly 2 miles long and, on an OS map, the line of stones marked across the fields to the east of the town is still visible. The original structure is believed to be Neolithic and stood for centuries before being demolished and removed as the region developed.

A painting from 1775, credited to Lady Lowther, shows a stone circle at the top and a broad avenue of stones sweeping away into the distance. The lack of preservation of the stones and their destruction without documentation, in large part by the rail company literally railroading their way through the centre of the stone circle, means that definite evidence for dating the stones or understanding what their function was is frustratingly absent. If you're interested in finding out more about them, there is a

Goggleby Stone.

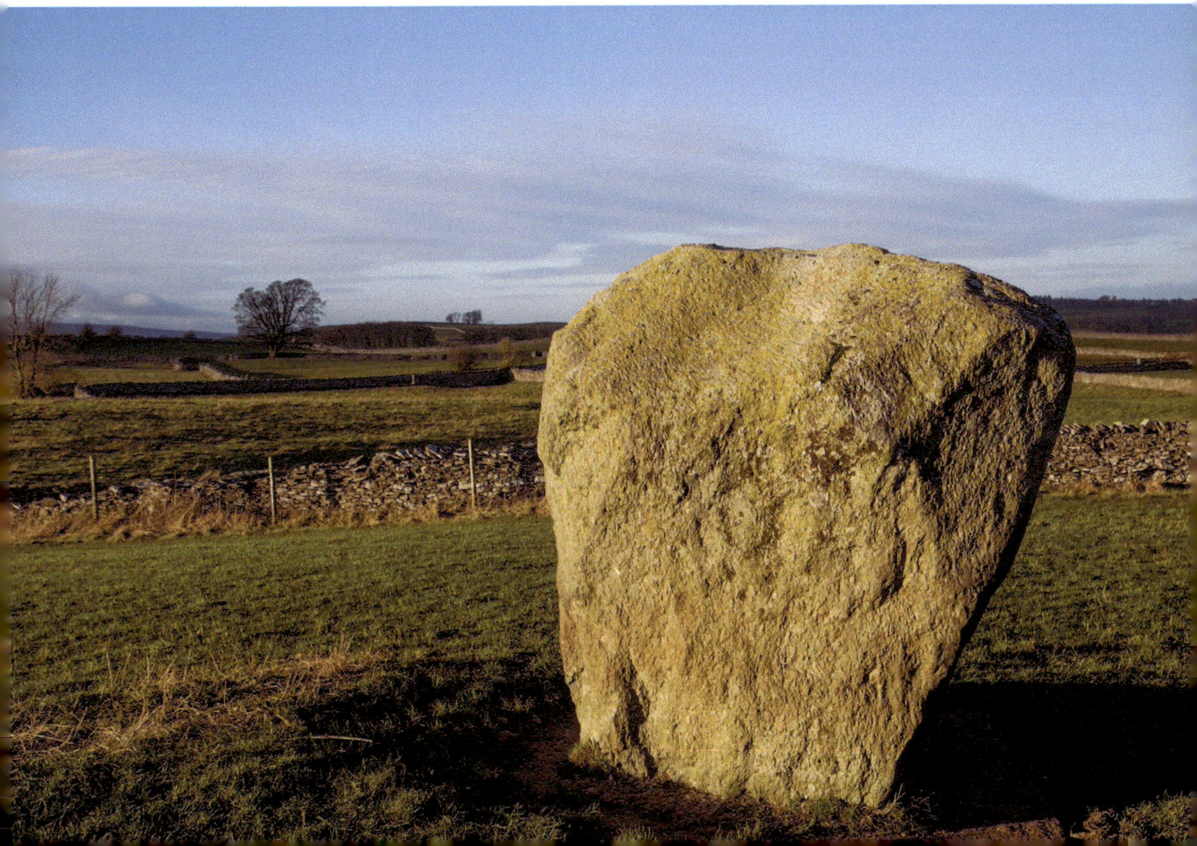

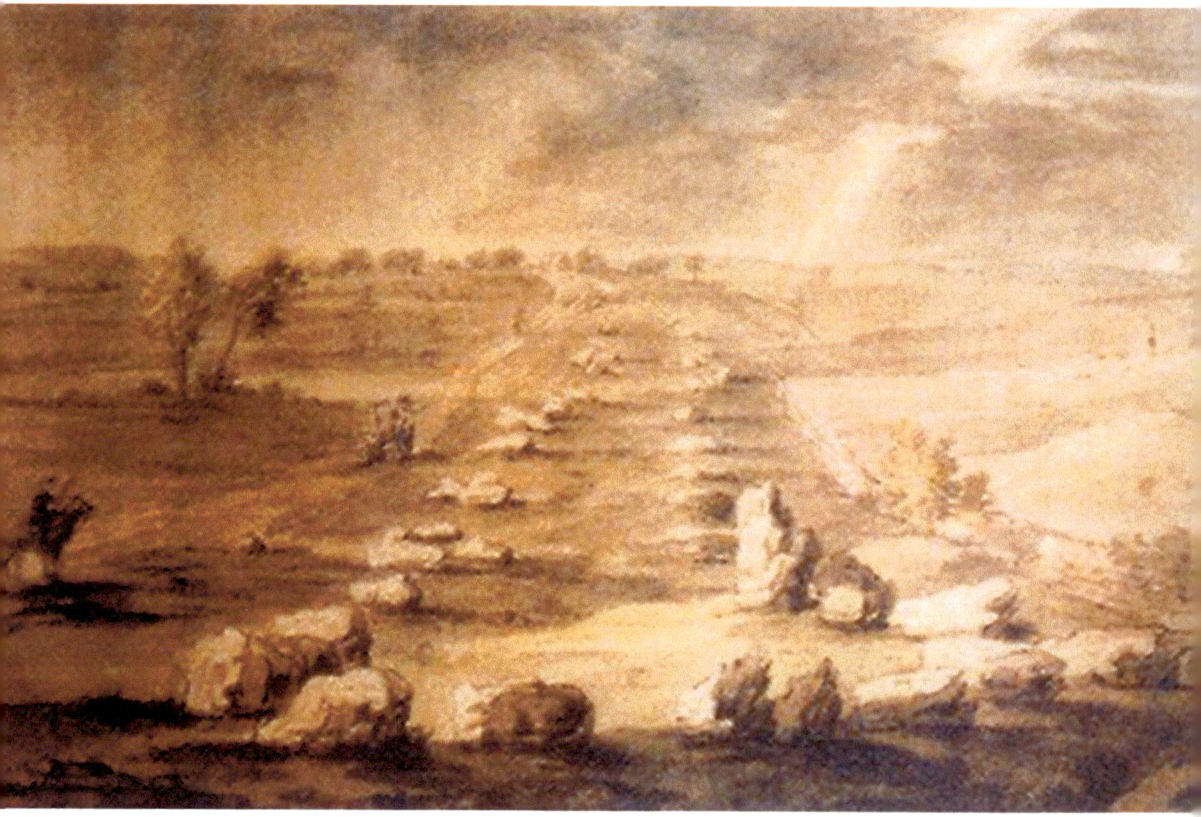

The Avenue of Stones, Lady Lowther.

fascinating paper on the Modern Antiquarian website (referenced in the bibliography), where the authors have tracked down many of the original stones, now incorporated into walls and gateposts.

Once you arrive in Shap, there are many historical places of note to visit. Wikipedia names over thirty listed buildings in the parish, including the Greyhound Inn, an old coaching inn, which dates back to the early eighteenth century and is reputedly where Bonnie Prince Charlie stayed. He was less than complimentary about the experience, but I'm sure it's now under new management.

The end of the Corpse Road is St Michael's Church, which predates the abbey by a hundred years or so, although it's thought there has been a place of worship on the site since AD 750. There's a monument in the churchyard to the men who lost their lives building the Lancaster to Carlisle railway, which is a sobering reminder that perhaps the introduction of health and safety regulations aren't an entirely bad idea.

Inside the church the only reminder of its ancient past are the Norman columns, the rest of the original building having been lost in a restoration in 1898. The Millennium Window depicts local scenes and land uses and was installed and dedicated in September 2000. It was designed by Adam Goodyear, who involved the local community to design something that reflected life in the parish.

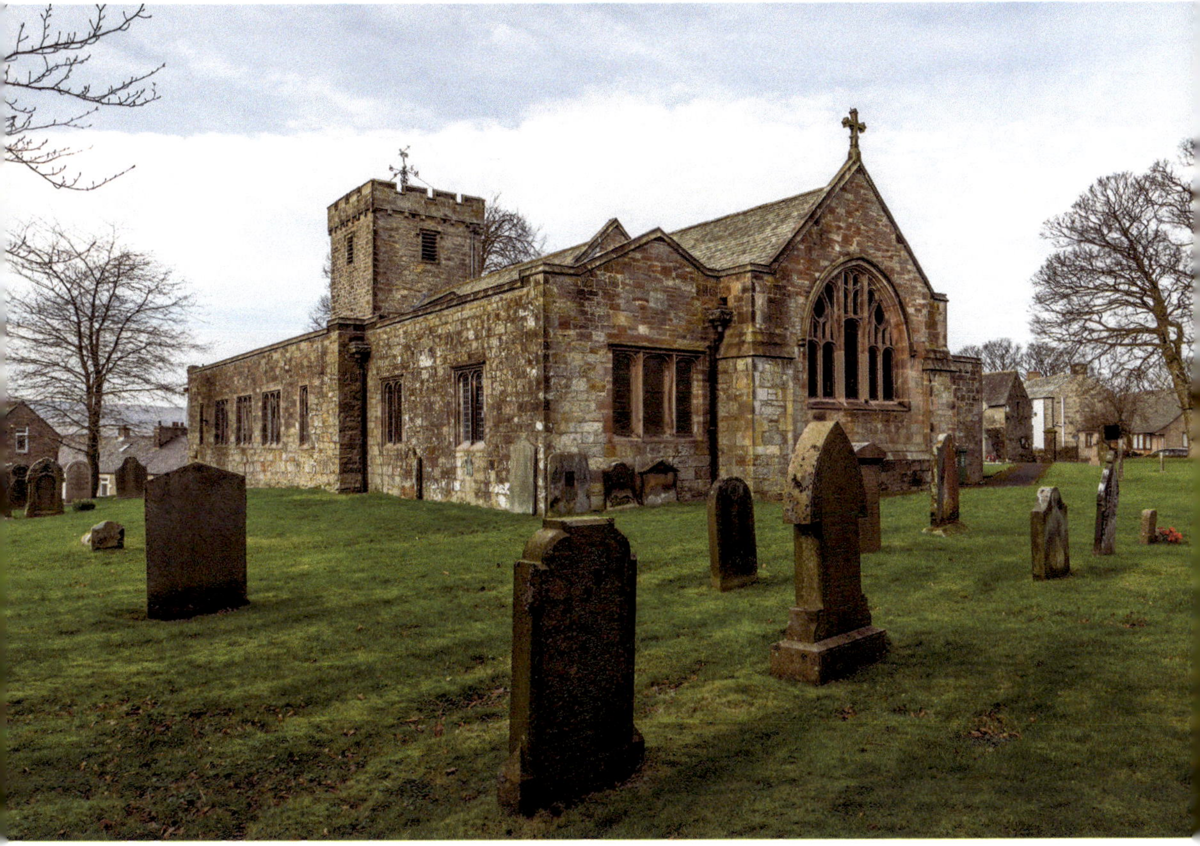

St Michael's Church, Shap.

In 2011 there were concerns that the church may have to close after thieves stole the lead from the roof and the insurance payment fell far short of what was needed to complete the work. The story was picked up by the national press and people from all over the country generously donated money, with United Utilities also adding a £6,000 grant to the funds, thus allowing the repairs to be carried out and the church to return to full use once again.

10. LONGSLEDDALE TO WET SLEDDALE – THE OLD QUARRYING ROUTES

Introduction

This is a combination of old quarrying routes and bridleways. As well as the main Longsleddale to Wet Sleddale route, we'll also take a short diversion along a track back to Swindale as it holds a wonderful surprise. Once you leave Gatescarth Pass, just after Wrengill Quarry the scenery changes dramatically from jagged soaring fells to a more rounded landscape, which is both beautiful and boggy. There are plenty of sheep around and you'll find plenty of Swaledales, Rough Fell sheep and Texels. Rough Fell and Swaledales look a lot alike but Rough Fell sheep have longer, more luxuriant fleeces, while Texels look like they might mug you.

The Route

The main route starts at Sadgill bridge and follows Gatescarth Pass up to Wrengill Quarry where you'll find a clearly signed path leading off to Mosedale and Swindale. At the fork,

View over Wet Sleddale Reservoir.

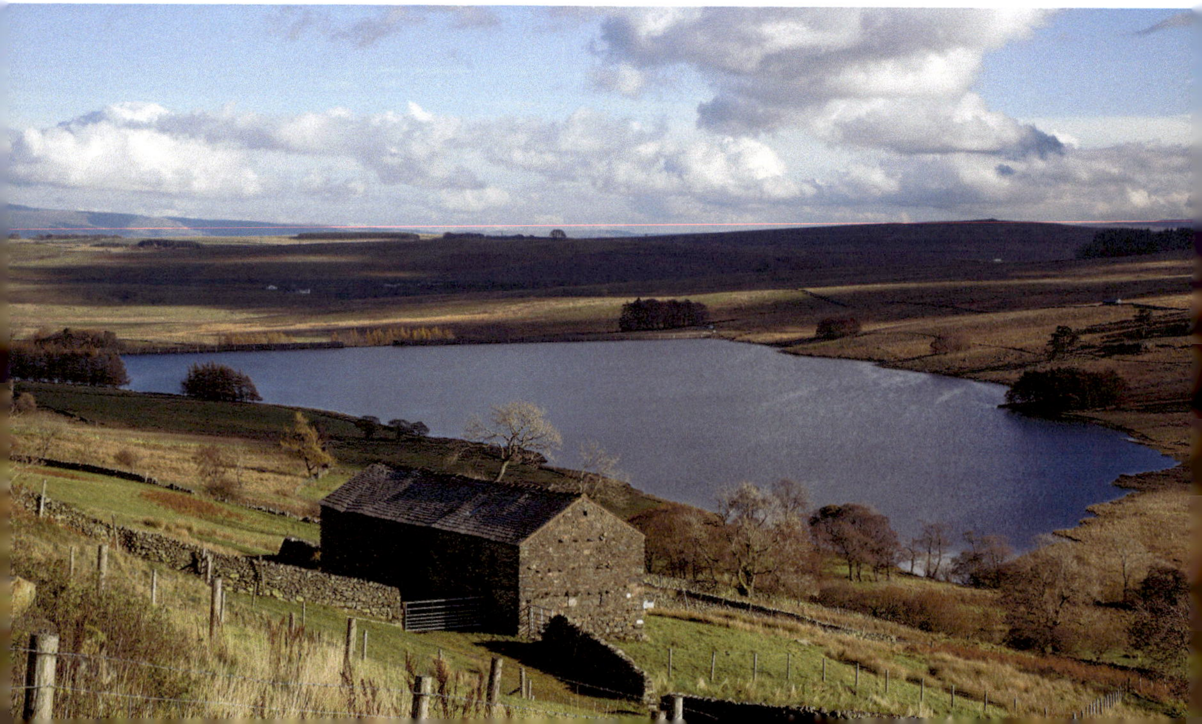

the left-hand route drops down to Swindale and if you don't fancy a there and back detour, it can be made into a looped route using the Corpse Road back to Haweswater. The right-hand route climbs a little to Scam Mathew where, if you turn around, there are lovely views back along Mosedale Valley. As you approach Wet Sleddale, the original track continues along Stackhouse Brow, but we opted to drop down via Sleddale Hall because it was more interesting and less boggy. You can then continue on to Shap, either along the nice solid A6 or via Steps Hall, where the going underfoot is generally swampy.

The History

First up, let me get contentious by taking Mr Wainwright and Miss Martineau to task. They both describe Mosedale Valley in less than glowing terms. Wainwright states that it is 'one of six upland valleys of that name in Lakeland, all being desolate wastes of marshy ground', while Martineau calls it 'the most desolate and dreary of all the vales'. Now there is no getting away from the fact that it is somewhat moist underfoot here and definitely one to avoid after prolonged rain, but desolate and dreary is just being plain mean. We walked it in November and February, and both times it looked absolutely lovely. For desolate read peaceful, deserted and tranquil, and for dreary read spacious, rolling and gentle on the eye. Lakeland beauty isn't just about the high fells; it's also about hidden away gems like this.

It wasn't always peaceful, quiet and deserted though. When both Wrengill and Mosedale quarries were in action, there was plenty of activity in the valley, and the presence of the quarries resulted in the hard tracks we see along the valleys.

Much-maligned Mosedale Valley.

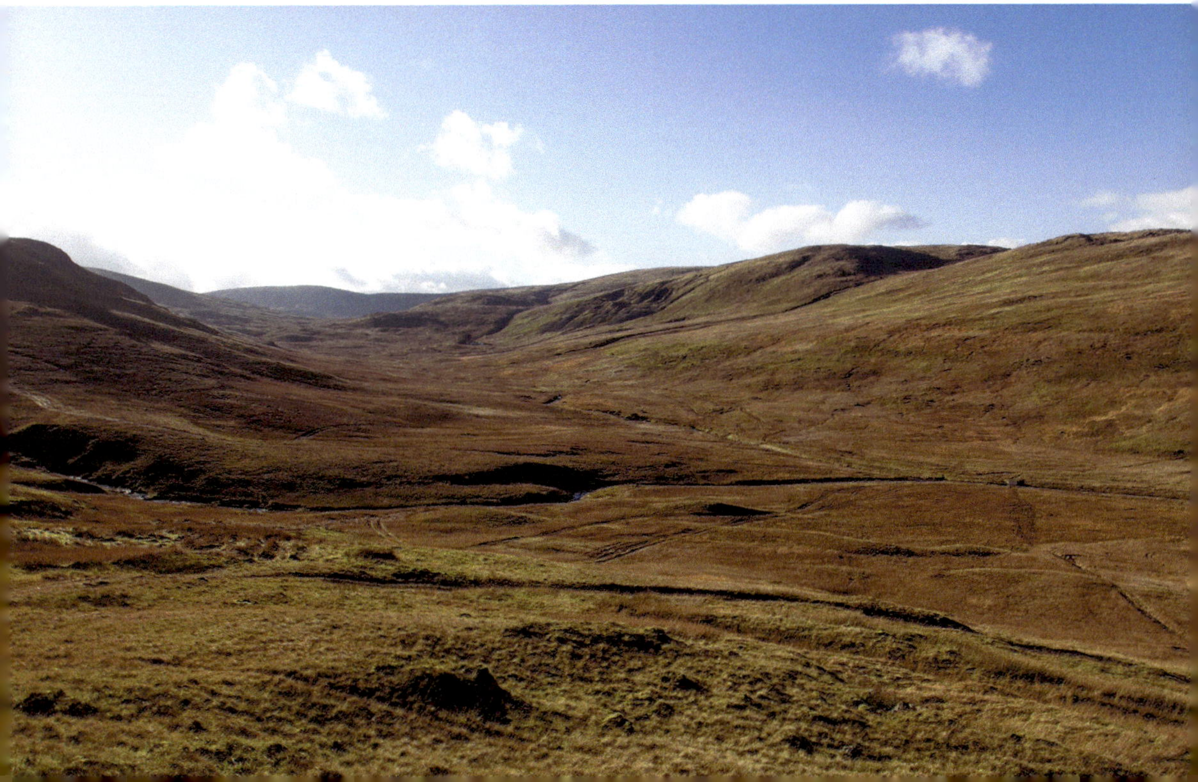

The approach to Wrengill Quarry passes over a small bridge with a dedication etched into the stone under it. The dedication simply reads 'Denys Beddard 1917 – 1985'. Denys, I discovered from a footnote on a blog by the 'Boot Boys', retired to the Lake District with his wife. He was the chairman of the Westmorland Geological Society, worked in medical administration and is cited in a book titled *Food Poisoning, Policy and Politics* (2005), which analysed the responses to the numerous food health scares of the 1980s. Remember that when you're sitting there tucking into a warm ham sandwich that has rattled around your rucksack for a few hours.

Wrengill Quarry must, like all disused quarries, come with a health warning: there is old machinery lying around and lots of sudden unfenced-off drops, so if you are going to explore, do be careful. Slate was mined there from 1729 to around 1847. Back then it was known as 'Rangle Quarry' and produced large quantities of 'fine blue slate', which was used in equally fine buildings of the period. The slabs of slate had to be removed from the quarry by pony all the way back down into the valley, where they could be loaded onto carts and carried away for distribution. This explains why the upper sections of the route up from Longsleddale are unusually metalled; it was to prevent the ponies slipping.

The quarry reopened briefly in the mid-nineteenth century and was allegedly worked by Italian prisoners of war during the Second World War. When they were sent home they put down their tools and left and the quarry was never worked again. Although this is hard to confirm, there was a POW camp called Merrythought near to Penrith (the site is now owned by DEFRA) and local landowners and farmers would regularly use prisoners as labourers, so it's not beyond the realms of possibility.

Opposite: Metalled track.

Below: Denys Beddard Bridge.

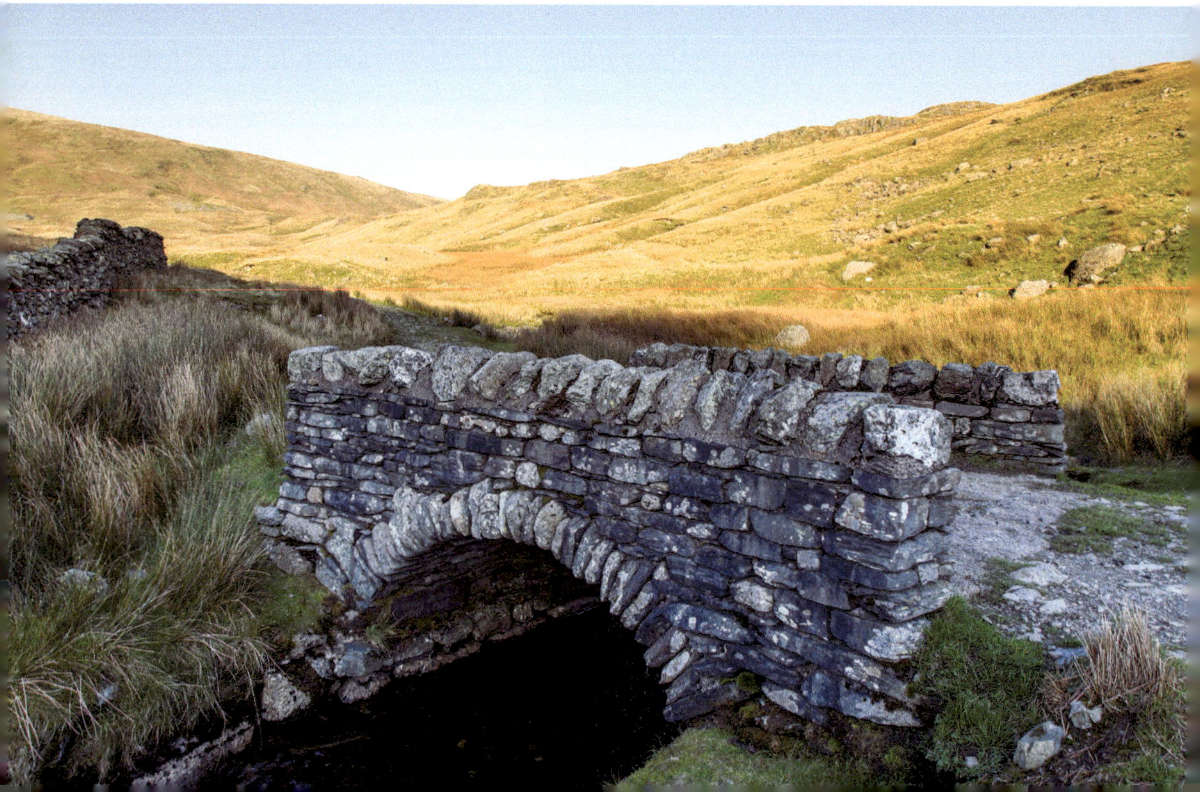

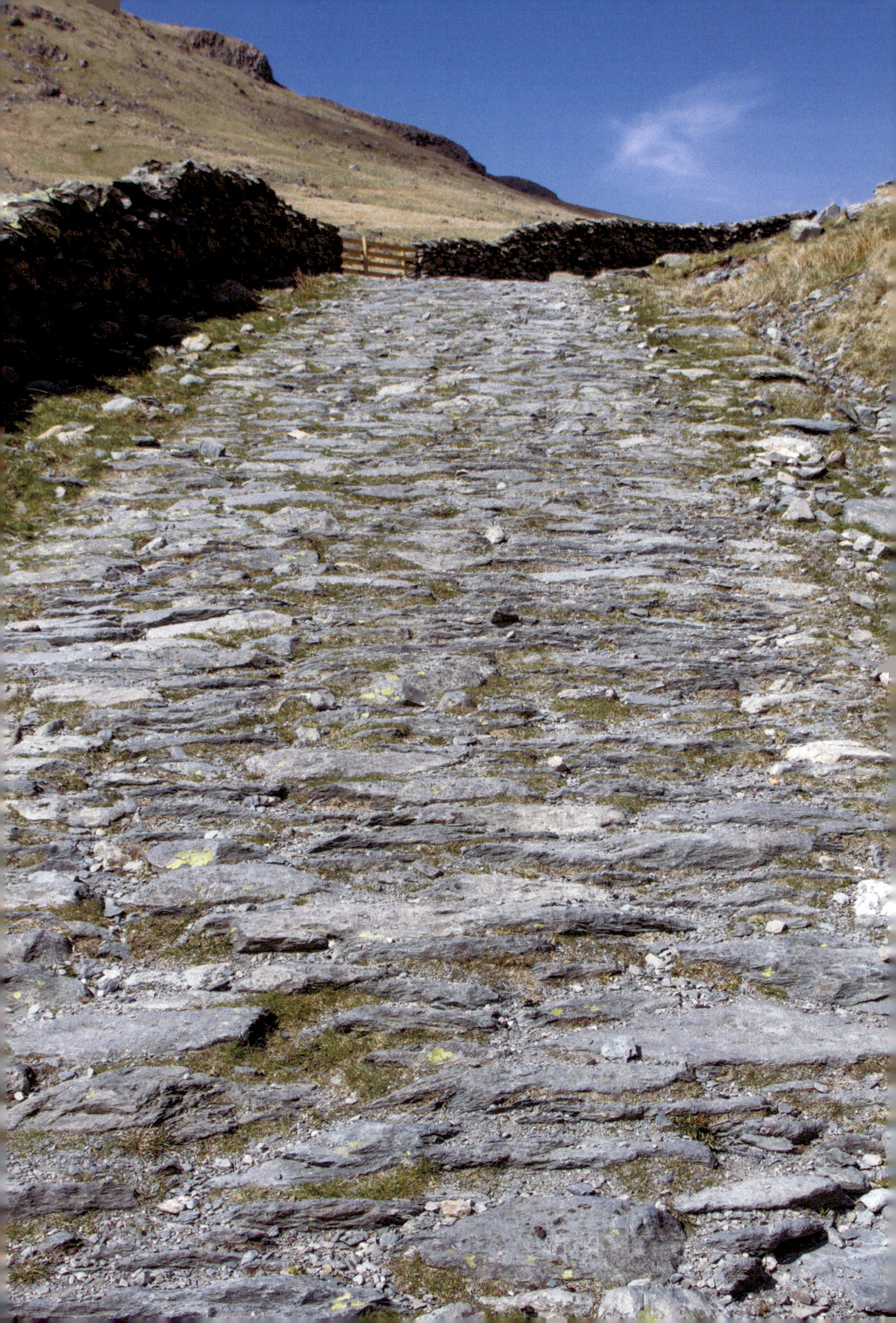

By far the finest image of the quarry is the one from 1835 drawn by Thomas Allom and engraved by J. W. Lowry. I love it because it captures an image of goings on there long before photography and also because it's exaggerated in the way artists of that time tended to do. The quarry is spectacular in a brutal, industrial way, but even though we've visited several times, we've not spotted the huge ravines or soaring packhorse bridges shown in the painting.

Mosedale Quarry mined exactly the same blue slate, but it's likely that rather than removing it down through Longsleddale, it was instead moved out of Swindale to the old road/A6. That section of the route is peppered with the remains of old buildings and, where it hasn't been lost, the track is broad and was clearly well laid initially. The spoil heaps still scar the landscape but slowly Mother Nature is claiming them back, and it won't be many years before they have vanished completely.

Mosedale Cottage, at the head of the valley, was once a permanent dwelling but was last inhabited in 1930. Previous census reports show a shepherd and his family living there but they were gone by 1861. Today the bothy is owned and looked after by the Mountaineering Bothies Association, and is free to stay in with no prior booking required. Although bothies can vary widely in their standards, this one is warm, cosy and has a decent sofa, which could be due to the fact that some of the outbuildings are locked and still used by the local shepherd who most likely still keeps a watchful eye on the place.

If you take the offshoot path to Swindale, be sure to loop back to see Forces Falls marked on the map. There is an excellent footbridge there now and the field opposite is part of the re-meandering project described in Chapter 9. The falls are one of Cumbria's glorious surprises and even Wainwright describes them as 'a spectacular ravine'. He was wrong about Mosedale but spot on about the forces; they are spectacular and were they to be anywhere more accessible, they would surely be swamped with visitors throughout the year.

Back on the main route to Wet Sleddale, the track passes by the curiously named Scam Matthew. The word 'scam' in its modern sense only came into use in the 1960s, but there's a map of the region from 1960 with Scam Matthew marked on. It's unlikely to have become a widely enough used term to have had a landmark named after it by then, so it's more probable that it's after the local dialect word 'scamb' meaning 'crack' or 'injury'. Sadly I've not been able to track down who Matthew was.

As you approach Sleddale Hall, on the opposite side of the valley is an old deer park, two oddly shaped fields immediately adjacent to the River Lowther. Anecdotal local history suggests that the monks at Shap Abbey used to fatten their deer here for venison, but there's not a lot of supporting evidence for that. Although many of the typically high walls of the old deer park remain, the last deer in the park were put there as an experiment by the 2nd Earl of Lonsdale in the 1860s.

These days Sleddale Hall is the stuff of local legend since it was used in the cult film *Withnail and I,* where it featured as Uncle Monty's cottage Crow Crag. Its early history is hard to pin down but as with many old local buildings, it may once also have been associated with the monks at Shap Abbey. In 1802 it was noted that although it had land covering around 250 acres, most of it was 'poorish meadow' or 'barren mountains' and was not highly valued. According to another source, the hall was the Sleddale family home, one of whom went on to become the first mayor of Kendal. The title was first given by Charles I in 1636, and the first mayor on the roll of honour is Thomas Sleddall, who had previously served as an alderman in 1617 and 1634, so if that's the case this could date the hall to at least the seventeenth century.

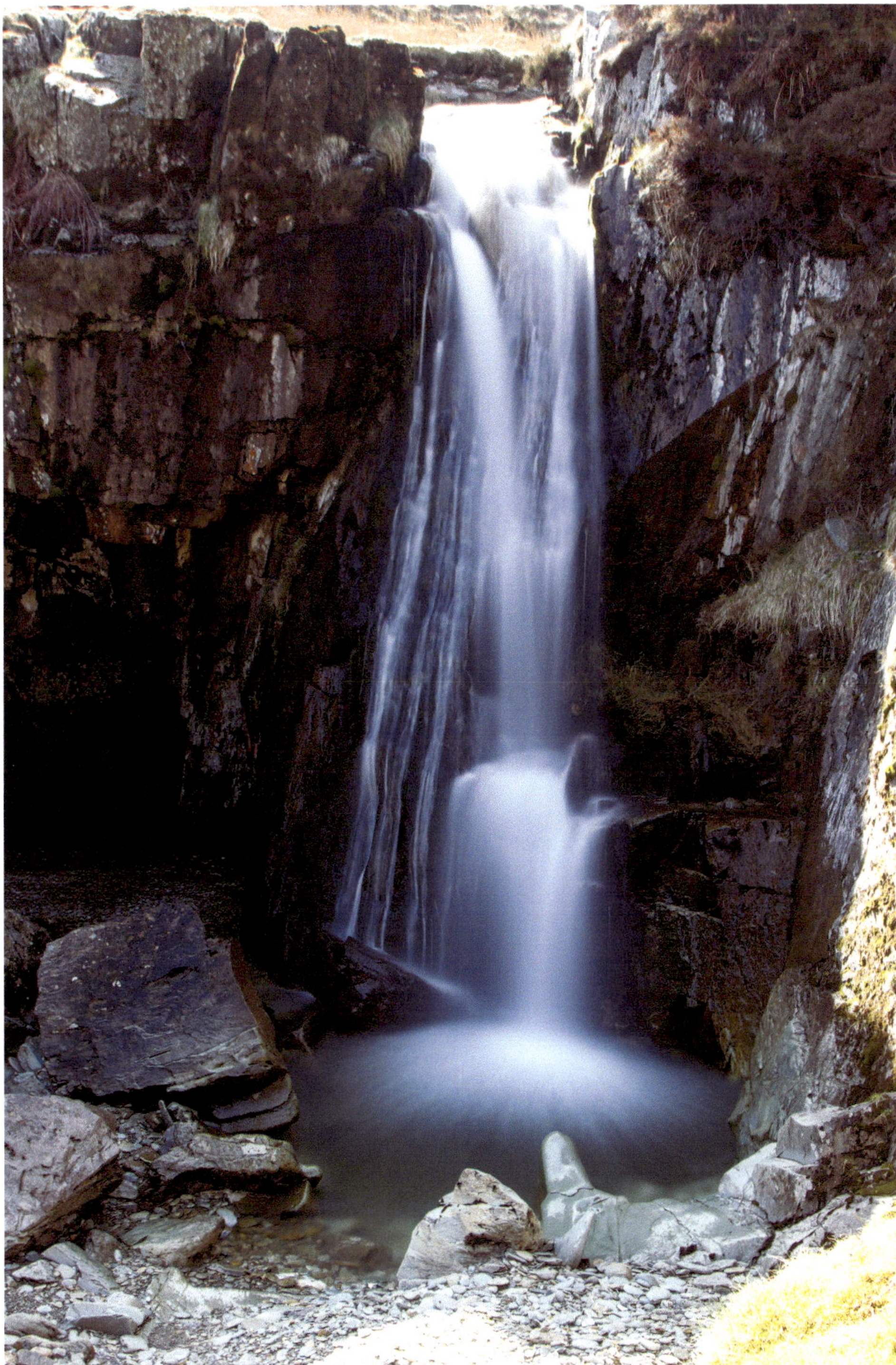

Waterfall, Wrengill Quarry.

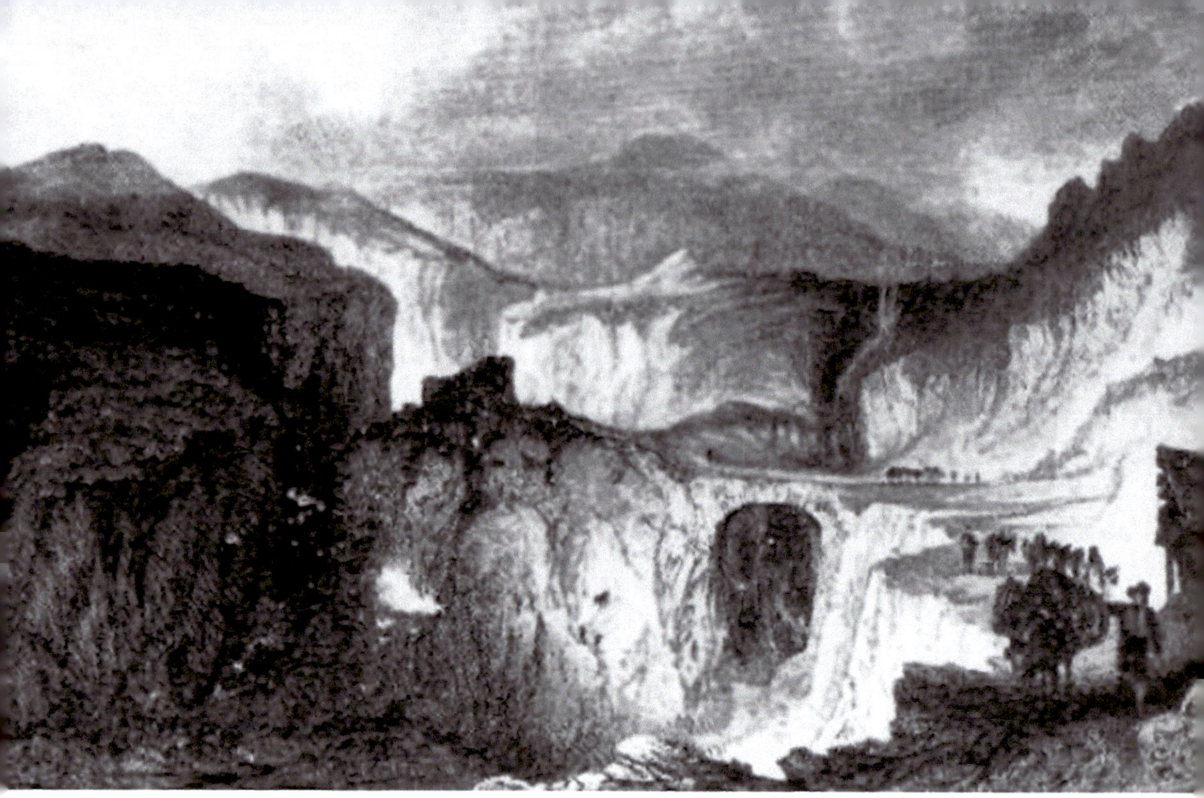

Above: Wrengill Quarry, Thomas Allom and J. S. Lowry.

Below: Mosedale Cottage.

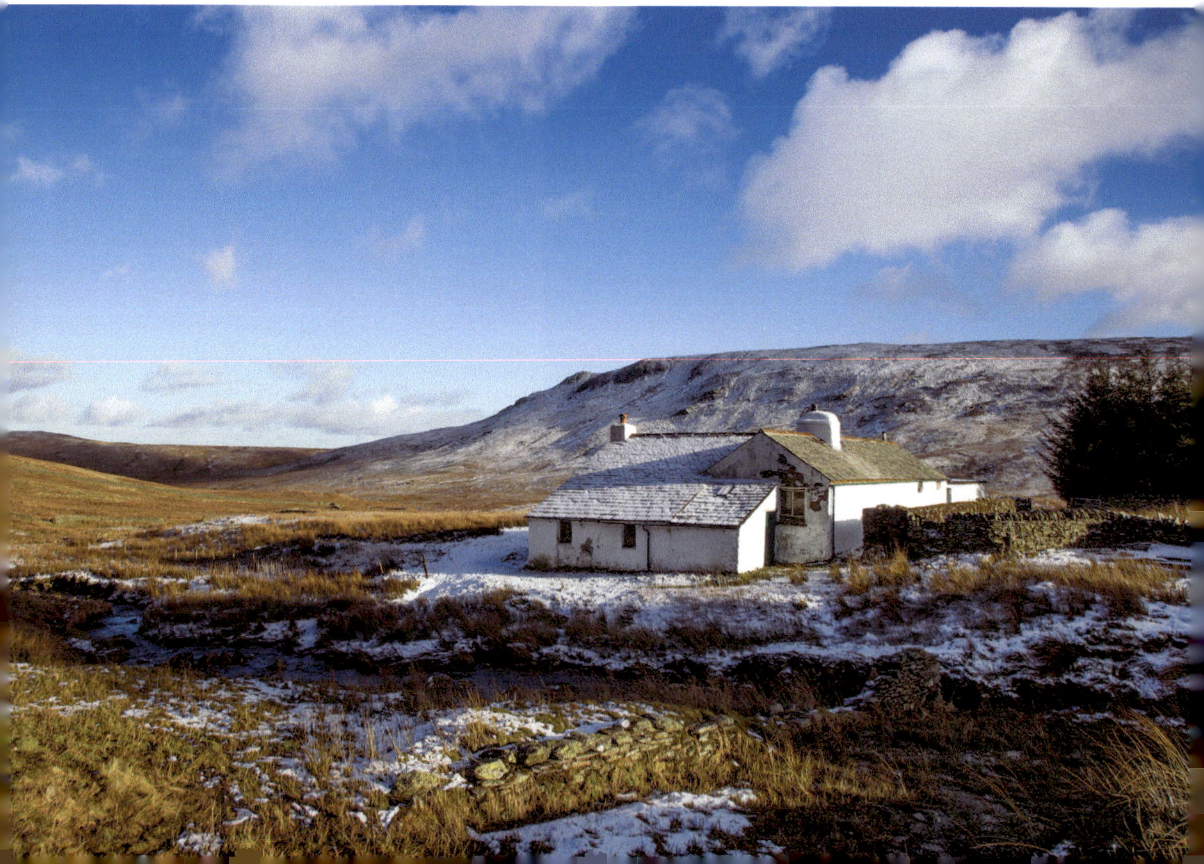

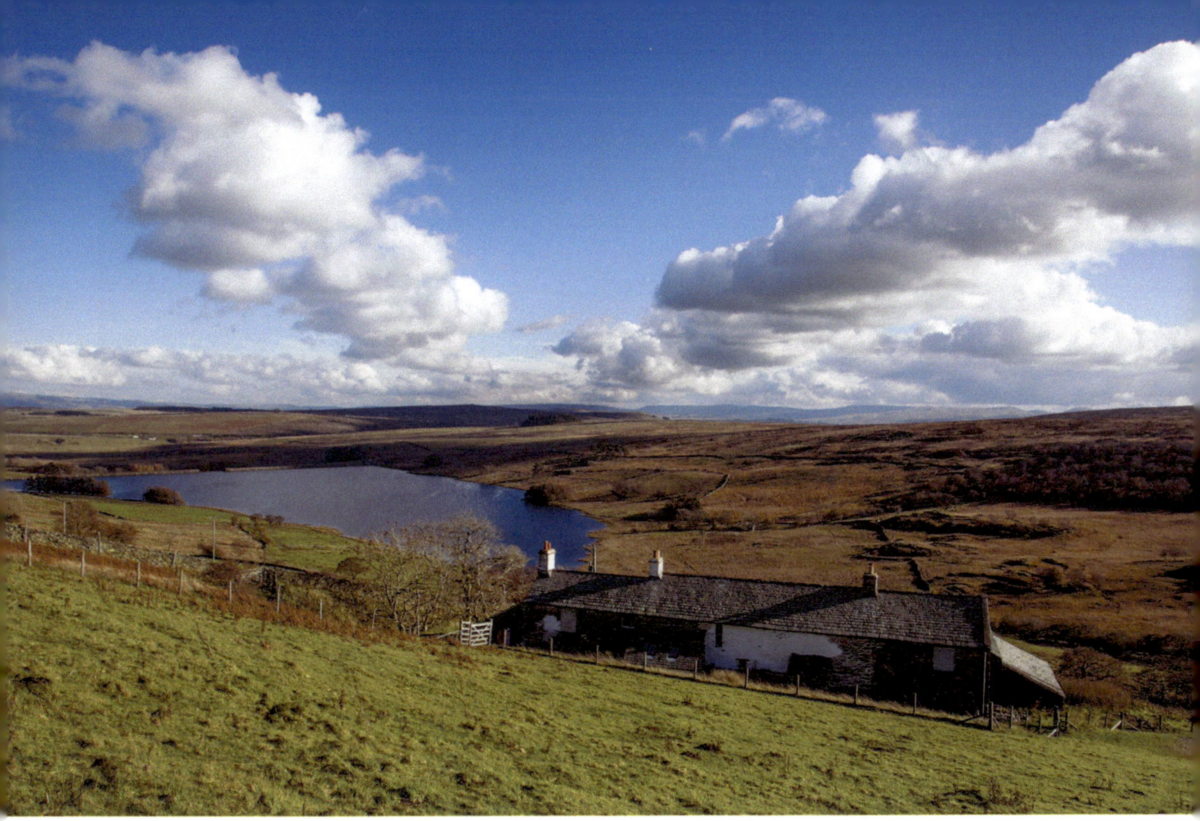

Sleddale Hall ('Crow Crag').

Only the downstairs rooms and the exterior of the hall were used during filming – the bedroom and staircase shots were filmed elsewhere. Despite its remoteness, the hall has long attracted fans of the film, many of whom have left graffiti on the outside of the building. The house was owned by United Utilities but the ownership of the hall hung in the balance for a while before it was eventually sold in 2009 to an architect and fan of the film, who vowed to restore it 'in a way that other fans of the film would approve of'. Certainly from the outside it looks much as it did in the film, although somewhat tidier.

Wet Sleddale Reservoir is another of the local reservoirs built to supply Manchester. It was completed in 1966 and the water is moved via tunnels to Haweswater and then on to Manchester. The dam wall is 21 metres (69 feet) high and is very impressive to see, especially when the water overflows down the front. If you don't fancy a long hike, there is ample public parking near to the dam wall and a lovely footpath circling the reservoir. One year while we were enjoying a walk there we heard the first cuckoo of the year calling in the nearby woods.

The building of all the reservoirs in the region may have been one thing that spurred the Friends of the Lake District into existence. They first met in Keswick in July 1934 (the national park wasn't formed until May 1951) and early members were required to pay 2*s* 6*d* per year. The original press release stated that (among other things) they aimed to 'mobilise local and national opinion' and create a fund to assist local authorities. The initial signatories to this press release included Eleanor Rawnsley (wife of Canon Rawnsley), Gordon G. Wordsworth (grandson of William) and Geoffrey Winthrop Young, climber, poet and mentor to George Mallory, whose attempt to summit Everest left the world with an enduring mystery that may never be solved.

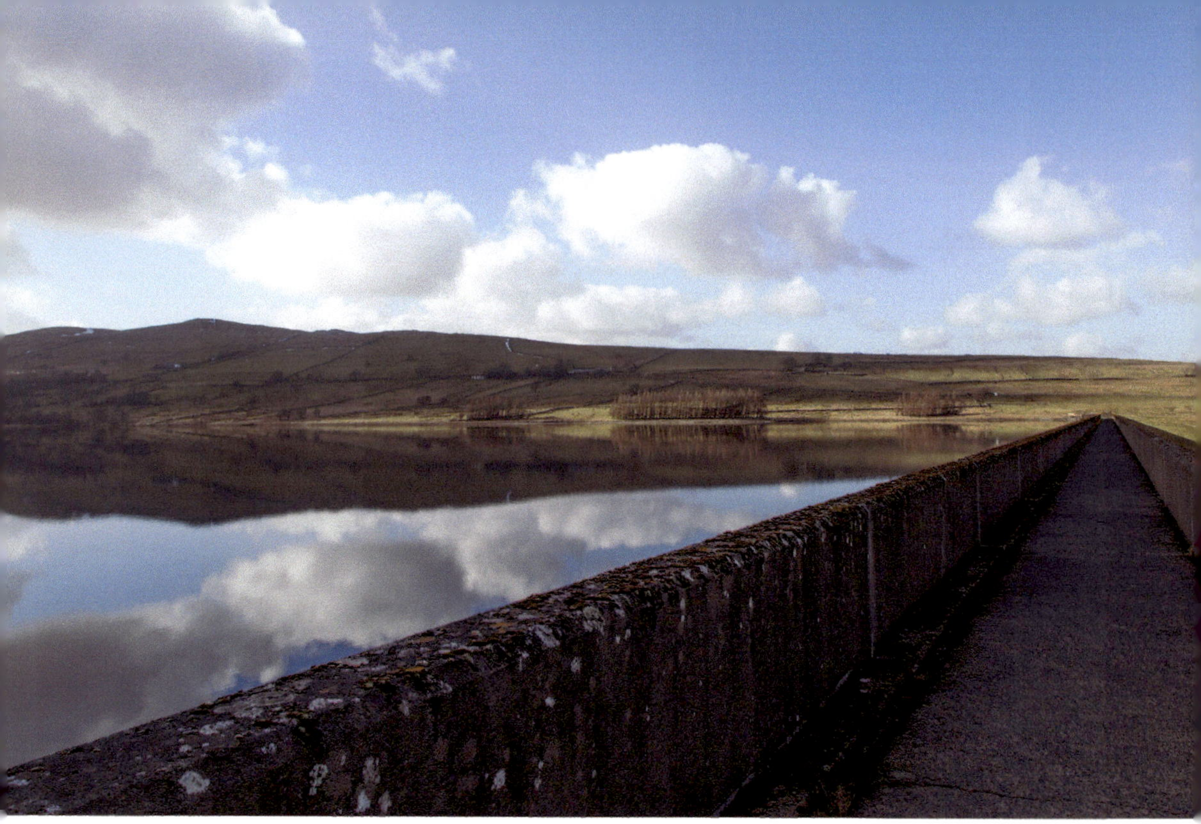

Above: Wet Sleddale Reservoir.

Below: Red deer.

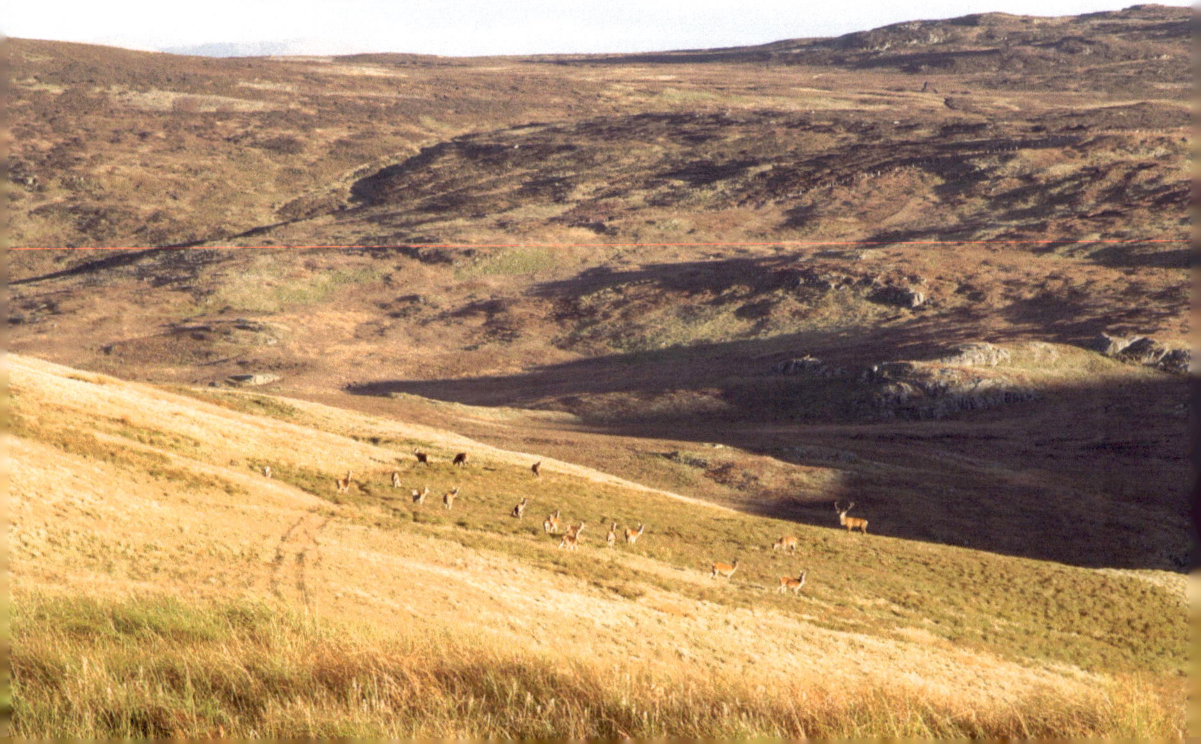

BIBLIOGRAPHY

Books

Baddeley, M. J. B., *The Lake District* (Ward, Lock & Co., 1940)
Brodie, Ian O., *The Cistercian Way* (Carnegie Press, 1989)
Budworth, Joseph, *A Fortnight's Ramble to the Lakes* (Cadell and Davies, 1810)
Burnett, T. R., *Friends of the Lake District* (Journal of Fell and Rock Climbing Club, 1934)
Cappelli, Tim, *The Thirlmere Way* (Sigma Leisure, 1992)
Collingwood, W. G., *Lake District History* (Titus Wilson & Sons, 1928)
Cooper, D. G., *The Crummock Water Aureole* (Journal of the Geology Society of London V145, 1988)
Dickinson, J. C., *The Land of Cartmel* (Titus Wilson, 1980)
Edmonds, Mark, *The Langdales* (Tempus Publishing, 2010)
Fletcher Buntin, Tom, *Life in Langdale* (Titus Wilson, 1993)
Fraser, Maxwell, *Companion into Lakeland* (London, Methuen and Co., 1937)
Gell, William, *A Tour in the Lakes Made in 1797*, ed. by William Rollinson (Frank Graham, 1968)
Harper, Charles G., *The Manchester and Glasgow Road* (Cecil Palmer, London, 1924)
Harris, Olwen, *The School in the Fells* (Mitre Press, London, 1969)
Hodge, E. W., *Old Maps* (Journal of Fell and Rock Climbing Club, 1934)
Honeyman, Neil, *Old Mardale* (Stenlake Publishing, 2012)
Howorth, Billy F. K., *Carlisle History Tour* (Amberley, 2018)
Hunt, Irvine, *Old Lakeland Transport* (Rusland Press, 1978)
Hurst, John, *Lakeland Reporter* (Sutton Publishing, 1996)
Lofthouse, Jessica, *Lancashire and Westmorland Highway* (Robert Hale, London, 1953)
Logan Thompson, Bruce, *A Deer Park in Wet Sleddale* (Transactions of the Cumberland and Westmorland Antiquarian and Archaeological Society, 1934)
Logoe, John, *Some Eskdale Rock Climbs* (Journal of Fell and Rock Climbing Club, 1959)
Martineau, Harriet, *The English Lake District* (Simpkin Marshall, London, 1876)
Murray, John, *A Tour in the English Lakes with Thomas Gray and Joseph Farington* (Frances Lincoln, 2012)
Nicholson, Joseph, *The History and Antiquities of the Counties of Westmorland and Cumberland* (Joseph Nicholson, 1777)
Ogilby, John, *Britannia* (1675)
Ramshaw, David, *The English Lakes* (Amadeus Press, 1996)
Richard, Guthrie, *A Tour Through Old Lakeland* (Stenlake Publishing, 1996)
Spence, Dr J. E., *An Early Settlement on Moor Divock* (Transactions of the Cumberland and Archaeological Society)

Wainwright, Alfred, *Old Roads of Eastern Lakeland* (Westmorland Gazette, 1985)
Walker, Peter N., *Folk Stories from the Lake District* (Robert Hale, London, 1993)
Watson, John, *The Annals of a Quiet Valley* (J. M. Dent & Co., 1894)
West, Timothy, *A Guide to the Lakes* (Richardson and Urguhart, London, 1778)
Williams L. A., *Road Transport in Cumbria in the Nineteenth Century* (Allen & Unwin, London, 1975)
Wilson Parker, John, *An Atlas of The English Lakes* (Cicerone, 2002)
Woods, Jack, *The North Road* (J. Woods, 1996)

Miscellaneous

Cumberland Official Guide 1962–1963
English Heritage Guidebooks: Hadrian's Wall, Carlisle Castle, Brougham and Brough Castles, Furness Abbey
Guide to Dalton Castle by Barrow Borough Council
Shap Abbey in Westmorland and the Chapel at Keld by Ronald Wentworth Taylor
Solway's Built Heritage by Solway Wetlands
Solway's Churches – leaflets by East Solway Churches
St Cuthbert's Parish Church, Kentmere by Staveley and District History Society
The Shap Fell Story by Shap Local History Society
Ulverston Leaflets (assorted) by Choose Ulverston

Websites

Archaeology UK, www.archaeologyuk.org
Archive, www.archive.org
BBC, www.bbc.co.uk
British History Online, www.british-history.ac.uk
English Lakes, www.English-lakes.com
Fell and Rock Climbing Club, www.frcc.co.uk
Historic Population, www.histpop.org
Kentmere Village, www.kentmere.org
Lakes Guides, www.lakesguides.co.uk
Modern Antiquarian Shap Avenue, http://www.themodernantiquarian.com/post/29979/weblog/british_isles.html
Patterdale Today, www.patterdaletoday.co.uk/history